A User's Guide to
Capitalism and Schiz

A User's Guide to
Capitalism and Schizophrenia
Deviations from Deleuze and Guattari

Brian Massumi

A Swerve Edition
The MIT Press
Cambridge, Massachusetts
London, England

© 1992 Massachusetts Institute of Technology

All rights reserved. No part of this book may be reproduced in any form by any electronic or mechanical means (including photocopying, recording, or information storage and retrieval) without permission in writing from the publisher.

An earlier version of "Pleasures of Philosophy" appeared as the foreword to Gilles Deleuze and Félix Guattari's *A Thousand Plateaus*. It is used here with the permission of the University of Minnesota Press.

Swerve editions are edited by Jonathan Crary, Sanford Kwinter, and Bruce Mau .

This book was set in Cochin at The MIT Press and printed and bound in the United States of America.

Library of Congress Cataloging-in-Publication Data

Massumi, Brian.
    A user's guide to capitalism and schizophrenia : deviations from Deleuze and Guattari / Brian Massumi. — A Swerve ed.
        p.   cm.
    Includes bibliographical references and index.
    ISBN 0-262-13282-6 (hc). — ISBN 0-262-63143-1 (pbk)
    1. Deleuze, Gilles. Capitalisme et schizophrénie. 2. Social psychiatry. 3. Schizophrenia—Social aspects. 4. Capitalism—Social aspects. 5. Psychology. Pathological—Etiology. I. Title.
RC455.M279   1992   91-30392
                                                    CIP
10 9 8 7

Contents

.

Pleasures of Philosophy

Two nouns, two books, two authors: *Capitalism and Schizophrenia* is the shared subtitle of Gilles Deleuze and Félix Guattari's *Anti-Oedipus* (1972) and *A Thousand Plateaus* (1980). The volumes differ so markedly in tone, content, and composition that they seem a prime illustration of their subtitle's second noun. It is hoped that the present book will be as much.

The "schizophrenia" Deleuze and Guattari embrace is not a pathological condition. For them, the clinical schizophrenic's debilitating detachment from the world is a quelled attempt to engage it in unimagined ways. Schizophrenia as a positive process is inventive connection, expansion rather than withdrawal. Its twoness is a relay to a multiplicity. From one to another (and another . . .). From one noun or book or author to another (and another . . .). Not aimlessly. Experimentally. The relay in ideas is only effectively expansive if at every step it is also a relay away from ideas into action. Schizophrenia is the enlargement of life's limits through the pragmatic proliferation of concepts.

Schizophrenia, like those "suffering" from it, goes by many names. "Philosophy" is one. Not just any philosophy. A bastard kind. Legitimate philosophy is the handiwork of "bureaucrats" of pure reason who speak in "the shadow of the despot"[1] and are in historical complicity with the state. They invent "a properly spiritual . . . absolute State that . . . effectively functions in the mind." Theirs is the discourse of sovereign judgment, of stable subjectivity legislated by "good" sense, of rocklike identity, "universal" truth, and (white male) justice. "Thus the exercise of their thought is in conformity with the aims of the real State, with the dominant significations, and with the requirements of the established order."[2]

Gilles Deleuze was schooled in that philosophy. The titles of his earliest books read like a who's who of philosophical giants. "What got me through that period was conceiving of the history of philosophy as a kind of ass-fuck, or, what amounts to the same thing, an immaculate conception. I imagined myself approaching an author from behind and giving him a child that would indeed be his but would nonetheless be monstrous."[3] Hegel is absent, being too despicable even to merit a mutant offspring. To Kant he dedicated an affectionate study of "an enemy."[4] Yet much of value came of Deleuze's flirtation with the greats. He discovered an orphan line of thinkers affiliated only in their opposition to the State philosophy that would nevertheless accord them minor positions in its canon. From Lucretius, Hume, Spinoza, Nietzsche, and Bergson there runs a "secret link constituted by the critique of negativity, the cultivation of joy, the hatred of interiority, the exteriority of forces and relations, the denunciation of power."[5] Deleuze's first major statements written in his own voice, *Différence et répétition* (1968) and *The Logic of Sense* (1969), cross-fertilized that line of "nomad" thought with contemporary theory. The ferment of the student–worker revolt of May 1968 and the reassessment it prompted of the intellectual's role in society[6] led him to disclaim the "ponderous academic apparatus"[7] still in evidence in those works. However, many elements of the "philosophy of difference" he had elaborated in them were transfused into a continuing collaboration, of which *A Thousand Plateaus* is the most recent product.

Félix Guattari is a practicing psychoanalyst and lifelong political activist. He has worked since the mid-fifties at La Borde, an experimental psychiatric clinic founded by Lacanian analyst Jean Oury. Guattari himself was among Lacan's earliest trainees and, although he never formally severed his ties with Lacan's Ecole Freudienne, the group therapy practiced at La Borde took him in a very different direction. The aim at La Borde was to abolish the doctor–patient hierarchy in favor of an interactive group dynamic that would bring the experiences of all to full expression in such a way as to produce a collective critique of the power relations in society as a whole. "The central perspective is . . . to promote human relations that do not automatically fall into roles or stereotypes but open onto fundamental relations of a metaphysical kind that *bring out* the most radical and basic alienations of madness or neurosis"[8] and channel them into revolutionary practice. From 1960, Guattari collaborated on group projects dedicated to developing this radical "institutional psychotherapy,"[9] and later he entered an uneasy alliance with the international antipsychiatry movement spearheaded by R. D. Laing in England and Franco Basaglia in Italy.[10] As Lacanian schools of psychoanalysis gained ground against psychiatry, the contractual Oedipal relationship between the analyst and the transference-bound analysand became as much Guattari's target as the legal bondage of the institutionalized patient in conventional state hospitals. He adopted the same stance toward psychoanalysis as he had earlier toward the parties of the left: an ultraopposition within the opposition. His antihierarchical attitudes anticipated the events of May 1968 and made him an early partisan of the social movements that grew from them, including feminism and the gay-rights movement.[11] *Anti-Oedipus*, his first book with Deleuze, gave philosophical weight to his convictions, and created one of the intellectual sensations of postwar France with its spirited polemics against State-happy or pro-party versions of Marxism and school-building strains of psychoanalysis, which separately and in various combinations represented the dominant intellectual currents of the time (despite the fundamentally anarchist nature of the spontaneous popular uprisings that had shaken the world in 1968). "The most tangible result of *Anti-Oedipus* was that it short-circuited the connection between psychoanalysis and the far-left parties," in which Deleuze and Guattari saw the potential for a powerful new bureaucracy of analytic reason.[12]

The book's polemical tone and the marks it bears of the authors' involvement in the political events of the period are often used as an excuse to dismiss it as an outdated, occasional work. The bulk of *Anti-Oedipus*, however, is given over to detailed analyses of the collective "syntheses" constituting a society and to the invention of a new typology of cultural formations. It is these positive and enduring contributions of *Anti-Oedipus* that the present work will attempt to foreground by tying its terminology to that of preceding and subsequent books by Deleuze and Guattari.

For many French intellectuals, the hyperactivism of post-May gave way to a mid-seventies slump, then a return to religion (*Tel Quel*) or political conservatism (the Nouveaux Philosophes). Deleuze and Guattari never recanted. Neither did they simply revive the old polemics. *A Thousand Plateaus* (1980), written over a seven-year period, is less a critique than a sustained, constructive experiment in schizo-phrenic, or "nomad," thought.

"State philosophy" is another name for the representational thinking that has dominated Western metaphysics since Plato, but has suffered an at least momentary setback during the last quarter century at the hands of Jacques Derrida, Michel Foucault and poststructuralist theory generally. As described by Deleuze,[13] State philosophy is grounded in a double identity: of the thinking subject, and of the concepts it creates and to which it lends its own presumed attributes of sameness and constancy. The subject, its concepts, and the "exter-nal" objects to which the concepts are applied have a shared, internal essence: the self-resemblance at the basis of identity. Representational thought is analogical; its concern is to establish a correspondence between these symmetrically structured domains. The faculty of judg-ment serves as the police force of analogy, assuring that each of the three terms is honestly itself, and that the proper correspondences obtain. In thought its end is truth, in action justice. The weapons it wields in pursuit of these are limitative distribution (the determination of the exclusive set of properties possessed by each term in contradis-tinction to the others: *logos*, law) and hierarchical ranking (the mea-surement of the degree of perfection of a term's self-resemblance in relation to a supreme standard, Man, God, or Gold: value, morality). The modus operandi is negation: $x = x = $ not y. Identity, resemblance, truth, justice, and negation. The rational foundation for order. The established order, of course: philosophers have traditionally been employees of the State. The collusion between philosophy and the State was most explicitly enacted in the first decade of the nineteenth century with the foundation of the University of Berlin, which was to become the model for higher learning throughout Europe and the U.S. The goal laid out for it by Wilhelm von Humboldt (based on proposals by Fichte and Schleiermacher) was the "spiritual and moral training of the nation," to be achieved by "deriving everything from an original principle" (truth), by "relating everything to an ideal" (justice), and by "unifying this principle and this ideal in a single Idea" (the State). The end product would be "a fully legitimated subject of knowledge and society"[14] — each mind an analogously organized mini-State morally unified in the supermind of the State. Prussian mind-meld.[15] Even more insidious than today's well-known practical cooperation between the university and government (the burgeoning military funding of research) was its philosophical role in propagating the form of representational thinking itself, that "properly spiritual absolute State" endlessly reproduced and disseminated at every level of the social fabric (nationalism and good citizenship). More insidious than its institution-based propagation is the State-form's ability to propagate *itself* without centrally directed inculcation (liberalism and good citizenship). Still more insidious is the process presiding over our present plight, in which the moral and philosophical foundations of national and personal identity have crumbled, making a mockery of the State-form—but the world keeps right on going *as if* they hadn't (neo-conservatism and cynical greed).

Deconstruction-influenced feminists such as Hélène Cixous and Luce Irigaray have attacked State philosophy under the name "phallogocentrism" (what the most privileged model of rocklike identity is goes without saying). In the introduction to *A Thousand Plateaus*, Deleuze and Guattari describe it as the "arborescent" model of thought (the proudly erect tree under whose spreading boughs latter-day Platos discharge their functions).

"Nomad thought" does not lodge itself in the edifice of an ordered interiority; it moves freely in an element of exteriority. It does not repose on identity; it rides difference. It does not respect the artificial division between the three domains of representation, subject, concept, and being; it replaces restrictive analogy with a conductivity that knows no bounds. The concepts it creates do not merely reflect the eternal form of a legislating subject, but are defined by a communicable force in relation to which their subject, to the extent that they can be said to have one, is only secondary. Rather than reflecting the world, they are immersed in a changing state of things. A concept is a brick. It can be used to build the courthouse of reason. Or it can be thrown through the window. What is the subject of the brick? The arm that throws it? The body connected to the arm? The brain encased in the body? The situation that brought brain and body to such a juncture? All and none of the above. What is its object? The window? The edifice? The laws the edifice shelters? The class and other power relations encrusted in the laws? All and none of the above: "What interests us are the circumstances."[16] Because the concept in its unrestrained usage is a set of circumstances, at a volatile juncture. It is a vector: the point of application of a force moving through a space at a given velocity in a given direction. The concept has no subject or object other than itself. It is an act. Nomad thought replaces the closed equation of representation, x = x = not y (I = I = not you) with an open equation: . . . + y + z + a + . . . (. . . + arm + brick + window + . . .). Rather than analyzing the world into discrete components, reducing their manyness to the One (=Two) of self-reflection, and ordering them by rank, it sums up a set of disparate circumstances in a shattering blow. It synthesizes a multiplicity of elements without effacing their hetero-geneity or hindering their potential for future rearranging. The modus operandi of nomad thought is affirmation, even when its apparent object is negative. Force is not to be confused with power. Power is the domestication of force. Force in its wild state arrives from outside to break constraints and open new vistas. Power builds walls.

The space of nomad thought is qualitatively different from State space. Air against earth. State space is "striated," or gridded. Move-ment in it is confined as by gravity to a horizontal plane, and limited by the order of that plane to preset paths between fixed and identifiable points. Nomad space is "smooth," or open-ended. One can rise up at any point and move to any other. Its mode of distribution is the *nomos*: arraying oneself in an open space (hold the street), as opposed to the *logos* of entrenching oneself in a closed space (hold the fort).

Capitalism and Schizophrenia is an effort to construct a smooth space of thought. It is not the first such attempt. Spinoza called nomad thought "ethics." Nietzsche called it "gay science." Artaud called it "crowned anarchy." To Maurice Blanchot, it is the "space of litera-ture." To Foucault, "outside thought."[17] Deleuze and Guattari also employ the terms "pragmatics" and "schizoanalysis," and in the intro-duction to *A Thousand Plateaus* describe a rhizome network strangling the roots of the infamous tree. One of the points of the book is that nomad thought is not confined to philosophy. Better, that it is a kind of philosophy that comes in many forms. Filmmakers and painters are philosophical thinkers to the extent that they explore the potentials of their respective mediums and break away from beaten paths. On a strictly formal level, it is mathematics and music that create the smoothest of the smooth spaces.[18] In fact, Deleuze and Guattari would probably be more inclined to call philosophy music with content than music a rarefied form of philosophy.

Deleuze recommends that you read *Capitalism and Schizophrenia* as you would listen to a record.[19] You don't approach a record as a closed book that you have to take or leave. There are always cuts that leave you cold. So you skip them. Other cuts you may listen to over and over again. They follow you. You find yourself humming them under your breath as you go about your daily business. *Capitalism and Schizophrenia* is conceived as an open system.[20] It does not pretend to have the final word. The authors' hope, however, is that elements of it will stay with a certain number of its readers, weaving new notes into the melodies of their everyday lives.

Each segment of writing, or "plateau" in the vocabulary of the second volume of *Capitalism and Schizophrenia*, is an orchestration of crashing bricks extracted from a variety of disciplinary edifices. They carry traces of their former emplacement, which give them a spin defining the arc of their vector. The vectors are meant to converge at a volatile juncture, but one that is sustained, as an open equilibrium of moving parts each with its own trajectory. The word "plateau" comes from an essay by Gregory Bateson's on Balinese culture, in which he found a libidinal economy quite different from the West's orgasmic orientation.[21] For Deleuze and Guattari, a plateau is reached when circumstances combine to bring an activity to a pitch of intensity that is not automatically dissipated in a climax leading to a state of rest. The heightening of energies is sustained long enough to leave a kind of afterimage of its dynamism that can be reactivated or injected into other activities, creating a fabric of intensive states between which any number of connecting routes could exist. Each segment of Deleuze and Guattari's writing tries to combine conceptual bricks in such a way as to construct this kind of intensive state in thought. The way the combination is made is an example of what they call "consistency" — not in the sense of a homogeneity, but as a holding together of disparate elements (also known as a "style").[22] A style in this sense, as a dynamic holding together or mode of composition, is not something limited to writing. Filmmakers, painters, and musicians have their styles, mathematicians have theirs, rocks have style, and so do tools, and technologies, and historical periods, even — especially — punctual events. Each section of *A Thousand Plateaus* carries a date because each tries to reconstitute a dynamism that has existed in other mediums at other times. The date corresponds to the point at which that particular dynamism found its purest incarnation in matter, the point at which it was freest from interference from other modes and rose to its highest degree of intensity. That never lasts more than a flash, because the world rarely leaves room for uncommon intensity, being in large measure an entropic trashbin of outworn modes that refuse to die.

The reader is invited to follow each section to the plateau that rises from the smooth space of its composition, and to move at pleasure from one plateau to the next. But it is just as good to ignore the heights. You can take a concept that is particularly of your liking and jump with it to its next appearance. They tend to cycle back. Some might call that repetitious. Deleuze and Guattari call it a refrain.

Most of all, the reader is invited to lift a dynamism *out* of the book and incarnate it in a foreign medium, whether painting or politics. Deleuze and Guattari delight in stealing from other disciplines, and they are more than happy to return the favor. Deleuze own image for a concept not as a brick but as a "tool box."[23] He calls his kind of philosophy "pragmatics" because its goal is the invention of concepts that do not add up to a system of belief or an architecture of propositions that you either enter or you don't, but instead pack a potential in the way a crowbar in a willing hand envelops an energy of prying.

The best way of all to approach a book by Deleuze and Guattari is to read it as a challenge: to pry open the vacant spaces the would enable you to build your life and those of the people around you into a plateau of intensity that would leave afterimages of its dynamism that could be reinjected into still other lives, creating a fabric of heightened states between which any number, the greatest number, of connecting routes would exist. Some might call that promiscuous. Deleuze and Guattari call it revolution.

The question is not, Is it true? But, Does it work? What new thoughts does it make possible to think? What new emotions does it make possible to feel? What new sensations and perceptions does it open in the body?

This volume is an introduction in the sense that an important part of its project is to relay readers back to Deleuze and Guattari's own writings. It is not an introduction in the sense of a succinct but complete account or an authoritative critique. The itinerary here is highly selective. Some key Deleuze–Guattarian terms do not appear at all. Some words they use in passing become key terms. The drift is as much away from the "originals" as toward them.

What follows is an attempt to play *Capitalism and Schizophrenia* the way its authors suggest. Not exactly like a record, though: with variations. Perhaps (I flatter myself) it will have created a monster.

The deviations from Deleuze and Guattari become more pronounced as the book plays on. Many passages are straightforward and explanatory in tone, many others are highly idiosyncratic. The idiosyncratic passages ought to be enough to destroy any misguided trust the reader may place in the authority of the explanatory passages.

The "scholarly apparatus" has been concentrated as much as possible in the notes. Readers interested in how developments in the body of the text relate to the "original" Deleuze and Guattari can turn to these notes for indications. Many digressions are also buried there,[24] evidence of overflow, of how hard it is to keep a text in departure from taking leave of itself.

meaning is
FORCE

Round One

"A phenomenon is not an appearance, or even an apparition, but a sign, a symptom which finds its meaning in an existing force."[1]

Take wood.[2] A woodworker who sets out to make a table does not pick just any piece of wood. She chooses the right piece for the application. When she works it, she does not indiscriminately plow into it with the plane. She is conscious of the grain and is directed by it. She reads it and interprets it. What she reads are signs. Signs are qualities[3] (color, texture, durability, and so on). And qualities are much more than simply logical properties or sense perceptions. They envelop a potential—the capacity to be affected, or to submit to a force (the action of the plane; later, the pressure of salt shakers and discourteous elbows), and the capacity to affect, or to release a force (resistance to gravity; or in a nontable application, releasing heat when burned). The presence of the sign is a contraction of time. It is simultaneously an indicator of a future potential and a symptom of a past. It envelops material processes pointing forward (planing; being a table) and backward (the evolution of the tree's species; the natural conditions governing its individual growth; the cultural actions that brought that particular wood to the workshop for that particular purpose). *Envelopment* is not a metaphor. The wood's individual and phylogenetic past exists as traces in the grain, and its future as qualities to be exploited. On a first, tentative level, meaning is precisely that: a network of enveloped material processes.

"A thing has as many meanings as there are forces capable of seizing it."[4] The presence of the sign is not an identity but an envelopment of difference, of a multiplicity of actions, materials, and levels. In a broader sense, meaning even includes the paths not taken. It is also all the forces that could have seized the thing but did not. It is an infinity of processes.

Interpretation consists in developing what is enveloped in the sign. The woodworker brings the qualities of the wood to a certain expression. His interpretation is a creation, not just of a physical object, but of a use-value, a cultural object, a table for steak and potatoes. Although the activity of the woodworker may seem to occur on a conscious level as a "will" or "intention" translated into action, it is no more subjective than the sign was merely objective. Only a Horatio Alger would say that it was by free choice alone that the woodworker-to-be became a manual laborer. The training he received is a particular institutionalization of craftsmanship formalizing knowledge accumulated over centuries by countless people. What product he makes from the wood is defined by the cultural needs and fashions of countless others. Interpretation is force, and an application of force is the outcome of an endless interplay of processes natural and historical, individual and institutional.

This gives us a second approximation of what meaning is: more a meeting between forces than simply the forces behind the signs. Force against force, action upon action, the development of an envelopment: meaning is the encounter of lines of force, each of which is actually a complex of other forces. The processes taking place actually or potentially on all sides could be analyzed indefinitely in any direction. There is no end, no unity in the sense of a totality that would tie it all together in a logical knot. No unity, but a region of clarity: tool meets wood. The meaning of an event can be rigorously analyzed, but never exhaustively, because it is the effect of an infinitely long process of selection determining that these two things, of all things, meet in this way at this place and time, in this world out of all possible worlds.

At first glance, this example might seem to reinforce traditional philosophical dualities: nature on the side of the sign, culture on the side of the interpreter; objective on one side, subjective on the other; matter, mind; raw material, production. None of these distinctions hold. The forces that brought the wood to the worker and the worker to the wood are a mixture of the cultural and the natural. A human body is a natural object with its own phylogenesis; from the point of view of the social forces that seize it, it is as much a raw material to be molded as is the wood from another perspective.

There is, however, a duality in play. The signs in the wood are not passive ("the thing itself is not neutral, and has more or less affinity with the force whose grasp it is currently in").[5] But they are less active than the tool. Their action is slower, their force weaker. They have an encounter with interpretation, and are overpowered. This is not to say that they are an amorphous substance given form by expression. Expression has no more a monopoly on form than content does on substance. There is substance on both sides: wood; woodworking body and tools. And there is form on both sides: both raw material and object produced have determinate forms, as do the body and tools.

The encounter is between two substance/form complexes, one of which overpowers the other. The forces of one are captured by the forces of the other and are subsumed by them, contained by them. "The value of something is the hierarchy of forces which are expressed in it as a complex phenomenon."[6] One side of the encounter has the value of a content, the other of an expression. But content and expression are distinguished only functionally, as the overpowered and the overpowering. Content is not the sign, and it is not a referent or signified. It is what the sign envelops, a whole world of forces. Content is formed substance considered as a dominated force-field.

The distinction between content and expression is not only functional, it is relative and reversible. Seen from the perspective of the dominating tool, the wood is a content. But from the perspective of the forces that went into it, it is an expression, of the water, sunlight, and carbon dioxide it captured and contains, of the genetic potential it did or did not pass on. The craftsman with hand to tool is an agent of expression, but from another angle he is the content of an institution, of the apprenticeship system or technical school that trained him. A content in one situation is an expression in another. The same thing can be both at different times or simultaneously, depending on which encounter is in question and from what angle.

The fact that the distinction between content and expression is relative and reversible does not mean that it is merely subjective, that we can have it any way we like it. Content and expression are indeed reversible, but the "perspective" according to which one becomes the other is not fundamentally the point of view of an outside observer. It is the angle of application of an actual force. Content and expression are reversible only in action. A power relation determines which is which. Since each power relation is in turn a complex of power relations, since each thing is taken up in a web of forces, the distinction may seem untenable. Complicated it is, but not untenable. The strands of the web can be unwound. We can follow the trajectory of a force across its entanglements with other forces (planing applied to a succession of woods, to different effect depending on the woods' qualities), and we can follow the trajectory of a thing as it passes from one knot of forces to the next (human body from technical school to workshop). Content and expression are in a state of what Deleuze and Guattari call "reciprocal presupposition." One does not exist without the other. They are mutually determining. And although they are always mixed in fact, they are distinct in nature.[7] Characterizing this distinction as "functional" might be misleading. The model is not one of utility but of struggle — a "hand-to-hand combat of energies."[8] The fact that armies always come in twos at least and soldiers by the brigade does not mean that a battle is unanalyzable. It may not be possible to know at every moment who has the upper hand, but the dust will settle. The distinction between victor and vanquished is real.

It is possible to make a further distinction by isolating the formal aspects of content and expression from their substance. The procedures of the woodworker have a method. This formal organization of functions could be called a "form of expression." Similarly, the qualities of the wood as raw material, the states they pass through as they become a table, and their condition as end product have an order and organization that could be called the "form of content."[9] The form of an expression or a content can be separated from its substance, but unlike the distinction between expression and content as a whole, the separation is only possible in thought.[10] A form — an organization of functions or qualities — is not materially separate from its substance. It *is* that substance, seen from the point of view of the actions to which it submits and the changes of state through which it passes. This time, the perspective is imposed from outside. The distinction, however, is a useful one. Dominating action (function) and change of state (change in quality) are two poles of the same process — the encounter between expression and content, in which each receives a determination in its struggle with the other. Distinguishing a form of expression from a form of content permits us to isolate that dynamic aspect of both formations at their determining point of impact. Thinking in terms of function and quality and bracketing the substances of expression and content is a way of evacuating the poles of dualistic processes. Rather than two irreducible formations, we have two edges of an interface. If we take the abstraction one step further and look at the interface itself—what happens *between* the form of expression and the form of content—we get a set of abstract relations between abstract points, the "diagram"[11] of a vectorial field: point (tool) bearing down at such and such an angle with so much pressure on point (wood) that yields to it to such and such a degree. . . . Form of expression and form of content fuse into the form of the encounter itself. We have extracted a unity from a duality. More precisely, we have created a unity that did not exist in actuality. That unity does not suppress the actual duality between content and expression, but exists alongside it, in thought. In fact, far from suppressing the duality, it replicates it. Our unity-in-thought is an expression enveloping the (double-edged) encounter as its content: a new content–expression duality, on a different, this time conceptual, level.

The form of the encounter we extract is not a "form" as we normally think of one. It is not static. It is a dynamism, composed of a number of interacting vectors. The kind of "unity" it has in no way vitiates that multiplicity—it is precisely an interaction between a multiplicity of terms, an interrelation of relations, an integration of disparate elements. It is a diagram of a process of becoming. Bracketing substance is a heuristic device that enables a real "translation" to take place (in the etymological sense of a "carrying across"): the interrelation of relations crosses from one substance (the thingness of tools and wood) to another (the ideality of thought). The dynamism is lifted out of one substance and incarnated in another. Thought repeats the interrelation in its own substance; it mimics the encounter, establishing a parallel network of vectors, but between different points (concepts instead of tools and wood). The dynamism can be rethingified, reactualized, by a further translation, into written or oral language (phonemes or written characters in their syntactical interrelation).

Meaning for Deleuze and Guattari is this process of translation. It involves a fundamental redundancy: what occurred once in wood is repeated in thought.[12] What occurred once as thought is repeated in written or spoken words. What occurred once as genesis (of a table) comes back inert (the flash of a thought, words that evaporate into the air, letters drying on a page).

Round Two

Meaning is not in the genesis of the thing, nor in the thought of that genesis, nor in the words written or spoken of it. It is in the process leading from one to the other. If meaning is as it has been described here — an interface between at least two force fields, or more specifically, between a form of content (an order and organization of qualities) and a form of expression (an order and organization of functions) — it stands to reason that there can be no direct causal relation between content and expression. An order of qualities (treeness, various stages of woodness, tableness) and an order of functions (being a person, being an apprentice, being a woodworker, making a table) have such different regimes of organization and lines of causality, and pertain to such different levels of reality, that on close inspection we see that between them there can be no actual "conformity, common form, nor even correspondence."[13] If we try to pinpoint the encounter, it slips from our grasp. The "hand-to-hand combat of energies" comes to a head when the plane shaves the wood. But many things intervene between what has been defined as the form of expression and the edge of the blade: a boss, a body, hands, technique, intentions, the handle of the tool. And between the blade and the form of content: a piece of wood, a customer order, rain, trucks, delivery, a tree. As we have seen, each of these elements is itself an encounter between force fields of content and force fields of expression, each with its own substance and form. Our original duality has fractured into countless new dualities proliferating in every direction, each encompassing clouds of heterogeneous elements without number. Expression can only cut through the fog and affect content by ceasing to be itself. It must become the content-tool in the dominating hand of the worker. It must surrender itself to the cut of the blade.

If this is true of the wood–tool encounter, it is also true of that encounter's encounter with the words we apply to it. Another infinite fracturing. Another interstitial void, sundering with brain waves and fingers and word processor keys and paper pulp and consonants. The expressiveness of thought getting packed into letters and phonemes, into forms of content which enter other causal circuits: speech, print, and electronic media. Thought surrendering itself to pen and pixel.

If meaning is a process of translation from one substance to another of a different order and back again, what it moves across is an unbridgeable abyss of fracturing. If meaning is the in-between of content and expression, it is nothing more (nor less) than the being of their "nonrelation."[14]

The *non* of the relation means that everything said earlier to support the fidelity of the diagram of meaning can be turned against it. If the diagram is indeed an integration of disparate elements which nevertheless retain their distinctness, and if it is struck with the same redundancy as the meaning-process it diagrams, but does not explicitly acknowledge that fact, then it is in a sense a sleight of hand. The only way out is to say that the diagram's deceptiveness is precisely what makes it faithful (and vice versa).

Replay: What the diagram diagrams is a dynamic interrelation of relations. The dynamism occurs twice: once as genesis in a state of things (tool to wood), and again in ideality (concept to concept).[15] The diagram combines a past (the working of the wood) and the future of that past (the thought of the woodworking), but it skips over its own genesis — the present of the content–expression encounter constitutive of thought (the unthought of thought). Actually, the dynamism occurs twice twice: after being translated into ideality (concept to concept) it is reexternalized in words (phoneme to phoneme; letter to letter) to resume its life among things in a new capacity. The diagram again combines a past (the thought of the woodworking) and the future of that past (pronunciation, publication), skipping over its own genesis, in this case the present of the content–expression encounter constitutive of speaking or writing (the unsaid of communication: afterthought). In each instance, the elided present, like the in-between of tool and wood, is at any rate a void. In skipping it, the diagram reduplicates the process it diagrams. The diagram is false, in that it contracts a multiplicity of levels and matters into its own homogeneous substance. But it is true, in that it envelops in that substance the same affect, and because it reproduces the in-betweenness of the affect in the fracturing of its own genesis. The expression of meaning is true in its falseness to itself, and false in its trueness to its content. Translation is repetition with a difference. If meaning is becoming, it is a becoming-other. It is the alienation of the same in the different, and the sameness of the different in its alienation from itself. The (non)relation is a *separation-connection*.

One more time: It is stretching things to say that the same affect is reproduced on both sides of the abyss of translation. The interrelation of relations between the wood and the tool bears no resemblance to that between concepts, which bears no relation to that between phonemes or letters: "no conformity or common form, nor even correspondence." The system of woodworking techniques is nevertheless unquestionably connected to changes in the wood's quality, and the words that envelop both are unquestionably connected to the bipolar process of woodworking, even if they are separated from it by an abyss or two. It is tempting to call these separation-connections parallelisms.[16] They are not: wood and tool are caught in their own circuits of causality and no sooner meet than are separated, one destined to be reimplanted in a kitchen, the other to gouge another wood; and no sooner do the words encounter that incision than they are swept away from both wood and tool, bound for circulation in a book. The separation-connection of translation is more an asymptotic relation than a parallelism. But it is a relation nonetheless. Meaning is the "relation of a nonrelation,"[17] the meeting, across a bottomless pit, of formations with skew trajectories.[18]

If meaning is a meeting between asymptotic lines of causality which have no common form or correspondence, who or what introduces them to each other? No one person or thing, but the infinity of forces, some willed, most fortuitous, that made that tree, brought it to that workshop, made that worker, brought her to that tool, made these words, brought them to these pages, made you, and—perhaps most mysterious of all—induced you to keep reading this interminably drawn-out example. What brings these formations together is the "abstract machine."[19] The abstract machine is interpretation. It is the meaning process, from the point of view of a given expression. Any sign, quality, or statement, as the trace of a process of becoming, can be considered a de facto diagram from which a formal diagram of the operative abstract machine could be developed. In the case of "meaning" as commonly understood (that is, as restricted to the conceptual or linguistic planes) the abstract machine is the subject of meaning (in the sense of the agency responsible for its unfolding), and the "meaning" is the formal diagram of forces extracted from the encounter in question. A diagram is a contraction of the abstract machine, which it envelops from a particular angle, recapitulates on a given level.

Deleuze and Guattari occasionally call meaning "essence" (Deleuze particularly, in such works as *Proust and Signs* and *The Logic of Sense*). It is called that because as the point of intersection between formations, it constitutes a point of contraction enveloping the entirety of their processes. The word "essence" should not be taken in any Platonic sense. The essence is always of an encounter; it is an *event*;[20] it is neither stable nor transcendental nor eternal; it is immanent to the dynamic process it expresses and has only an abyssal present infinitely fractured into past and future. The essence can be condensed into an integrated graphic representation of a vectorial field—a literal diagram, directional arrows between points (a favorite method in *A Thousand Plateaus*).[21] Or, as in *The Logic of Sense*, it can be stated as an infinitive: to-make-wood-into-table. Or, it can be spun out as the words of an expository analysis. Whatever form its diagram takes, the unity of the essence is always self-undermining. In the infinitive, the essence is resolvable into the verbal phrase "to make," and the noun phrase "wood-into-table." Even in its most deceptively homogeneous expression, the essence faithfully marks its own bipolar nature as a fragile integration of two "forms" separated by a hyphenated gulf. It is two-faced, suspended in the abyss looking to both edges at once. From the point of view of the form of content, this two-sidedness appears as an "attribute" (the tableness attributed to the wood). From the point of view of the form of expression, it is an "expressed" (the becoming table of the wood).[22] The attribute is not fundamentally a logical property assigned by an individual mind to a state of things. It is a real quality "attributed" to (produced in) the wood by the abstract machine, as enveloped in the infinitive. The expressed is not fundamentally a signified caught in an interplay of signifiers. It is a function involving a real transformation.

The envelopment in thought and language of a qualitative transformation in a state of things translates a dynamism onto a level at which different materials are in play and different modes of interrelation obtain. It adds and subtracts qualities, reattributing the attribution. The real transformation it effects is of a special kind. A conceptualization of woodworking makes it possible for the process to carry over into a set of verbal or written instructions. These in turn permit the process to carry over into an institutional framework. Institutionalization makes woodworking reproducible (through the training of woodworkers; through their insertion into a system of work in which they can be ordered to repeat the process as needed) and perfectible (through the accumulation and dissemination of technique). The infinitive is an especially apt form in which to express an essence: translation on the level of thought and language catapults the inexhaustible complexity of each unique encounter's conditions of emergence into an indefinite circuit of reproduction and systematic variation. Translation adds another level of definition (de-finition) to an event's dynamism. It repotentializes it, makes it repeatable, multiplies it. But the multiplication of the event is also its domestication. Its dynamic potential is simultaneously carried to a higher power and dulled, diffracted, captured in a regularizing network of forces. Since the action of this reproductive network of forces is qualitatively different from that of the productive network of forces from which the event arose in all its sharpness, it deserves another name: "power." Force culminates a boundless potential. It takes the uniqueness of the event to its limit. Power delimits and distributes the potential thus released.[23]

The institutional dimension of reproducibility does not imply a firmness under foot or fixity of connection. Since every repetition of a process repotentializes it, adding and subtracting qualities, there is always the possibility that the event will be carried far enough afield that it will fall from its accustomed framework. The event remains on uncertain ground. A diagram gives us a handle on it by expressing it as a bipolar integration. Still, if we move out from cutting edge of any particular occurrence of an encounter forward or backward in time or in any direction in space, the formations in interaction—from one point of view so unified in their effect (a table is born)—crumble beneath us. As we have seen, the content was, is, and will be many things. The expression was, is, and will be many functions. The things were, are, and will be many functions. The functions were, are, and will be many things. Fractured, all. Every step falls in a void. No sooner do we have a unity than it becomes a duality. No sooner do we have a duality than it becomes a multiplicity. No sooner do we have a multiplicity than it becomes a proliferation of fissures converging in a void. The fact that an event can be reproduced (the fact that the dynamism is connectable, can be reinserted into states of things) does not belie its utter uniqueness (its separation or difference from all other events; the absolute singularity of the conditions of occurrence of any given reinsertion). For re-production is translation, a transformational carrying-over to another site or substance. In itself, the event has only extinction. Its accomplishment is its evaporation in the infinite interplay of its seething components. The uniqueness of the event means that its happening is always also its undoing. Its reproducibility means that it will nevertheless come again to be undone: to each event, many happening returns.

Meaning is the contraction of difference and repetition in a self-expiring expression. Power is the resuscitation of meaning.

In the separation-connection of the act of meaning, the separation runs deeper than the connection. For Deleuze, the essence of meaning, the essence of essence, is best expressed by two infinitives: "to cut," "to die."[24] A person is either still alive or already dead. The moment of death is ungraspable. When sword sears flesh—on second thought, let's stick with our example—when plane gouges wood, you cannot pinpoint any contact. Zeno's paradox. Halve the distance between the blade and the surface, halve it again, and again . . . the blade will never reach its goal. Yet it cuts. The event of the gouging is empty, instantaneous, insubstantial. The wood is always about to be cut, or has just been cut. The cutting has no present, only the scintillating abyss of a future-past.[25] It is a meaning, but a meaning without depth, only multiplying surface (the surface of blade and the surface of the wood; the surface of the blade and the two surfaces of the wood after incision). It is an event, but in the infinitive, with no recognizable tense. It can be enveloped in words, but that doesn't make it any safer. Words can cut, in a manner of speaking—someone *told* the woodworker to make that table. The boss's words did not physically gouge, but gouge they did, like an incorporeal blade crossing the void between the inertness of sounds evaporating into the workshop air and the formative action of a tool in all its material density. The same words and tool may have combined in the past, and may combine again. Has cut, will cut. Definite tenses keeping company in time. In the slash between their future and their past: "to cut," as always timeless and alone.

The complexity of the event leads inevitably to the kind of paradoxical formulations in which Deleuze delights in *The Logic of Sense*: essence as instantaneous and eternal, different and the same, unique and repetitious, chance and destiny, active and extinct ("sterile," evaporative),[26] surface and depth, absolutely particular and superhumanly abstract, empty and overfull, sense and nonsense, the unity of a multiplicity, and so on. The paradoxes should not be taken as mere frivolities. They are serious attempts to pack meaning into the smallest possible space without betraying it with simplification. The meaning can always be unpacked, in precise and useful ways. A paradox is not a contradiction. A paradox abolishes contradiction. It does not negate, it compounds. The unity, duality, and multiplicity of meaning are not mutually contradictory. They are moments or aspects of a process. They are mutually determining, in reciprocal presupposition. But they can be unraveled. Each has its expository efficacity, as *Anti-Oedipus* and *A Thousand Plateaus* set out to show. They may be thought of as levels, or "plateaus." We can operate on whichever level seems adequate to the problem we are dealing with, and can choose to emphasize that level's connection to or separation from the others (the relation or the *non*). We must remember, however, that the ground is ultimately unstable, and should be prepared to jump at any moment.

Each of these levels is real. The multiplicity is a real heterogeneity of sites and substances. The duality is a real distinction between the overpowered and overpowering formations those materials are taken up in. The unity is a real "diagram" enveloping the real dynamism of a duality and depositing it, perchance, on a page. The unity is something else again: the real monism of matter. For there is only one world, one nature, and—below the quantum level of matter and beyond the synapses of our brains—one unified field.[27] Which never ceases to divide into a multiplicity of singular elements and composite materials, into dualities of content and expression, into unifying conceptual and linguistic contractions. The unity is before, as "cause," lost in the gritty "depths" of the genesis of matter, and it is after, as "effect," evaporating in the "sterile" atmosphere of thought and language. It is twice. In between: the future-past event of meaning.[28]

Meaning as local fissure and cosmic contraction. Paradox and the laughter of the gods.

Round Three

Being is fractal. In non-Euclidean geometry, a fractal is a figure with a fractional number of dimensions; for example, something between a point and a line, a line and a plane, or a plane and a volume. The easiest fractal to understand is one between a line and a plane. Start with a straight line, measure it into thirds, build an equilateral triangle with the middle segment as its base, remove the base segment, repeat the process on the resulting four segments, repeat the process on the resulting sixteen segments, and so on to infinity. Now start with an equilateral triangle and perform the same operation on all three sides simultaneously. What you end up with looks like a snowflake. But the apparent interiority of the figure is misleading. The outline is endlessly dividing and is therefore infinitely riddled with proliferating fissures. The figure can nevertheless be assigned a precise value: it has 1.261859 dimensions. It is a specific figure that can be accurately described, and even has a name (the Koch curve). In spite of its infinite fissuring, it *looks like* and *can function as* a unified figure if we adopt a certain ontological posture toward it: monism as produced meaning, optical effect. On close inspection, it is seen to be a network of bifurcation: duality. On still closer inspection, it becomes a web of proliferating fissures in infinite regress toward the void. Such a figure can be expressed as an equation (paradox with precision). Like the directions above, the equation does not strictly speaking describe the figure, as one would describe the contours of a static form. Instead, it maps a procedure (the equation is an "abstract machine" as the principle of a becoming).[29] The equation is a set of potential operations (affects; vectorial relations between points; abstract dynamism) that comes "before," as "cause," but is not a sufficient cause, since it needs someone or something (another abstract machine) functioning on a different level of reality to actualize it by writing it down or working it out in a diagram (expression jumping the abyss and moving into content through the intervention of an asymptotic line of causality). The diagram is drawable, but only if the fissuring is arbitrarily stopped at a certain level (produced meaning as evaporative end effect; monism as the redundancy of the inert double; momentary suspension of becoming). We can operate on any of these levels, depending on our purpose. Monism (contraction-integration), duality (cut), and approach-to-the-void (the unreachable limit toward which the process tends; death) are in mutual presupposition but are really distinct, and are therefore capable of being unraveled and minutely analyzed (even death, as Blanchot has shown).

We skipped multiplicity. In one sense, it is the reproducibility of the fractal, the potential for generating from the same equation a variety of diagrams, each of which would be different depending on when the process was stopped. But as we have seen, there is a multiplicity inherent to every meaning encounter taken separately, in that each diagram envelops a number of heterogeneous levels. This aspect is missing in this example because the fractal proliferates according to a principle of self-similarity. The transformations are identical, so any two segments on any level are symmetrical. What is missing is chance. If chance variations are thrown in (the "throw of the dice" in *The Logic of Sense* and *Nietzsche*), the endless snowflaking will deviate into a truly random figure in which no two segments are the same, but which is still mathematically describable. As it proliferates, it will snake in and out on itself, creating a formation resembling a shoreline with islands. If randomization is taken one step farther and the chance variations of line-draw and cut are freed from the constraint of a triangular starting point, the fracturing will fill more and more space, eventually producing a unified plane-effect. This is called a "random walk." The "plane" of Life itself (the "cosmos"; nature-culture; the abstract machine in its widest connotation; monism in its other aspect, as generative matter-energy, an abstract dynamism at a level at which it *is* a sufficient cause) is a "space-filling fractal" of infinite dimension. Computer graphics employs fractals generated by controlled stochastic procedures (programmed deviations) to simulate natural formations.[30] But nature is never effectively controlled (causing but uncaused; founding but unfounded). Every moment in life is a step in a random walk. Uncannily familiar as the shore may seem, looking back reveals no Eden of interiority and self-similarity, no snowflake state to regain. Ahead lies nothing with the plane reliability of solid ground. You can never predict where the subatomic particle will appear, or what will flash across the synapse (pure instantaneous event). Once thrown, however, the dice are destiny.

God as a drunken gambler. Dionysus snickering at fate as he steals an extra turn.[31]

Pause

What do we have so far? A slew of slippery concepts. They seem to congregate into two groupings. One set is best suited to a semiotic analysis of local encounters: affect, quality, function, form and substance of content, form and substance of expression, reciprocal presupposition, redundancy, contraction-integration, asymptotic causality, diagram. The other to far-reaching speculation: meaning, nonsense, chance, destiny, being, becoming, immanence, cosmos, void. Putting the two together is the most fun.

Neither set, taken alone or together, is meant to add up to a system or a universally applicable model. In fact, they are specifically designed to make that impossible. On the speculative level, they self-combust in playful paradox. Since no two people's sense of play is alike, no two people will find a given formulation satisfying. Pick any local encounter and apply the semiotic set to it. You will find that you cannot use the concepts without changing them or the way they interrelate. Every situation is unique and requires a specially tailored repertory of concepts. The concepts were formulated to help meet the challenge of thinking the unique. That is, to meet the challenge of thinking—for there is nothing in this world *but* uniqueness. They are less slippery than supple. They should under no circumstances be crystallized into a methodology. Like all of Deleuze and Guattari's concepts, they are logical operators or heuristic devices to be adapted as the situation requires. Deleuze and Guattari themselves cannot be accused of making a method of them. No two books muster the same array. In *Proust and Signs*, for example, Deleuze describes four Proustian "worlds" with very different semiotic organizations. In *Cinema I*, he describes no less than sixteen different categories of cinematic signs, none of which would be especially welcome in any world of Proust's.[32] When Deleuze writes solo he tends to use different kinds of conceptual mixes and concentrates on different aspects of problems than Guattari.[33] Everything is up for continual reinvention.

Focusing in on another localized encounter will illustrate this conceptual variability, and lead us by a different route back to broader questions of language and meaning.

Round Four

Take a person in an institution, a high school for example.[34] What is the content? It is not, as common sense might dictate, what is taught in the school. That, as any graduate knows, is largely irrelevant. The answer becomes obvious if the question is rephrased: What goes into a school? The content is the students. More precisely, it is human beings of a certain age and a certain level of ability. More precisely still, it is the human potential of those beings, for as we have seen, content is ultimately a bundle of forces both actual and potential, and is not reducible to an object. Since content receives form only through its encounter with expression, and since the bundle of forces that is content is a dominated one, the most final formulation of school content would be: a selected set of humanoid bodies grasped as a biophysical matter to be molded. There are actually two levels of content in play here. Deleuze and Guattari distinguish between "substance of content" and "matter of content." A "substance" is a formed matter (the thing understood as an object with determinate qualities), and a "matter" is a substance abstracted from its form, in other words isolated from any particular encounter between content and expression (the thing as all the forces it could embody in all the encounters it could have, either as content or expression). Thus "human beings of a certain age and a certain level of ability" (the entering students as formed by primary school) is the substance of content, and "humanoid bodies grasped as a biophysical matter to be molded" (the students' human potential) is the matter of content.[35]

What every student body as substance of content enters is a school. Thus the form of content is the architecture of the school itself. What is the form of expression? If a form of expression is an order and organization of functions, then in this case it is the complex of administrative rules, laws, and traditions that determine how a school is laid out and what it does; the substance of expression is the phonemes and letters embodying those functions. What a school does as an overall process is its "essence." What might that be? Ask any politician what a school is for, and the answer will be: To build good citizens. The essence, therefore, is "to-make-young-body-docile." We saw before that the infinitive expressing an essence can be split in two. This time we will make them gerundives: from the angle of expression, the essence is "the making of a docile worker" (future aspect); from the angle of content, it is "the making docile of an adolescent" (past aspect). The changing placement of the "of" takes us from the pole of expression to the pole of content by switching the emphasis from the function, "the making," to the quality, "docile," from action to passion.

The interrelation between these terms is quite different than in the woodworking example. Content and expression are relatively disengaged. The school board's rulings are not literally hammered into the students. Substance of content and substance of expression do not come to a head in the way they did when tool met wood. The substance of content is not embedded in the form of content, but walks the halls and even out the door. The gulf between content and expression is wider, making the fractal bifurcations of the process more immediately visible. A student, for example, has a form to walk around in, so there are in fact two forms of content, each relating to the matter of content in different ways. The definition given earlier of the form of content as an order and organization of qualities applies to the student form, but not to the school, for which another definition would have to be invented. Student and school join in the same content formation, but belong to very different lines of causality, having been determined as content by different forms of expression for different lengths of time (a school never graduates). This example has more levels or "strata" and more causal lines directly involved in the actual encounter. The terms of the analysis have to be multiplied and modified accordingly.[36]

We need to ask one final question: What is the subject of the expressive process of schooling? Out of all possible contents, something selected human beings of a certain age and ability. Out of all the potential in the human body, something selected its capacity to be a docile worker. Out of all the ways a body can be docile, something selected the particular kinds of docility our schools develop. This selective agency is the subject. The subject is not psychological, it is not contained in any one mind. It is in the interactions *between* people. Which is not to say that it is simply interpersonal: it is also in the technology that defined the kinds of productive work our docility serves. Which is not to say that it is simply socioeconomic: it is also in the raw materials at the basis of that technology and in the genes that define the physical and intellectual potential of the human body. Which is not to say that it is material in any deterministic way: genes result from chance mutation. The subject is a transpersonal abstract machine, a set of strategies operating in nature and spread throughout the social field. It is a whole world composed of an infinity of causal lines on countless levels, all fractured by chance. Although it is a whole chaotic world, it is our world—and from the very precise angle of the very localized event of a high school graduation. That event lies in a region of relative stability and clarity. With the proper conceptual tools, we can unravel its several strands.

That the subject of meaning is transpersonal is perhaps easier to accept for an expression of woodiness or studenthood than for one, say, of commitment. Linguistic expression per se is psychological, yes? Meaning in the strictly linguistic sense is in the mind, no?

We must adapt our terms again. The form of expression on the most general level is composed of words and their combinations. The substance of expression is the phonemes of speech, or the letters on a printed page, or for that matter the electronic zeros and ones of machine language or the oscillations of radio waves—it is the materiality of the medium. The form of content is the state of things within which the words themselves are generated (the content–expression encounter enveloped "vertically" in the linguistic form of expression), *and* the more distant and autonomous state of things with which the words are coupled—if there is one (woodworking; schooling: the content–expression encounter enveloped "horizontally" in the words applied to it). Since words can and do couple with nonexistent things, or simply forgo any pretense of horizontal encounter, the "vertical" form of content is the crucial one. The substances of content are the respective states of things of the two forms of content considered in their materiality. The content as a whole is two forms-substances of content considered as force fields, *and* the relations of force obtaining between them.

The subject is the agency that selects which words are generated and coupled with which states of things. It is an abstract machine which, as always, is immediately bipolar: on one side it organizes a form-substance of content, and on the other a form-substance of expression. On the side of content it is called a "machinic assemblage"; on the side of expression it is called a "collective assemblage of enunciation." Both are abstract machines in their own right. The (non)relation by which the overall abstract machine brings the content formed by the machinic assemblage and the expression formed by the collective assemblage of enunciation into an asymptotic encounter is called a "double articulation."[37] A subject which is bipolar, each pole of which is a subject in its own right, and so on—no psychological unity here. Even considered as a diagram enveloping the abstract machine(s), the linguistic expression has no subjective interiority, only a redundancy of outsides: the meaning-effect as evaporative double, and the dynamic in-between, or interrelation of relations, that it transformationally duplicates. Of course, conscious thoughts and intentions play a part in the process, but only as one line of causality among the many proliferating in the fractal void.

A classic example: saying "I do" at a wedding ceremony.[38] There is no horizontal content with which the words "I do" couple. The expression "I do" does not diagram a more or less distant encounter. It exists only in relation to its vertical content, to the dynamic state of things within which it is generated. Its relation to its vertical content is one of culmination: it is the end effect of an interrelation of relations that it envelops as its own genesis. Once spoken, the words "I do" evaporate irretrievably into the air. They have no afterlife; they are not written down; they are not retranslated into content to cut like a blade. They expire with the breath that speaks them. Yet in their very evanescence they have lasting repercussions. They do not couple with or insert themselves into another encounter: they couple bodies in their own encounter. They coincide with (double) and culminate (trans-form) the very state of things that generates them. Say "I do," and your life will never be the same. Your legal, social, and familial status instantly changes, along with your entire sexual, psychological and financial economy. You have been pronounced man and wife. You may file a joint tax return.

"I do" is a connector: it binds two bodies. And it is a component of passage: it transfers those bodies into a new network of power relations, in a kind of leap in place.[39] Before you open your mouth you are one thing. By the time you close it you have landed in another world. Nothing touched you, yet you have been transformed. "I do" effects an "incorporeal transformation" (another name for event).[40]

A particular man and a particular woman say "I do." Their words undoubtedly have personal meaning for them in their heart of hearts. But their personal intention is not in itself responsible for the magical transformation that has touched their lives. What has brought them to say those words and what makes those words effectively transforma-tive is too big to fit into a single mind. It is a complex interplay of laws, customs, social pressure, and tax law. That is the subject of the enunciation: a transpersonal abstract machine contracting countless levels and enveloping many matters. The stereotypical nature of the expression is an indication that it is fundamentally impersonal. "I do" is not a particularly original thing to say at a wedding. If it expresses an individual subjectivity, it is a remarkably dull one. The "I" is not a person. It is a social function.

"I do" as a form of expression can be reiterated in another wedding, in which case it repeats the incorporeal transformation. But there is one proviso: the words must be spoken by a different couple. Same event, different bodies. A variation on a theme. As real as the variations are, the overall diagram remains the same. Roughly the same interrelation of relations is actualized. Roughly the same social function is fulfilled. The same "I" speaks—only through a different body. Demonic possession would be a more fitting model for this process than personal expression. Ripe young bodies animated by secondhand words. People speaking without being fully conscious of the inhuman agency that speaks through them. Ghoulish indirect discourse. Glossolalia.

There are ghosts in the machine. In the abstract machine, as uncaused cause of expression: the abstract machine of marriage cannot make the essence without making it essentially redundant. It cannot say "I do" just once. Marriage would be meaningless if only one couple did it. The stereotypical nature of the culminating expression does not detract from the event. It is of its essence. The abstract machine must bring a parade of bodies to stand in the same enunciative position. Into the ears of each new bride and groom it whispers an incantation spoken through the ages by legions of our dead. Ancient words, lent new life, brush across poised lips. Bodies leap in place in ritualized dance.

Who has the salt? I do. The form of expression "I do" can be reiterated in a way that does not repeat the same incorporeal transformation. The same words, two entirely different meanings. Or, to use Foucault's terminology, two entirely different "statements."[41] What makes them different is not of a grammatical or logical nature. On those levels they are identical. The determining factor is most immediately the state of things within which the words are spoken.

The "I do" of marriage is a prime example of what the linguist J. L. Austin calls a "performative" statement: words that directly accomplish an act and change a state of things merely by being said. The performative is often understood as a special category of statements. That is how Austin himself saw it when he began his investigations. In the end, however, he was led to conclude that the performative is less a special category than the most manifest instance of a transformational "dimension" within every statement.[42] Every statement conveys, in addition to any meaning it may have in the narrow sense of semantic (in our vocabulary, "horizontal") content, a commanding "illocutionary" (nondiscursive) "force" responsible for its pragmatic success (or lack thereof, in the case of an "unhappy" outcome of language-culminated force). Deleuze and Guattari go even further. Following Oswald Ducrot, they question whether it is possible to separate semantic content from the nondiscursive force in any rigorous way.

A simple example illustrates the point: "Paul suspects John's arrival." The semantic content of the statement bears on a mental act of Paul's concerning John's location. In order to convey that meaning, the statement tacitly posits that John has in fact arrived or is arriving. In other words, it immediately conveys a presupposition without which the literal semantic content could not be expressed, but which is not itself manifestly stated. The literal meaning is simultaneous with and indissoluble from this "implicit presupposition"; both are couched in a single grammatical sequence. To emit an implicit presupposition, Ducrot says, is to say something in such a way that it need not be said.[43] Every presupposition of this kind is also simultaneously and indissolubly an existential act: to say something in a way that makes it go without saying is to *do* something. Even if that something is only to direct or deflect a conversation, that in itself is a lot: to make things *go* without saying could stand as a definition of "ideology" as a motor of social relations. But that term obscures an essential point about incorporeal transformations: the doing of a saying is not determined by or primarily aimed at the level of ideas ("ideo-"). Which logical presupposition embedded in a particular grammatical sequence at any given moment is in no way determined by a "logos" ("-logy"), or unifying groundwork upon which an enduring referential truth may be asserted or a system of belief built.[44] Every meaning encounter, as we have seen, is a groundless becoming, not an assertion of being. What becomes of a meaning encounter is attributable to its unique and contingent "context," the nondiscursive network of forces within which particular speaking bodies are positioned and which ordains what those bodies say-do and thus where-how they subsequently go. "Context" is an infinitely complex concertation of forces, the logical unity of which can only be conceived as one of movement: the direction in which a speech-driven body is impelled. Impulsion is a general function of language.

Unity-in-movement is the only unity language knows. Extralinguistic yet internal to language, it should rightfully be the object of linguistics. Language by essence includes extraverbal factors.

"Context" is what has been identified here as "vertical content": a dynamic formation whose encounter with expression effects a transformation guided by an abstract machine and culminating in a statement. It is imprecise to say that the unity-in-movement produced by the "context" and culminated by a statement is "internal" to language. If our description has been accurate, language has no inside. If it involves two basic formations (of content and expression), and if those formations are force fields, in other words sets of relations between points of pressure and resistance, and if the encounter between them is therefore an interrelation of relations, then what brings them together is best described as a field of exteriority: a relating of interrelations of relations (in a nonrelation). It is more accurate to say that context is "immanent" to rather than "internal" to language. As we saw earlier, the dynamism of a meaning encounter, the unity-in-movement produced by a context, may be captured and inducted into a network of repetition (variation) called "power." Context is the juncture at which force is translated into power, in a shared field of exteriority.[45]

If context is immanent to language, language as a whole is nondiscursive. Meaning is only secondarily what the words say literally and logically. At bottom, it is what the circumstances say, in other words — and outside words. The head of the house says "Who has the salt?" (read: Don't just sit there, for Christ's sake, hand it to him). The minister says "I now pronounce you man and wife" (read: Be fruitful and multiply, for Christ's sake). The principal says "Here's your diploma" (read: Get a job, sucker). Every meaning encounter conveys an implicit presupposition which more or less directly takes the form of a parenthetical imperative. One whispered by an inhuman agency that borrows for a moment a pair of lips.

Deleuze and Guattari call the repetition-impulsion of this imperative function immanent to language the "order-word."[46] "Order" should be taken in both senses: the statement gives an order (commands) and establishes an order (positions bodies in a force field). The order-word culminates transformations that place the concerned body or bodies in a position to carry out implicit obligations or follow a preset direction.

In everyday language, the French term for order-word, *mot d'ordre*, means "slogan." "I do" is the slogan for marriage and salt. Man and woman are transformed by "I do" into the sacred procreative partnership of husband and wife, in accordance with the laws of God and the State. Eater of food is transformed by "I do" into polite family member, in accordance with the laws of etiquette.

You do?—then do it—it's as good as done. Implicit presupposition / existential imperative / incorporeal transformation. The trinity formula for meaning in motion.

The ordering force of language is most readily apparent in conventional situations, especially explicit rituals marking a life transition.[47] But as the John–Paul example indicates, not all words that accomplish an act by being said change a state of things so dramatically. Many statements require other words or physical actions to complete any transformation that might transpire. For example, one effectively asks a question by saying "Is . . . ?," but the change in a state of things induced by the question is only consummated after receiving (or failing to receive) an answer. The dinner-table "I do" effectively states a willingness to accept a responsibility, but actually only positions one to be polite, and fails in its mission if not followed by the salt shaker. The transformation into polite family member thus effected is of a different kind than the marriage transformation: it is repeatable for the same body and easily reversible, and in the history of a family most likely is repeated and reversed many times. It is less punctual, but no less an order-word for that. Earlier, we glossed over the status of what is taught in the schools. It is indeed irrelevant from the point of view of its intellectual content. But it does play a role. It conveys myriad mini-order-words, later summed up in the students' mute gesture of taking their diploma. Who has the answer? *I do*. I can make the required distinctions. I know what is masculine and feminine, in conduct as in grammar. I know who's boss, historically and in class. I know what "democracy" is. I'm ready to go out and exploit or be exploited. Although the teacher does not hammer, the content of school courses is indeed the analog of the woodworking tool. What is taught is a subsidiary form-substance of content in which the form of expression of schooling must necessarily alienate itself in order to effectively interface with the primary content of the students and do its job of making them mouth the endless incantation of social acceptability. The principal's graduation speech envelops this lengthy incorporeal brain-carving process in an implicit presupposition: the duty and right to enter the wonderful world of work.[48]

Language is an endless high school. Every utterance, innocuous as it may seem, takes place in a social or institutional context that inflects it with an imperative, however indirectly. Every utterance is struck, however faintly, with the redundancy of an anonymous murmur.[49] Every society reproduces standardized contexts within which every word spoken echoes those spoken in all the others. Every word is laden with the implicit presupposition of what "one" says-thinks-does in such a circumstance. "I" is not an expressive subject, only a linguistic marker indicating what body is addressed by the whispered imperative immanent to that particular position within that particular state of things.[50] What effectively speaks is the transpersonal agency that creates the context by orchestrating a local encounter between content and expression and by bringing that body to the "I" of that site. The "I" does not inhabit the body, but is attached to the place of enunciation. It insinuates itself into the body tapped for possession by the "one" haunting the premises. I mouths one's words. Every body has as many "I"s as there are "ones" in the world it moves through. The first person only repeats here and now what the anonymous third person of the abstract machine has already said elsewhere in the mists of time, and will undoubtedly say again. Free indirect discourse—reported speech not attributable to an identified speaker—is the fundamental mode of language.[51]

A summary: A meaning is an encounter between force fields. More specifically, it is the "essence" (diagram, abstract machine) of that encounter. Its own essence (the meaning of meaning) is the incorporeal transformation, which comes in many varieties. At its most incisive, it is as instantaneous and as localized as the cut of the knife. But it can also be spread out (across many a classroom) and drawn out (over grades and years) without losing its character. Even at its most diffuse it still participates in the mystery of death. Either you are or you aren't. (Even though you can never put your finger on the specific answer that made a young body into a willing worker.)

The order-word as existential imperative (standardized function of existence) is the motor of the incorporeal transformation. It is the unsaid doing of a saying. As enveloped in an actual statement it—not the phoneme, word, or proposition—is the elementary unit of language.[52] At its most potent, it is a connector that couples bodies and at the same time a component of passage that instantly transfers them from one set of power relations to another (thus culminating the incorporeal transformation, of which it is the operator). It too comes in many varieties. It can be a connector but not a component of passage, or vice versa. It may be a summation of many a mini-order-word (correct answers). Even at its most cumulative, it does not lose its character as an implicit presupposition, or anonymous command immanent to a state of things: do it.

Pause

Before we do, we need to take a look at what is probably the most pivotal, and is certainly the least understood, concept in Deleuze and Guattari's philosophical vocabulary: virtuality. Its importance is rivaled only by the complete lack of interest in it thus far displayed by the (admittedly few) commentators who have written on their work.

At several turns in the preceding remarks we have observed phenomena of redundancy, and all along the way have been fighting an apparent ambiguity or doubleness in the terminology itself. "Order-word," for example, did double duty, designating both a given statement culminating an incorporeal transformation and a social function. An incorporeal transformation was a change in a state of things and the diagram of that change. The diagram was a literal drawing, verbal formulation, or equation, but also the essence enveloped in these. Essence was on paper and in thought, as well as being an abstract machine in the depths of matter. The "I" spoke, but only as spoken by a "one" splattered across the social field.

The distinction between the dual aspects of these concepts was expressed variously as the difference between an evaporative effect and a generative process marshaling cosmic energies. It was implied that the same distinction was also between the particular and the abstract. These formulations are of only limited usefulness: under certain conditions an evaporative effect can be reinserted into a state of things and convert into a cause, and a fully adequate abstract expression of any phenomenon must be tailored to its uniqueness and is thus absolutely particular to it.

Finally, the distinction was presented as the difference between something actually in existence and a potential for existence. This is getting closer to the mark, but only if it is borne in mind that "existence" is not a static presence (being is a fractalization, the present an abyss), and that a potential is not a possibility. The first point is a generally accepted premise of poststructuralist thought, but the second might still sound strange. Understanding how a potential differs from a possibility is the key to Deleuze and Guattari's concept of the virtual, and a passport to the adroit use of Capitalism and Schizophrenia.[53]

Round Five

Back to the fractal. We have seen that a fractal has three levels or dimensions: the monism of its optical effect, the dualism of its mode of composition and the void of its infinitely proliferating division. These are strictly simultaneous and mutually determining. In other words, they are in reciprocal presupposition. In spite of their inseparability, the fractal as such can only *exist* on the second level, in the dualism of its composition. As a unity, it has ceased to be a fractal to become a snowflake or a plane. In the void, it is pure division, an insubstantial cutting function that does but does not be. A thing can exist only in relation to at least two dimensions that belong to it yet lie beyond its being. As a first approximation, and in affront to their simultaneity, those dimensions can be thought of as dimensions of time: the future of the fractal's reception (it can effectively be a plane if observed from the proper perspective), and the abyssal past of its genesis.

An important aside: The future "perspective" in question is not reducible to a subjective point of view on an object. It is a perceptual event which, like every meaning encounter, is an interrelation of relations between two dynamic formations, one of which overpowers the other and adapts it to its own ends. The becoming-plane of the fractal is a potential for transformational capture inherent in its essence, and in that of the observer. It is a perspective in Nietzsche's sense: an "objective perspective" that includes both observer and observed, but on their outside edges, in the actual interaction between their essences.[54] A fractal "in itself" (that is, prior to a particular encounter) is never a plane, but it can "function as" a plane because the human visual apparatus will grasp it as such to certain effect at a certain point in the fractal's unfolding. The same corrective should be applied to the "outside perspective" discussed earlier in relation to the logical extraction of forms of content or expression from their substances. Logical analysis, like any thought or perception, grasps its "object" from a particular angle, and attributes it potentials that it did not previously have (being in a book; being part of a system of institutional inculcation and practice). The thing "in itself" is only the sum total of the graspings to which it lends itself, a set of angles of potential intervention by outside bodies. All thought and perception are therefore partial, in the double sense that they are never all-encompassing, and that they follow upon a constitutional affinity, or mutual openness, of two bodies for one another. Partiality does not preclude objectivity.[55] Thought-perception is always *real* and always *of the outside*. The thinking-perceiving body moves out to its outermost edge, where it meets another body and draws it into an interaction in the course of which it locks onto that body's affects (capacities for acting and being acted upon) and translates them into a form that is functional for it (qualities it can recall). A set of affects, a portion of the object's essential dynamism, is drawn in, transferred into the substance of the thinking-perceiving body. From there, it enters new circuits of causality. Thought-perception is a foray by one body into another's essence in such a way that the second is carried outside itself. Thought-perception reaches into things, launches them up through the atmosphere of language, and in the same motion returns them, altered, into the depths of matter.[56]

To continue: future reception, past genesis. The fractal proper is in-between. To pass into its future as a plane it must cease to be itself. But to remain in its dynamic present it must continue to divide, rushing impossibly into the void of its own past. Two thresholds, two ways of passing: a relative limit above which a thing ceases to be itself but gets a new lease on life in a different mode; and an absolute limit below which no thing can go but upon which all things tread. A threshold leading across the synapses toward a new being, and a foundation of nonbeing. The dimension of the future mode and past genesis are absolutely real for the fractal but are not it; it cannot exist without them, but they do not exist with it. To avoid the paradoxical formulations the use of temporal expressions force upon us, Deleuze and Guattari say that these dimensions are "virtual." The virtual is the future-past of the present: a thing's destiny and condition of existence (as one—the second meaning of monism again). To avoid philosophical baggage, they are more likely to say that a thing is "actual" than that it "exists." To drive it home that actuality is dynamic they use the word "becoming" in place of "being." A thing's actuality is its duration as a process—of genesis and annihilation, of movement across thresholds and toward the limit. The virtual is real and in reciprocal presupposition with the actual, but does not exist even to the extent that the actual could be said to exist. It *subsists* in the actual or is immanent to it. The element of immanence—thought-matter—could be called eternal, but not without introducing an unwelcome religious or Platonic tinge. Nietzsche's term, "untimely," suits it best.[57]

There was one other way in which a fractal can cease to be, but this time without ceasing to be itself. It can come out the far side of thought and be diagrammed at a point before it becomes a plane. The resulting diagram is the outcome of a fractal process, but one that no longer moves. It is a fractal, but a dead one: before a fractal can be drawn and reinserted into a state of things, its infinite division must be stopped in thought. Actualization is always death: a becoming-other, or a staying the same but inert.

A fractal process can be stopped and diagrammed at any point in its dividing. Every stop will yield a different diagram, each of the same fractal. Since the process is infinite, the number of potential diagrams is also infinite. Even as itself, even between its two limits, the fractal is multiple and boundless. All the potential diagrams are immanent to the many levels of any one, as potential effects of the same process. The overall identity of the fractal is enveloped in each diagram, but is not manifestly present in it. It cannot be, since the fractal's identity (becoming) is one with the generative process that must end for a given diagram to be produced. A mathematical equation or verbal instructions on how to construct the fractal are "diagrams" that express its latent identity-in-process more adequately than a static representation. All of the diagrams derivable from the same equation (abstract machine) subsist in each actual diagram produced (repetition as an inherent dimension of difference).

Thus between the limits there subsists a multiplicity of potential fractals. This in-between constitutes a level of virtuality lower than that of new being or nonbeing: what could be called the fractal's realm of "possibility." Possibility is a restricted range of potential: what the thing can become without ceasing to be itself (how the process can end without ending up outside). In theory, the derivable equations could be actualized one after the other and laid out in a series moving from its beginning as a line toward the point where the fractal could be taken for and effectively function as a plane. The fractal proper can therefore be described, for convenience, as a continuum of variations leaving one relative limit (its birth as a line) and approaching another (its transformation into a plane) as well as simultaneously leaving and approaching a dual absolute limit (genesis-in-division/abyss). In reality the relative and absolute limits toward which it tends are one and the same: the further the generative dividing process is taken, the more the fractal snakes in on itself and begins to approximate a plane; but the same motion furthers its fissuring, bringing it all the closer to the void. The difference between the two kinds of limit is that one can be crossed (if the process is captured by outside forces and thereby saved from itself) and the other cannot. The way in which the equation as a process contracts the future and the past into itself is called "complication," because of the paradoxical noncoincidence (discontinuity) of those two inseparable dimensions in reciprocal presupposition with the actual. The way in which a given diagram as evaporative effect contracts within itself all the other derivable diagrams is called "implication," because the continuity of the series of variations is a diagram's most accessible level of latency.[58] Returning to the John-Paul example, the presupposition of John's arrival is "implicit" in the statement; the existential act of deflecting a conversation is "complicit" in it (both can be said to be "immanent" to, or "enveloped" in, the statement). The implicit presupposition can engender a series of logical propositions in continuity with one another (for example, if the phrase is spoken by a spy, a number of clues as to John's actual whereabouts and what the speaker is doing in implying his arrival could be derived from it). The existential act (a deception to lure the listener into a murderous trap?) is a singular and unreproducible movement in space-time (maybe even into the next world). What is implicit in a speech act can be made explicit. It can be unpacked, translated into a logical proposition (meaning as the "expressed" of the statement) engendering a series of other propositions constituting a chain of logical possibilities. What is complicit is a physical potential that does or does not come to pass (meaning as "attribution"). It cannot be made any more explicit than the singular and unreproducible movement that it is. It can only be actualized, and if it is, its passing sweeps the body in question toward a limit at which it is transformed into something other than what it will have been. A statement's existential imperative is always a death sentence.[59]

Back to marriage. Every wedding is an actualization of the marriage process, its culmination in a statement as evaporative effect. "I do" holds all marriages past and future in implication; marriage in general subsists in it as the whispering "one" without which the wedding would have no meaning. That meaning, the essence of marriage, could be expressed as a continuum of variation: a series, in principle infinite, of all the ways different bodies can be joined in matrimony in different places by different authorities for different reasons to different effect (what the wedding could have been; its realm of possibility).[60] The marrying "I," like every "I," is not sufficient unto itself. To wed, it needs to be possessed of the "one," to repeat a stereotypical incantation that makes the body to which it is attached coincide with a standardized function (social equation). Miss X becomes the Bride, Mister Y the Groom. The "I do" is a component of passage that transforms the engaged bodies into something other than what they have been, carrying them across one relative threshold (being single) toward another: the implicit presupposition (go forth and multiply) of the "I do" marks the Bride and Groom's departure on a journey leading inexorably toward the "do us part" of divorce—barring the intervention of an outside force strong enough to defy every wedding's statistical destiny (love? religion? boredom?). Thus in addition to implicating a continuum, an essence complicates a discontinuity: the outside limits of marriage, singledom and divorce, are an integral part of every wedding, the boundaries without which it would have no shape. They are also of its essence, but belong to a deeper level of virtuality than the potential marriages implicit in the slogan "I do." The absolute limit of marriage is even more profoundly virtual: it is literally death (unless of course the newlyweds are Mormon), an experience no one can ever have (an experience only "one" can have). The subject of the wedding is the social equation of which "I do" is the de facto diagram (the sign of the culmination of a process, an index from which a formal diagram, for example a discursive diagram consisting of a series of logical propositions, could be developed). The subject of the wedding is the abstract machine of marriage in its *linear* functioning, expressible as a realm of possibility: the connecting in actuality of one body to another as part of a life progression; the serialization of wedding after wedding over an implicit time span subsisting in each present connection. More broadly, the subject is the abstract machine is the insubstantial process of division enveloped by the equation: the incorporeal cut between singledom and marriage and between marriage and death or divorce, the discontinuity haunting every connection, the inescapable complicating factor of the void. A void is inexpressible and has no particular shape, but since the linearity of expression springs from it (as enduring matter does from quantum energy[61]) it is described as "superlinear."[62] Superlinearity (complication; complete envelopment), linearity (implication; serialized development), and surface (explicitness; evaporative optical or auditory effect) are the three moments of the abstract machine. There are other designations for them: • untimely genesis-destiny / durational procedure / present diagram; • insistent nothingness / active becoming / inert being; • pure virtuality / virtuality in the process of being actualized / actualization arrested. A single philosophical term (essence; meaning; order-word) can be used to straddle all three moments or dimensions for the very good reason that in their multiplicity they are one.

This way of thinking about things might seem bleak. If the order-word as the basic unit of language is the culmination of a standardizing social function that makes a body do what "one" should do, then we ("I and I") are imprisoned by the impersonality of language. This imprisonment is less an immobilization than a stereotyped progression, since the order-word acts to carry a body from one predefined set of potential relations to another. Everyday language does not entirely straitjacket our potential, but it does restrict us to the lowest level of our virtuality. It limits the dynamism of our becoming to the stolid ways of being deemed productive by an exploitative society. It takes us from one bland realm of possibility to another. It delivers us to power.

Bleak it is at first glance. But it is ultimately joyous. For if Deleuze and Guattari are right, discontinuity has the final word. Every step in time is a fissure. Every step in the world of possibility skirts the impossibility of a generative void. Outside the limits of marriage: not the singles scene, not divorce, but as yet unimagined ways of bodies moving together, beyond boredom, beyond religion and taxes, maybe even beyond "love" (that most potent of all Western order-words). Outside productive work: invention. Outside school: halls without walls, a universe free for the learning. In every order-word there is indeed an implicit presupposition of funereal normality, the echoed refrain of the walking dead. But perhaps lost in the zombied murmur of social acceptability there are presuppositions so implicit we don't know how to hear them, "one"'s so impersonal we don't know how to place them in our "I," deaths to breathe new life into our lungs.[63] The order-word of Deleuze and Guattari's philosophy is the anti-order-word of the call of the outside: listen closely for existential imperatives which, rather than limiting I and I's realm of virtuality, take it out of bounds. Don't toe the line — be superlinear. Don't plod the straight and narrow path down the aisle — marry the void. Rewrite the slogan of the United States Army: dare to become all that you cannot be. Complicate, and chortle.

Pause

Some ways in which Deleuze and Guattari's theories of language differ from more familiar linguistic and semiotic approaches:

1. Language is not a transparent medium of communication. If it is a medium in any essential way, it is in the occult sense. What language conveys are fundamentally redundant order-words, not clear and distinct messages. Information is vital to this function, but only as the minimum semantic content necessary for the transmission of an imperative (the difference between "hire" and "fire").[64] Language as storage and retrieval of pure information (the cybernetic model) is a recent invention paralleling the rise of the computer. No matter how cybernated society gets, information processing will always remain a derived, secondary function of language.

2. There are no constants of language. Language is no less fractalized than any other thing. It is forever fragmenting into dialects, idiolects, and jargons that often coexist in the same speaker. The Saussurian concept of "*langue*" and the Chomskian concept of "competence" petrify living language into a structure. These approaches are inherently prescriptive, for any departure from the rules laid down by the

linguist for a given dialect can only be conceived of as a deviation from a norm. This is an invitation for a dominant dialect imposed by one group of speakers on others to become the linguistic "standard" against which the others are measured. *Langue* and competence are bedfellows to linguistic terrorism in the cause of uniformity. For Deleuze and Guattari, change (incorporeal transformation), not petrification, is the essence of language. A linguistic expression implicitly presupposes a continuum of variation between and across thresholds of meaning that are simultaneously thresholds of social functioning. Any given language is a dialect among others, in a network of power relations marked by grammatical formations standing as signposts to a site of everyday conflict. Each dialect in the network varies at the same rate as the functions its order-words effectuate, in other words endlessly. Linguistics should be a *pragmatics* that opens language to the vagaries of "context," indexing grammar to relations of power and patterns of social change. Its tasks should be to lay out a continuum of variations of the acts of saying-doing immanent to grammatical forms of expression, to analyze the mechanisms determining which virtual variation is actualized where, and to describe the mechanisms of passage from one continuum of virtuality to the next. The operative concept is "continuous variation."[65]

3. The Saussurian concepts of synchrony and diachrony are useless. The problems of periodization nagging structuralist-influenced disciplines testify to the constitutional inability of this framework to think in terms of becoming. At what point does one synchronous system end and another begin? Is the shift gradual or sudden? How does it occur? A synchronous structure is by definition a closed system of permutations, and is therefore logically inconsistent with the open-ended progress of diachrony. The terms of the problems forbid their solution. It gets us nowhere to say that synchrony is an instantaneous cross-section of diachrony. A cross-section of the present will not hit stable ground, but descend into levels of deepening complication forking infinitely into the future and the past. The concepts of virtuality and actualization allow us to think in the present and past-future tenses at the same time, to conceive of the same and the different together (continuous variation as the repetition of difference; the order-word as transformative redundancy). A synchronous structure defines the *logical conditions of possibility* of statements *in general* (What standard

permutations can the system produce? What can it do without ceasing to be itself?). The challenge is to conceptualize the *real conditions of production* of *particular* statements (How does the system move from one unique permutation to the next? How is it forever becoming other than itself?). In the first case, the assumption is stasis and movement is introduced as an afterthought, if at all. In the second, stasis exists only relatively (as a lower degree of difference: the repetition of different statements within the same relative limits of becoming), and the world is recognizable as the chaotic one in which we live. This does not mean that synchrony has simply disappeared in favor of diachrony. The untimeliness of the virtual in its reciprocal presupposition with the actual takes us entirely outside the false structure–history dilemma into a new dimension of fractal spatiotemporality. Deleuze and Guattari do not fault linguistics for being too abstract, but for not being abstract enough to account for change — and its conditions of emergence, in the same stroke.[66] Linguistics would do well to follow physics into the twentieth century by venturing beyond the artificial calm of mere possibility, beyond the implicit, into the unstable realm of the virtual in all its immanence.

4. Virtual and actual do not correspond to *langue/parole* or competence/performance. First, because all enunciation is collective and there is no individual subject to do the speaking-performing; second, because the generative agency, the abstract machine behind the order-word, is itself a variable in continual variation, changing with each actualization. A language does not exist in some pure and eternal realm outside the speech acts it produces. It subsists locally but globally in each and every one.

5. The relation of the signifier to the signified is not constitutive of language.[67] The essential relation is that of a statement to the generative process of "vertical content" (the statement as order-word). The term is a misnomer: the process is more multidimensional than "vertical," enveloping many levels and lines of causality, in relation to which the statement stands less as a "content" than as a culmination, an evaporative end effect, a landmark pointing to a geologic past. Theories of the signifier replace this "complicated" asymptotic causality with an unabashedly perpendicular one according to which the statement lies at the intersection of two sets of rules, one governing a

"horizontal" axis of combination, the other a "vertical" axis of substitution. The "horizontal" combination of signs within a sentence and of sentences within a discourse does, of course, obey certain rules of formation. These syntagmatic rules are not, however, a given statement's efficient cause, even together with a set of paradigmatic rules. Paradigmatic rules define which "vertical" substitutions *can* be made at each point in the "horizontal" flow of signs across the page or of sentences through time, but they cannot explain why one substitution rather than another was effectively made or why the same statement is repeated in different instances (let alone how it varies functionally across those repetitions). Syntagmatic and paradigmatic rules describe how a statement is generated as a form of expression. In other words, they diagram its formal cause as an abstract linguistic or semiotic machine. By bracketing the statement's real conditions of social emergence, however, they cut it off from its efficient cause: the overall abstract machine that pragmatically determines the substance as well as the form of both content and expression in their double articulation. Theories of the signifier reduce language to expression and expression to its form. In so doing, they unmoor language from its "vertical content," from the realm of virtuality constituting its real becoming as a hand-to-hand combat of energies. The lurch of language, its "leaping" between dimensions and emplacements, appears as a tranquil metonymic progression along an unbroken horizontal. The infinite division separating every expression from the next and fissuring each internally is simply glossed over, transforming the surface level of actualized statements (effects) into a nice smooth linguistic line, purified of cut and struggle. Signs that have dropped below that horizontal axis supply a second smoothed-over dimension. The complicated existential potentials enveloped in unactualized statements are simplified into a pool of possible substitutions: metaphor as the latency of signifiers turned signified. A neat two-dimensional symbolic structure emerges. Its dual causality (syntagmatic/paradigmatic, horizontal/vertical) is logical and tidy. But it is also an illusion. A kind of optical illusion, or objective perspective like the fractal's afterlife as a plane. Signification is inscribed in the essence of language as one of its own potentials: the potential for becoming other than it is (flat). An outside force must intervene to extract that potential and actualize it. Theories of the signifier are useful to the extent that certain societies, most notably "modern" ones, do indeed extract the symbolic potential of language. Baudrillardian "postmodernity" goes one step further and unmoors the "horizontal" line from the "vertical," creating an objective illusion of unanchored slippage from signifier to signifier, pure unmotivated metonymy in a one-dimensional world without metaphor. Both of these processes do indeed occur. It is crucial, however, to remember that their occurrence is caused: the detachment from the virtual is *produced* by determinable social functionings within a real network of power relations. In order to grasp the conditions of existence of these phenomena it is necessary to reattach them to their obscured "vertical content" in all its fractal glory. This is precisely what Lacanians omit to do in their treatment of the unconscious as a metonymic–metaphorical deep structure, and it is what Baudrillard refuses to understand in his celebration of late capitalism as shimmering metonymic surface. Both approaches reduce "vertical content" to a signified (which Baudrillard then claims has been abolished). What I have called "horizontal content" (a second state of things or force field with which certain classes of overpowering expressions are coupled) is either dismissed as a "referent" lying irretrievably outside language understood as a closed system or two-dimensional form of interiority (a typically modern move); or, once language comes to be seen as a senselessly replicating one-dimensional gene, it is discounted as nonexistent (a typically postmodern move). Deleuze and Guattari reinstate content. But for them content is *neither a signified nor a referent*—a possibility that does not seem to have occurred either to modernists or postmodernists. Deleuze and Guattari's reintroduction of content should in no way be interpreted as the addition of a third dimension of romantic "meaning." That time-worn strategy is simply a denial of "modern" society's inescapable two-dimensionality, a desperate humanist attempt to inject a comforting sense of significance into the seasonal reruns of our culture's stereo-typed symbolism. What Deleuze and Guattari are after is a real perception of the superhuman becoming immanent to human being, a pragmatic embrace of meaning in its infinite but fractional dimensionality.

6. A corollary to this is that the binarism of the signifier/signified relation is a produced, secondary characteristic. Language necessarily presents many binarisms (content / expression being the primary one),

but they are produced by nonbinary mechanisms. Signifying structures arise from nonsignifying processes comprising a multiplicity of
virtual spatiotemporal levels and actual materials in reciprocal presupposition. Language produces linear series of signs and statements, but
is itself superlinear.

7. The virtual is not hidden in the sense of a repressed signified or lost
referent. It is occulted, but as part of a necessary clearing. For a
statement or thought to appear in all its apparent simplicity and clarity,
its complicated genesis must recede into the abyssal shadows from
which it came. The virtual is the *unsaid* of the statement, the unthought
of thought. It is real and subsists in them, but must be forgotten at least
momentarily for a clear statement to be produced as evaporative
surface effect. "The statement is neither visible nor hidden."[68] The task
of philosophy is to explore that inevitable forgetting, to reattach
statements to their conditions of emergence. As Foucault repeatedly
contends, a statement needs no interpretation, but a "stand" (*socle*) may
be fashioned for it (its "archive" of implicit presuppositions may be
recreated by "archaeology") in order to bring back to light its realm of
virtuality (the immanent "strategies" that produced it). Under certain
conditions of signifying capture, the statement and its "vertical content" will in fact be doubled by a repressed signified. The forgetting will
then be recast as a symbolic structural unconscious which will function
in addition to (as a unity apart from and in reciprocal presupposition
with) the primary causal strategies, into which it will be reinserted to
serve as a new, secondary line of causality. It will function, but
according to different rules and at a lower level of virtuality. That
inferior degree of potential is not in this case the realm of logical
possibility (although its mechanisms are logically describable) but—
equally bland—an "imaginary."[*]

---

[*]As the frequent references to Foucault were meant to indicate, Deleuze and
Guattari's theories of language are closer to Foucault's than to any other contemporary thinker's. Reading Deleuze and Guattari in terms of semiotic frameworks they
explicitly reject—in particular Saussurian-derived systems—is the most common
source of the consistent unreadings that have plagued their work. The same is true
of Foucault. To be read to best effect, they should be read together.[69]

HABIT

is the ballast that chains the dog to his vomit[1]

Deleuze and Guattari are sometimes accused of coldness. The previous chapter may have reinforced that perception. There were "humanoid bodies," husbands, wives, and zombies, but not a recognizable human being in sight. If it was chilling, it may be because in Deleuze and Guattari's opinion human consciousness and identity are on the order of an "I do," empty effects that culminate a transformation whose complicated causality lies at other levels. Our "humanity" is to us as a plane is to a fractal: an objective illusion.

Yet Deleuze and Guattari pepper their books with the word "intensity" and, almost alone among poststructuralist writers, reserve an important place in their thought for the concept of "sensation." Protestations in favor of "human warmth" betray an inability to feel an ardor of a different kind. Stirrings that are not just prepersonal, but impersonal, bodily but inhuman, outside intentionality, open irrevocably to chance.[2] How there can be sensation without a unified subject, or how inhuman intensities can produce humanity-effects are questions of *synthesis*: the joining of separate elements through chance encounters into an enduring, apparently stable, more or less reproducible conglomerate capable of being taken in by its own objective illusion of identity. "Synthesis" figures prominently in earlier works, in particular *Différence et répétition* and *Anti-Oedipus*. If the word all but disappears in *A Thousand Plateaus*, it is not because the concept is absent, but because it has become ubiquitous. "Abstract machine" is another word for synthesizer.[3]

On the way to identity:

Muck

Something comes along. Something else comes along. They collide and stick. They stay together, perhaps combine with something else again to form a larger combination. This is called a "connective synthesis." An example is sediment.[4] A grain comes to rest. Another joins it. Many grains follow from a variety of sources, brought to a point of accumulation by chance. Not brute chance. Chance discrimination: the accumulating grains are in the same size and weight range and share certain chemical properties. Not all grains answering to the description join the gang. Given a particular grain, no one, however savvy in sedimentation, can predict whether it will be one of the select. All that can be said is that a number of like particles probably will be. A statistical process of this kind, combining chance and approximate necessity, can be called "selection." A selection is an act of perception, since something, in this case a set of natural laws, "perceives" the grains that come together in a layer. The resulting muck is an "individual."[5] An individual is singular—the element of chance assures that no two mucks are exactly alike—but nonetheless multiple: a muck deposit envelops a multiplicity of grains composed of a multiplicity of atoms, all of which followed multiple paths to their common agglomeration. In addition, each individual is enveloped in others. Layer accumulates upon layer, stratum upon stratum. Under the proper conditions, the greater individual of the deposit is selected, or captured, by another set of discriminating forces (another perception). Over time, under pressure, sediment folds and hardens into sedimentary rock. The originally supple individual has been transformed, without ceasing to be itself. The fluctuating muck has rigidified into a stable formation. Certain potentials come into clear expression, while others are selected out. Oozing, for instance. In principle, the ability to be supple is still in the particles, but it is locked out of any future transformations (for example, the mining of the rock to build a courthouse): it has returned to the virtual. One set of potentials has been deducted from the muck, or deactualized; others carry over (basic chemical properties); still others are added, or actualized (the ability to withstand gravity). The basic change is in the "mode of composition" or "consistency" of the individual, in other words in the way in which the particles hold together. The statistical accumulation started as a shifting mass brought together by fragmentary processes operating particle by particle through strictly local connections, or in a manner that could be called "molecular." The resulting multilayered individual was then grasped as a whole by a set of outside forces working in concert and molded into a well-defined superindividual or "molar" formation.[6]

The connective synthesis of the statistical accumulation of particles and their folding and condensation into rock was a "production of production," the creation of an individual as if from scratch. The end of this two-part connective synthesis is the beginning of a new synthesis, this time a "production of recording":[7] once the particles and their geologic pasts have been registered in a stable formation, more regulated perceptions and more elaborate captures become possible: the deposit is quarried. It is inscribed in the balance books, recorded in the economy of capital. The acts of perception involved in this are not just local selections of physical presence. The activity of quarrying is preceded by an apparatus of knowledge that classifies the rock by kind and grade. Long before the first bulldozer arrives, mineralogy has abstracted a set of properties common to any number of distant deposits (inventing a category), has subdivided those properties (into types), and has defined the appropriate type for the application. Prospectors have found the deposit and judged it according to these distinctions. Only then was the particular deposit selected. The first synthesis was gregarious: find and lump together. It was selective, but the selection came first and was in the interests of a congregation. In the second synthesis, separation is the goal: divide and quarry. In keeping with its divisive nature, it is called a "disjunctive synthesis." In this case, it is an "exclusive" disjunctive synthesis: it divides all but only quarries some. It employs a classification system of mutually exclusive identifications — nominal identities — and chooses only the ones judged suitable. Muck is a supple individual (existing locally and fragmentarily, with fluctuating boundaries). A rock deposit is a superindividual (existing locally but globally, with delimited boundaries). Sedimentary rock as a raw material is the content of a universal category; it could be called (not without ulterior motives) a "*person.*"[8]

The connective syntheses that made the muck and turned it to rock were passive. No concerted action by an isolable agent was involved. The disjunctive synthesis that made it a building was active. It was a product of self-reproducing cultural activities drawing on a store of memory, or knowledge, and directed toward more or less utilitarian ends. As different as the disjunctive synthesis is, it cannot be separated from connective syntheses: another case of reciprocal presupposition. A disjunctive synthesis can be active because it has connective syntheses to act upon. It swoops down to capture connective syntheses, but also rises from them: its human agents are the result of connective syntheses both biological and psychic, and their standardized knowing and quarrying procedures are the outcome of a diversity of cultural sedimentations. Finally, the disjunctive synthesis leads to a new connective synthesis, this time an active one. The disjoined rock is methodically reconnected to itself in order to actualize a new potential: block by block, a wall is built. Three walls join it. The courthouse they frame is the site of a third and final synthesis. Rocks are not the only things that come to these premises. A courthouse is more than a building. It is also a conjuncture of judges, handcuffs, law books, and accused. Any number of disjoined things, each the result of a unique combination of connective and disjunctive syntheses, follow their separate paths there, conjoin in a less permanent way than mortar, and then continue on. This "conjunctive synthesis" is also "consumptive," but not in the sense that it physically consumes its things (the two earlier syntheses were more consumptive in that respect). Its captures are essentially incorporeal: the pronouncement of a sentence instantly makes a man a criminal. But legal capture through incorporeal transformation is only of consequence if preceded and followed by physical action (of police and jailors), and if acquiesced to by the public. That such cooperation and complicity is normally forthcoming implies that value is collectively attached to the judge above and beyond his[9] immediate attributes. His power is far in excess of his physical prowess. This excess takes such intangible forms as respect for the law and its representatives, awe, and intimidation, and is not unrelated to the impressive appearance of the former muck within which the judge presides. The accomplishment of an incorporeal transformation is necessarily accompanied by production of the incorporeal excess, which is on the order of a global sensation emanating from the courthouse conjunction. The sentence strikes like lightning. The excess radiates diffusely from the scene of the judgment. It is more like static electricity, a feeling in the air, a general effect, than a sealing of fate or a searing of flesh. The collective consumption of an intangible excess and the consummation of a punctual process of transformation are the two aspects of the conjunctive synthesis: evaporative excess-effect and the crossing of a threshold.[10] For the public, satisfaction that justice has been served. For the convict, a trip out the door in handcuffs. The "evaporative" excess can in fact be converted into a cause. It can join with others of its kind and lead, for example, to the election of a law-and-order candidate whose disciplinary attentions would then be lavished on the connective syntheses of the populace: more handcuffs. Any time a transformation on one level produces an excess-effect that bifurcates into a higher level causality, we say that the transformation has created a "surplus value."[11]

The story of the muck retold: The individual of the first connective synthesis was the outcome of repeated acts of erosion and flow ending in an accumulation of muck. A pattern of repeated acts is a "code." A code is always of a "milieu," or relatively stable, often statistical, mixing of elements (here, climatic and geologic).[12] A code is the same as a "form" in the sense discussed above (an order and organization of functions).[13] The muck, a form of expression in relation to its milieu, would later become a form of content for operations of quarrying and construction. But only after being transformed by a second connective synthesis. The supple molecular code governing wind- and water-borne particles is replaced by a new geologic pattern acting on the muck as a whole: the individual is "recoded" as a molar formation. That recoding consisted in a condensation and folding resulting in a rock deposit with rigid frontiers: an "interior" (bounded) milieu has separated off from the exterior milieu through infolding.[14] This is the "double articulation" of the last chapter, but in its simplest form (two moments of the same passive process occurring on a single level, rather than an active placing in relation of two heterogeneous levels).[15] The superindividual of the rock deposit is an enduring "territory." Its capture by cultural forces was a two-pronged movement. On the one hand, it was a "deterritorialization" (an uprooting of the individual) and "decoding" (a change in the pattern of actions affecting it). And on the other, a "reterritorialization" (the rock's reimplanting in a building), and (re)recoding (the imposition of new patterns of connection with itself and its surroundings). The recoding was directed by a disjunctive synthesis that swooped down on the unsuspecting rock from a higher level of organization and applied a grid of identifications to it, in a categorizing overlay of its individuality. To distinguish this recoding from its geologic precursor, it can be called an "overcoding."[16] The overcoding gave the rock a nominal identity, facilitating its insertion into a whole new level of synthesis: a conjunction with numerous other categorized individuals, or persons, in a complex assemblage of thunderbolt judgment.[17]

Any object we care to interrogate, however humble, proves to be a multilayered formation of staggering complexity. The muck's odyssey featured interlocking syntheses involving climatic, geologic, biological, and cultural strata, each of which is itself multilayered and recapitulates the same mechanisms in its own unique way. For example, the chemistry of the living cell is based on the propensity of certain molecules to connect end to end (statistical accumulation; individual) then automatically fold in on themselves (double articulation; supple individual) to form three-dimensional structures (molar individual as the result of passive connective syntheses), which then interact with each other as such (causal bifurcation; surplus value). In the proper medium, the interaction between macromolecules forms feedback loops allowing one variety of macromolecule to reproduce itself by breaking down and recombining others (perception-capture; passive exclusive disjunctive synthesis). The cell itself is an infolding of that process within a membrane (bounded molar superindividual; second capture) and its regularization in a molar code (DNA). Cells join with other cells to form organs (inclusive disjunctive synthesis; molar supersuperindividuals), and organs join with other organs to a form a molar supersupersuperindividual capable of global sensations, some of which are preferred over others (overall conjunctive synthesis; overall surplus value; value "judgment"). The whole process is the result of evolution (natural selection) and constitutes an infolding of that aleatory outside.[18] If we look below the level of the cell, even below the grain of muck, down to the very smallest (and largest) level of all, we still find the basic mechanisms repeated, most intriguingly:

Quarks & Company

The paradoxes of atoms and the menagerie of particles inhabiting them are well known: particle or wave, matter or energy. Test it one way it's a particle, test it another way it's a wave. If you know its velocity you don't know its position, if you know its position you don't know its velocity. Quarks and things have the nasty habit of failing to obey the law of noncontradiction. This has led certain logical people to deny their existence.

"Realists" make the unabashedly illogical assertion that yes, they are real, but no, they are not either/or: they are *both and neither*. They are both particle and wave, both matter and energy, and therefore have neither assignable position nor velocity. They are everything and everywhere, a *superposition* of what are "normally" mutually exclusive states. In other words, they are virtual. They are real but subsist in a dimension where our objective "laws" do not apply: "abstract yet real."[19]

When scientists use their instruments to try to pin down a subatomic phenomenon, their intrusion transforms it. "The quantum void is the opposite of nothingness: far from being passive or inert, it contains in a dimension of potential all possible particles." Scientific perception *actualizes* a virtual particle.[20] It changes the mode of reality of its "object," bringing into being one of the states the quantum phenomenon holds in virtuality. It simplifies a complication. This "reduction" of the phenomenon is called a "collapse" of its "wave-packet": many virtual states which subsist everywhere and in everything are contracted into a here and now.[21] Which state is selected to be here now is not arbitrary. It depends on the form the intervention takes. The particle is produced in an encounter between two realities: it is cocaused. The result is not entirely predictable. It is only statistically consistent because half the cause, the quantum half, does not obey our laws and is apt to elude us. We can never know its reality directly or completely, but we can be sure that it has reality outside our perceptions of it—if only because we are not the only things that "perceive" it. Even an isolated atom is perceived: it is bathed in an electromagnetic field that "perturbs" it as surely as a scientist does, and can coax one of its states into existence.[22] All of matter, the whole stratified world, is one giant perturber of virtuality. It has to be, otherwise it would return to the quantum void from which it came. For it has no other place to be but in that crowded void. It has no firm foundation on which to rest. Our world is not static. It is an eternally recommenced creation. Its existence, like that of the living cell, depends on a constant infolding, or contraction, of an aleatory outside that it can only partially control. The world is stable only to the extent that the strata working in concert can regularize their infolding of chance; it is stable only within certain limits. The strata can envelop chance but not abolish it, confine it but not banish it. Their judgments strike like fate, but since Einstein we know that they are only relative. We should thank God (or rather the lack thereof) that the objective indeterminacy of the virtual world that cocauses our becoming renders total control impossible. If it were possible, that continual chance-ridden creation, that eternal return of difference, would be an eternity of the same. It might get boring.

Pause

The upshot is: the assertion in the last chapter that be(com)ing is fractal is not a metaphor. The physical and cultural worlds are an infinite regress of interlocking levels. Each level or stratum recapitulates mechanisms from the last on a larger scale, and adds new ones of its own. Every bifurcation to a new level has an essential element of randomness, giving our universe the diverging symmetry of a fractal figure. With one difference: there is no adequate equation for our lives.

Once again, we have a slew of concepts. They do not fit together in a neat system. This is not a package deal. They are offered as a repertory to pick and choose from, to recombine and refashion, in the hopes that they may be found useful in understanding processes of structuration: the integration of separate elements into more or less regular stratified formations, from a basis in chance.[23] Connective, disjunctive, conjunctive syntheses; accumulation and folding; perception and capture; contraction and collapse; surplus values and causal bifurcation; double articulation, coding, and overcoding. Levels on top of levels within levels, overlapping and interlocking, but each with its own consistency. Between them, a continual motion of mutual adaptation in a hand-to-hand combat of energies. This is the cosmic fractal cut that sunders all things and holds them together: separation-connection.[24]

A few observations:

1. It is crucial for understanding Deleuze and Guattari, and what follows here, to remember that *the distinction between molecular and molar has nothing whatsoever to do with scale*. Molecular and molar do not correspond to "small" and "large," "part" and "whole," "organ" and "organism," "individual" and "society." There are molarities of every magnitude (the smallest being the nucleus of the atom). The distinction is not one of scale, but of mode of composition: it is qualitative, not quantitative. In a molecular population (mass) there are only local connections between discrete particles. In the case of a molar population (superindividual or person) locally connected discrete particles

have become correlated at a distance. Our granules of muck were an oozing molecular mass, but as their local connections rigidified into rock, they became stabilized and homogenized, increasing the organizational consistency of different regions in the deposit (correlation). Molarity implies the creation or prior existence of a well-defined boundary enabling the population of particles to be grasped as a whole. We skipped something: the muck as such. A supple individual lies between the molecular and the molar, in time and in mode of composition. Its particles are correlated, but not rigidly so. It has boundaries, but fluctuating ones. It is the threshold leading from one state to another.

2. When we say that a molarity is grasped as a whole, the emphasis is on the *as*. The particles are still there, no less numerous than before. A molarity remains a multiplicity—only a disciplined one. For a population to exist *as* a whole, it must be grasped as such by outside forces. The unity of the individual exists *in addition to* its multiplicity, as imposed on it from a higher level than the one on which the individual existed up to that point (concerted geologic action surrounding and compressing the muck; concerted cultural action swooping down on the rock and sweeping it away).[25] A molar individual is the dominated term in a relation of power (a content for an overpowering form of expression). A contained population is called a "subjected group."[26] The unity of a molarized individual is transcendent (exists only from the point of view of the forms of expression to which the individual is subjected, and on their level) and redundant (doubles the individual's multiplicity in a supplemental dimension to it; constitutes a surplus value).[27] A molarized individual is a "person" to the extent that a category (cultural image of unity) has been imposed on it, and insofar as its subsequent actions are made to conform to those prescribed by its assigned category. A person is an incarnation of a category, the actualization of an image of unity (diagram of regularized actions) in a substance other than thought. Actualization is always translation: conformity to the assigned actions will always be approximate (the deviations skipped over in the process of generalizing the individual mark a residual heterogeneity). The individual's particularity remains, in addition to its generalized functioning on the personal level. There is always some level of resistance to total regularization inherent in the

new substance (geologic imperfections; criminal tendencies; "perversions").

3. The syntheses and their products can be labeled "passive" or "active." These are only approximate terms, because every process of synthesis involves a mixture of forces that could be characterized as active or passive, again in an approximate way. Wind is active, but is part of the passive connective synthesis of sediment. Gravity is active, but less so than wind, and acts to induce passivity. In sedimentation, gravity wins out over wind. Passive and active are *evaluations*: they assign a value to the outcome of a synthesis on the basis of which constituent force dominates and what the product's intrinsic potential for action is (the pragmatic "meaning" of the synthesis). Rocks are active to the extent that they can be made into a wall that resists gravity, but are passive to the extent that they need an outside agency to do so. "Entropic" or "negentropic" would be better terms because they emphasize that the object of evaluation is a process involving relations of motion and rest in an interplay of energizing or deenergizing forces (the celerity of quarrying versus the gravity of rock; uprooting and reimplantation).[28] Action itself is multivalent and must be evaluated before the pragmatic meaning of a synthesis can be fully accounted for. There are two kinds of action. *Reaction*: gravity is active, but can only *re*act to the presence of a body; quarrying is active but involves a disjunctive synthesis which *re*duces a number of individuals to their shared properties, *re*cognizes a given individual as belonging to a type, and judges that individual on how well it *re*peats a model; husbands are active but only in order to *re*produce; a judge actively transforms individuals but only insofar as he is *re*presentative of the law. Reaction, reduction, recognition, repetition, reproduction, representation. Re: habit. *Affirmation* is nonreactive action. So far we have seen no examples of it.[29]

4. Each kind of synthesis has an inclusive and an exclusive usage. A synthesis is inclusive when it multiplies. An inclusive connective synthesis adds an accumulation or a repeatable collision to the world (this *and* that; distinct muck deposits). An inclusive disjunctive synthesis creates diverging series of individuals that may deign to coexist but in principle do not mix (this *and/or* that; different biological species). An inclusive conjunctive synthesis takes the *and* of the inclusive

disjunctive *and/or*. It joins divergent individuals in a network of potential mixtures in which no individual is precluded a priori from going from any given point to another (*both* this *and* that; different species converging in "unnatural" couplings).[30] A synthesis is exclusive when it subtracts. Only a disjunctive synthesis is fundamentally exclusive. It creates series of diverging individuals whose only fully authorized mode of coexistence is in the abstract, in a categorical grid composed of mutually contradictory types. Even when its usage is inclusive, it is exclusive in its operation: one category is applied at a time in a divisive action or judgment (this *or* that). Its version of *and* is a succession of *or*s. The disjunctive application of the category limits the ways in which the target individual can connect with the individuals and objects with which it coexists concretely (mortar; handcuffs). Not only is the disjunctive synthesis fundamentally exclusive, it invades the connective syntheses, imposing limitative usage on them. Once begun, the invasion tends to accelerate. The segregative conjunctions into which exclusively disjoined individuals are led (courthouse; justice) produce a surplus value sensation that can convert into a cause (election of a law-and-order candidate) that multiplies limitative connections and segregative conjunctions with utmost efficiency (discipline). Exclusive usage spreads like a cancer. It is not only reactive but imperialist by nature.

5. An individual, supple or molarized, is stable only within certain limits. All living things die, rocks crumble, genes mutate, universes are created and destroyed. Even within the limits of its stability, an individual is always changing. Muck rises and recedes, an atom's electrons leap to and fro unpredictably, new laws are passed every day. A structure is at best *metastable*: stable on the whole (statistically) or as a whole (from the regularized point of view of its molarity). Stability is not fixity. It is variation within limits. Electrons unpredictably leap too far, fly off into space, and atoms combine to form a molecule. A law is broken and the perpetrator goes to jail. A judge is bribed and a corrupt official goes free. Enough individuals mutate, and a new species arises. Not enough individuals mutate, and no new species arises. An unusually wet season washes away part of a sediment deposit. *A structure is defined by what escapes it.* Without exception, it emerges from chance, lives with and by a margin of deviation, and ends in disorder. A structure is is defined by its *thresholds* — the relative limits

within which it selects, perceives, and captures, more or less consistently (its margin of deviation); and the absolute limits beyond which it breaks down (chance, chaos). A structure is a regularized infolding of an aleatory outside. The closest thing there is to order is the approximate, and always temporary, prevention of disorder. The closest thing there is to determinacy is the relative containment of chance. The opposite of chance is not determinacy. It is habit.

Warm Water

The preceding discussion was a cover-up. It ignored a basic problem running through all of its formulations: the supple individual was presented as the in-between of molecularity and molarity, but it was utterly passive. The most active process in evidence was transcendent, it swooped down on unsuspecting mucks to sweep them away to a future of walled oppression. How can forces become active enough to be reactive? If a human body's activities are limited by categorical judgment, doesn't that imply that it was active but not molarly limited before being judged? All structures, it was said, arise from an infolding of chance. Doesn't that ignore the fact that the sedimentation of a muck deposit and the geologic action that molarized it involve deterministic forces, such as gravity?

Only half of the story has been told. There is a missing link. There must be supple, nonmolar individuals that are active, but according to an immanent principle and despite the presence of deterministic constraints. Only then would supple individuality truly be the in-between needed to explain the combination of passive and reactive forces we see around us, as well as providing an escape route from that same double-pincered domination: it would be what we called "affirmation," or free action.[31]

The missing link is known.[32] It can be found as close to home as warm water. Heat is applied to a tranquil liquid. It is perturbed. Its lower layer, closest the heating source, becomes hotter than the upper layer. The liquid's equilibrium has been upset, and it endeavors to regain its former state of rest. In classical thermodynamics, a physical system tends toward maximum entropy—the highest degree of stability and homogeneity it can achieve given existing conditions. Faced with a disturbance, it carries out the minimal activity necessary to return to that maximally entropic equilibrium state. That means conduction. As the liquid's molecules absorb the heat, their movements increase, causing them to collide with one another. Their collisions diffuse the heat upward and out the upper surface. The liquid has lost its stability, but retains it homogeneity: every part of it is equally chaotic; no pattern of activity distinguishes one part from another. In theory. In practice, something else happens. If the heat is increased at a certain rate, a threshold is reached at which order spontaneously arises out of chaos. The liquid differentiates. Certain regions turn in on themselves, "nucleate," form fluid boundaries. Whirlpools form: convection currents. These vortexes appear because the liquid is under another constraint besides the command to regain equilibrium through thermodiffusion. That second constraint is gravity. The heat increases the motion of the molecules in the bottom layer, causing a given volume in that layer to become less dense and therefore lighter than an equivalent volume in the cooler upper layer. As a result, the cooler molecules descend and the warmer ones rise, creating a swirling pattern. The system has moved farther from entropic equilibrium: it is now not only unstable, it is no longer homogeneous. Regions have differentiated. It has become ordered, exhibiting a higher level of systemic activity than either thermodiffusion or gravity acting alone would have allowed. This phenomenon of spontaneous self-organization cannot be sustained. The probability of order surviving under these unstable conditions is virtually nil. In theory. In practice, if the heat continues to rise at the right rate, a second threshold is reached at which the vortexes multiply to cover the entire volume of the liquid — and continue indefinitely. The liquid will display a tendency to conserve its patterning, reacting to any further disturbance *as a system* (rather than molecule by molecule). Structural stability has been achieved under conditions of extreme instability.

No law of nature has been defied. Gravity is respected, and the vortexes create an efficient pattern of circulation from the heat source to the cooling surface, accelerating the heat dissipation called for by the Second Law of thermodynamics. All the liquid has done is break the rule that maximum dissipation necessarily means minimum systemic activity and differentiation. It has contravened the scientific wisdom that there is no such thing as a spontaneous dissipative structure.[33]

It did this not by breaking natural laws, but by combining them in such a way as to end up with more than the sum of their parts. It exploited a *differential* between them. Gravity alone would entail less motion and a higher density of molecules on a liquid's bottom layer. Thermodiffusion, since it requires molecules to absorb heat and pass it on, entails greater motion and a lower density nearest the heat source. When the liquid's bottom layer was heated, the requirements of gravity and heat diffusion entered into tension. Combine the requirements, and you get a swirl. Nothing so unusual about that. However, both laws agree that the liquid should be maximally stable and inactive at equilibrium, and unstable and active when equilibrium is disturbed. When the liquid combined their requirements, it became stable *and* active—each in a new sense. Stability no longer meant maximum systemic homogeneity, but order—sustained patterning, differentiation. Activity no longer meant increased molecular chaos, but an ability to change patterning by responding systemically to further disturbance. The laws said "Be this and that" (stable and inactive) *or* "Be this and that" (unstable and active). The liquid responded by being this *and* that, giving both a new meaning. It obeyed the laws, to new effect. It did this, of course, without ceasing to be this *or* that—turn off the heat, and it's back to the *or*. This *and/or* that: an inclusive disjunctive synthesis. The clash in constraints was a differential that was also a *potential*, which the liquid exploited to invent a new synthesis. The liquid contracted two virtual states into its actuality rather than one: it collapsed its "wave-packet" less reductively than it was called upon to do by either constraint alone. In the process, the liquid became "sensitive." The effect of gravity on a liquid at rest is normally negligible, but in its agitated state, the liquid suddenly "perceived" it and was transformed.[34]

Call a state toward which a system tends an "attractor."[35] In this example, there are two: the constraint to dissipate heat and return to thermal equilibrium, and the constraint to lose momentum to gravity and return to kinetic equilibrium. Call the differential potential created by the contradictory motion and density requirements of the two attractors an "intensity," and the new level of responsiveness accompanying the perception of the intensity a "sensation." While passing from stability to instability under heat duress, as it was trying to follow its tendency to dissipate the heat and return to equilibrium, the liquid "perceived" another attractor. It added that attractor to the first, yielding a new level of sensitivity. "*Both* this *and* that": the inclusive disjunctive synthesis of the qualities the laws entail is an inclusive conjunctive synthesis of the attractors governing the laws. The resulting state of active stability is a hybrid between the two attractors and the qualities they imply. This new equilibrium is undecidable—both one and the other, this and/or that. It is off on a tangent deviating from both attractors. Call the new equilibrium a "singularity," and the tangent the liquid followed to reach that state a "becoming." The liquid's new state is stable, but only within certain limits (it is metastable, to extend a term applied earlier to molarity). If the heat is turned off, or if it is turned up too high, the liquid returns to its former chaotic self and rejoins the paths set out for it by its attractors. Order, the turbulent order of a dissipative structure, is a tangential passage between two thresholds.

The singularity the liquid becomes is actually much more than a simple hybrid. It obeys the terms laid down for it by its attractors and at the same time transcends them. It redefines the terms of its existence (within certain limits), effecting a synthesis that places it in irreducible excess of the causal principles governing its own genesis. This excess takes the form of a sensation accruing to the liquid: a surplus value. The sensitivity the liquid exhibited toward gravity carries over into the liquid's new existence as an actively differentiated system, and is in fact multiplied. Each vortex is a population of locally correlated molecules—a supple individual. The particles in one vortex are correlated at a distance with the particles in all the others. The liquid is a correlated population of correlated populations—a supple superindividual. Because the liquid is doubly correlated, any chance disturbance that might occur in one area will immediately be "felt" everywhere. It will *resonate* throughout the liquid, affecting the correlations within each and between every vortex. The disturbance's effect will be *amplified* instantaneously from the local to the global level.[36] Any disturbance will be sensed separately by the individual nucleations and simultaneously, in excess of them, by the superindividual as a whole.

The liquid's global responsiveness is not the kind that would qualify it as a molarity. Its suppleness has not been suppressed. The liquid has not surrounded itself with a fixed or self-reproducing boundary. Its local and global levels are completely interfused. Although the liquid's responsiveness involves all of its regions in their individuality, it is not confined to any one of them. It is produced by the differential relationships among the local subpopulations or nucleations, and the differential relationship between those differentials and the global sensitivity they add up to at every instant: it is *local–global*. The local–global resonation regulating the liquid's responses are immanent to it (even if it infolds disturbances from outside). The liquid has bifurcated into a new causal dimension (double articulation) enveloping new potentials (different vortex patterns, depending on what disturbance is received when). The supplemental local–global dimension is strictly consubstantial with the molecular. Each level offers possibilities for action that the other does not, but the levels have combined without clashing. The component molecules have effectively retained all of their molecular potential and can instantly return to their attractors if conditions change. The potentials of the two levels are "compossible" (lie within the realm of possibility of the same actual formation).[37]

In its antiattractor states, the liquid is a "supermolecule":[38] singular yet differentiated, multiple yet capable of concerted action, more than molecular but not molar—that magical in-between.

Some disturbances reaching the liquid from outside may resonate against the vortexes, in which case the system of compossibility between levels will crash and the liquid will return to its original path moving to and from molecular entropy (death). Other disturbances may resonate with the vortexes, or be *recognized* by them.[39] The vortexes will adjust their shape to the disturbance and retain that shape for as long as the disturbance is sustained. If this happens, a new active equilibrium is created, this time through the absorption of chance. A new singular state of local–global interfusion is induced. What its nature will be is not entirely predictable.

In the presence of a disturbance, or "noise," the supple structure will either move toward a new order or back to its disordered past. A double bifurcation: life or death, and if life, this state or that. The path selected is a function of the interaction between the particular disturbance and the particular correlations the liquid has developed. In other words, it is a function of its past as enveloped in its locally–globally correlated substance and the future arriving from outside. At the precise moment of impact, as the amplification of the noise is occurring, the liquid's state is indeterminate. It is in crisis. It could go either way. It is still ordered by its past, but its future has already arrived. The *either/or* of past and future is momentarily an *and* (a new conjunctive synthesis), and the future itself is an *either/or*. Past *and* future *or*: *and/or*. The crisis is an inclusive disjunction of two exclusive disjunctions. The liquid now envelops more tensions. Its intensity is heightened. The exclusiveness of the disjunctive syntheses of the laws of thermodynamics has returned at a higher level, translated into a choice between obedience to them and a future choice. The system can return to the low-intensity, low-order, stable attractor state, or it can opt for living dangerously as a high-intensity, high-sensitivity, ultimately unstable, active order (a metastable supermolecular system). Which path it will take cannot be predicted a priori and cannot be induced with accuracy even after long trial and error. Probabilities can be assigned, but the system will always exhibit a certain "degree of freedom."[40] The liquid has contracted more virtual states into its actuality than can be deterministically manipulated. It has tapped the creative turbulence of its pool of virtuality. It is capable of free action. A supermolecular population capable of free action is called a "subject-group."

Indeterminacy has arisen out of determinacy, freedom out of the constraint of law. The trajectory leading from effective attractors to an self-organizing individual or subject-group goes against the grain of the passive syntheses predicated on chance encounters that led, in our earlier example, to muck and other things. Throughout our first version of structuration, determinacy arose from indeterminacy. Now we see that indeterminacy can arise from determinacy. That is the other half of the story: *cocausality*. One thing does not lead to another as a full cause to a simple effect. To begin with, there were two full causes (attractor states). Their line of cocausality then joined in cocausality with another causal line —constituted by chance. The supermolecular subject-group lies at a doubly cocausal crossroads of chance and determinacy.[41] Off on a tangent: a singular in-between state of cocausal local–global self-organization, with no assignable destiny.

We have presented the actively self-organized individual as a special case. As tangential or singular as such individuals may be, the inventors of the science of dissipative structures insist that they are in fact the rule.[42] It is instead the kind of fixed or self-reproducing molarities we were concerned with earlier that are the exception. The constraints of personhood, unlike those of warm water, are essentially limitative and reductive. The overlay of a category confines an individual to prefabricated trajectories and discounts its particularities—but never totally. Molarity limits individual deviancy but never entirely suppresses it. When we said that a molar structure was defined by what escapes it, that chance was knocking at the doors of the courthouse, it was a way of saying that nothing is ever successfully molar. Every person is a dissipated individual squirming in handcuffs waiting to escape. Stability is always actually metastability, a controlled state of volatility. No body can really *be* molar. Bodies are *made* molar, with varying degrees of success. The reactive agents of molarization—the world's judges and petty gods incarnate—are dissipative individuals gone bad. They are dissipative individuals who have been subjected, and resentfully subject others in turn.

There is a crucial difference between the dissipative structures that fill our lives and the structure we have analyzed thus far: there were only two attractors in the liquid system, and they were whole. The system had a whole dimensionality of two (it had two independent variables: the tendencies determined by the attractors). If life is an infinite fractal, it must have one monstrous *fractal attractor*. Cases like the one we just saw would only exist in controlled settings, the kinds of settings molarizing forces try to create. A new definition of molarity suggests itself: the imposition of *whole attractors* on a far more complex reality. That the presence of whole attractors (tendential stable equilibriums) cannot prevent the irruption of indeterminacy—however scrupulously controlled the experimental situation may be—is more evidence of just how special a case molarity really is. It is so special that it only exists as the objective illusion of a line of adequate causality that is always in fact deflected into cocausality by interference.

Fractal or "strange" attractors are just becoming available to scientific investigation. The details are not important here, but a brief sketch of the concept is. A whole attractor can be visualized as a distinct point at the end of a line. At both ends, actually: in classical thermodynamics, molecular instability departs from an entropic equilibrium and eventually returns to it. The process is reversible. The attractor state is virtual insofar as the instability that departs from it and tends toward it is concerned, but in theory it is actualizable. A fractal attractor, by contrast, must be visualized as a mixed set of points—"*dense points*," infinitely dense points.[43] Each point corresponds to a potential global state of equilibrium (stable or metastable, classical or dissipative). Say that every region of the system, however small, includes every kind of dense point. In other words, in every possible state of the system, every one of its regions — down to the tiniest molecule — has the potential to resonate with the others in such a way as to actualize any of the global equilibrium states corresponding to a given dense point. The intensity of a dense point may vary by region (not every part of the system will display the same inclination to join the move toward a particular equilibrium). But the dense points are still there, however far we go, even if we dip below the molecular level. They are still there even beyond our ability to probe: they are virtual particles. A mixed set of infinitely dense virtual particles is a singularity in much the same way we defined an actual singularity: a differential local–global resonance.

The whole attractor guiding a tendency toward entropic equilibrium is weak. It pertains only to one potential state expressed as a destiny, which it cannot fully actualize. The cocausal tendency expressed by the singular threshold state of an active equilibrium is more dynamic. It pertains to more than one potential state, and can effectively contract them into its actuality in the form of inclusively disjoined bifurcating choices. The whole attractor is virtual, but weakly so: it resonates one dense point corresponding to one global state, but at too low an intensity to be entirely effective. The singular threshold state effectively resonates several dense points at a high enough intensity that more than one global state is materially present (in a highly differentiated but undecidable mix). The supermolecule interacts more extensively with the fractal attractor comprising the totality of dense points; it is closer to the virtual. The fractal attractor *is* the virtual. No actuality can effectively contract all of the fractal attractor's states into its bifurcations, or overlap with it entirely. Some potential states drop out of each global state's actuality, but they go on quietly resonating in another dimension, as pure abstract potential.

The virtual and the actual are coresonating systems. As the actual contracts a set of virtual states into itself at a threshold state, the virtual dilates. When the actual passes a threshold, bifurcates toward a specific choice, and renounces the other potential states, the virtual contracts them back and the actual dilates. When one contracts (resonates at a higher intensity), the other dilates (relaxes). Each side has its own internal local–global correlations: resonances and tensions between nucleating subpopulations that respond individually and together. The local–global correlation of the actual and that of the virtual interact as subpopulations of a single individual. The universe is a double-faced supermolecule, each face of which is a supermolecule in its own right. They peacefully resonate together, or, if the tensions on one side or the other reach turbulent proportions, they clash. In that case, the turbulent side sends shock waves of crisis that amplify through the other, which is forced to infold the disturbance into its local–global correlation as best it can. The universe as a cosmic dissipative system.

To every actual intensity corresponds a virtual one. Actual intensity has extension (form and substance), virtual intensity does not: it is a *pure intensity*. The virtual has only *in*tension. This is not to say that it is undifferentiated. Only that it is indeterminate in our spatiality. Every one of its dense points is adjacent to every point in the actual world, distanced from it only by the intensity of its resonance and its nearness to collapse. This means that it is also indeterminate in relation to our temporality. Each of its regions or individuals is the future and the past of an actual individual: its system of contractions and dilations; the states it has chosen, will choose, and could have chosen but did not (and will not). All of this is always there at every instant, at varying intensities, insistently. The virtual as a whole is the future-past of all actuality, the pool of potential from which universal history draws it choices and to which it returns the states it renounces. The virtual is not undifferentiated. It is *hyperdifferentiated*. If it is the void, it is a hypervoid in continual ferment. The fractal attractor of the world cannot be represented as a reversible line with two distinct end points. Its only directionality is the jagged, superlinear line of becoming and debecoming leading from its virtuality into our actuality and simultaneously back again in a local–global interference pattern. The actual fractal, or our world, is the only destination the virtual has. Its only end is an endless becoming-actual of immanence through *ex*tension into our dimension and its mode of spatiotemporal composition. Conversely, the only end the actual world has is the constraint to rejoin its plane of immanence. It is destined, as the Taoists say, to pace the void (or as the mathematicians say, to take a random walk).[44]

No system is a closed system. Some, however, appear to be. Our liquid, for example, was in a vessel. But the vessel was in the world, which does not have two independent variables. A system can be controlled within certain limits, and within those limits it can be described as closed and as having whole attractors. Not adequately, but adequately enough, as long as the controls hold. The whole attractors attributed to the liquid system were abstract images of two of the fractal attractor's dense points. Any singular states or thresholds embodied by the system corresponded to other of that attractor's dense points. In the limited deterministic context, these singularities are not deemed attractors because they arise intrinsically from the "determined" system — are *invented* in the course of its history. This is precisely what makes them of such interest: they are unexpected effects that spontaneously arise from deterministic constraints, producing an enigmatic cocausal context much closer to the actual situations we find outside the laboratory. A cocausal dissipative structure of this kind can be treated, again for practical purposes, as a less limited, open system with a strange (fractal) attractor all its own, one capable of creating singular, deviant becomings that go off on a tangent to their nominal constraints. (This is the context in which we will approach the human body in what immediately follows, wherein we fill it with warm liquid.) When a system is treated as though it were guided by a fractal attractor of its own, only the dense points that most actively resonate in its vicinity are taken into account. The potential tensions and trajectories defined by that set of dense points is the system's plane of immanence or consistency: its level of virtuality. Scientists express a phenomenon's plane of consistency as its "phase space": the sum total of the system's movements and moments contracted into the same set of diagram coordinates. Each coordinate axis corresponds to an independent variable, and each coordinate to a potential state combining those variables. Coordinates around which potential states cluster are dense points, or attractor states. For example, the dense point corresponding to the attractor state of gravitational rest lies at the intersection of three axes — time, space, and velocity — and expresses a tendency for velocity to approach zero. The dense point expressing the tendency of a liquid system to self-organize as a dissipative structure would appear with the addition of axes corresponding to the independent variables of heat and density. The number of independent variables defines the system's dimensionality to the nearest whole. As we have seen, interference between attractors adds an element of chance, meaning that the actual dimensionality is always fractional. The integration of the phase space (the equation or diagram expressing the pattern of potential states and paths between states that the phase space envelops) is always an approximation (it is an*exact*). It can never grasp the real indeterminacy of the everywhere-all-the-time density of the virtual, which ultimately forbids any system, however controlled, to have a whole dimensionality and entirely predictable behavior. No system is a fully integrable system. Fractionality (fractality) is the measure of a system's deviation from the law.[45]

The important thing is that any theoretical analysis or "diagram" of a phenomenon is an incomplete abstraction designed to grasp from a restricted point of view an infinitely abstract monster fractal attractor that is alone adequate to the complexities of life. Whole attractors (governing closed deterministic systems) and fractal attractors (governing probabilistic, or cocausal, open systems) are valid conceptual tools within certain parameters. No presentation envelops a complete knowledge of even the simplest system. This is not because information is lacking and needs to be found. Complete, predictive knowledge is a myth. The perpetual invention called "history" paces a void of objective indeterminacy. All we can do is experimentally perturb it as we walk our life's path, and see what comes. We cannot even begin to understand the richness and surprises of life — and the possibilities it offers — without at least acknowledging that line of cocausal becoming between the actual and virtual worlds. It can be frustrating because our calculations will always be off. But it is also encouraging: it throws *their* calculations off as well. Judges and petty gods incarnate, take heed: The world is an infinite(simal)ly strange double-headed monster fractal attractor. Step lightly. Your judgments dance on the brink of a teeming void.

Burp

A baby is a vortex. Observe a smiling infant's toes. The joy of eye-to-eye contact with its mother resonates through its body and comes out the far end in a kick. Every impulse travels instantly in waves from the point of impact to every region of its body, where it is translated into an action that amplifies or muffles it. A baby is a supermolecule. It has differentiated body parts, but every local excitation brings a global response. Every body part, every time it is stimulated, sends out vibrations to every other part. The baby as vibrator. The globality of its responses does not diminish its local differentiation; on the contrary, differentiation increases. The vibrations a given part receives are more or less intense depending on their origin. The impulses it receives most directly are most intense of all. Each local part is a unique superposition of potential response-states of varying intensity. Each part will register every state, but to a different degree and translated into an action of which no other part is capable (no one can kick joy in the eyes). Interference patterns develop which vary the degree and the actions of the same body part. The supermolecule sees its father and the smile is translated into a curl of the toes; it sees its mother and kicks. It is hungry. Its stomach has modulated the toe response. The toes are developing a repertory. They not only receive vibrations of varying intensities from other parts, but they vary the intensity of their response to the same vibration. The baby develops increasingly nuanced local reactions which translate increasingly complex global interactions. Differentiation on one level goes toe in toe with differentiation on the other.

A baby is a local–global integration of vibrations. Each of its parts is a collection of potential modulations of impulses originating somewhere else in the body. Every part transmits the impulses it receives for modulation by all the other parts. Some, like the eyes, receive their impulses from an aleatory outside. Others, like the stomach, from a genetically determined "inside" (which is ultimately an infolding of the aleatory outside of natural selection). A cocausal dissipative system. Impulses following either trajectory are infolded to some degree by every part, and those infoldings combine to create a singular state or overall intensity. Each singular state is a threshold state composed of a set of potential responses. The interference pattern reaches a point of bifurcation at each of its local destinations: it will be translated into one action or another. That bifurcation in turn bifurcates: the action is executed to one degree or another. The local bifurcations add up to an instantaneous global response. The next singular state is an interaction of that global response and a new impulse. A new threshold is reached. The baby flails its way from one threshold to the next. Its life is an endless succession of crises, some major, some minor. The interferences are modulated in such a way that the singular state is an actively stable one more often than not. Behavior patterns develop. Certain responses are favored. Certain parts associated with those responses are privileged over others. The system gets so complex so quickly that in spite of habitual patterns responses cannot be accurately predicted even in the youngest of supermolecules. It is hungry, and kicks at its father even though he is a nice married man of the sort who would never dream of picking up a baby bottle. The mother comes, and only gets a curl. Who knows what is going on in the convolutions of its brain?

The infant is a supermolecular supple individual. Call it a "body": an endless weaving together of singular states, each of which is an integration of one or more impulses. Call each of the body's different vibratory regions a "zone of intensity." Look at the zone of intensity from the point of view of the actions it produces. From that perspective, call it an "organ." Look at it again from the point of view of the organ's favorite actions, and call it an "erogenous zone." Imagine the body in suspended animation: intensity = 0. Call that the "body without organs" (or BwO, as D & G like to write it).[46] Think of the body without organs as the body outside any determinate state, poised for any action in its repertory; this is the body from the point of view of its potential, or virtuality. Now freeze it as it passes through a threshold state on the way from one determinate state to another. That is a degree of intensity of the body without organs. It is still the body as virtuality, but at a lower level of virtuality, because only the potential states involved in the bifurcation from the preceding state to the next are effectively superposed in the threshold state. The disjunctive synthesis constituted by the bifurcation can still be considered inclusive: although only one alternative is actualized, it includes vibrations from all the other states at different degrees of intensity, and none of those states is excluded a priori from being actualized next. As behavior patterns develop, the disjunctions become increasingly exclusive: for each threshold reached, another state can be expected to follow with a high degree of probability. Fewer states are effectively superposed: the body's potential ("power," "degree of freedom") has diminished. If you freeze it at the threshold state now, the vibrations of all the states but the one just left and the one about to come are muffled to the point that they are almost imperceptible. The vibrations associated with two of its states are amplified, but the body's overall intensity is lower. Since the body is an open system, an infolding of impulses from an aleatory outside, all its potential singular states are determined by a fractal attractor. Call that strange attractor the body's plane of consistency. It is a subset of the world's plane of consistency, a segment of its infinite fractal attractor. It is the body as pure potential, pure virtuality (its phase space). The body without organs is a subset of the body's plane of consistency: the attractor segment containing the repertory of potential states among which it effectively chooses. An organ corresponds to each point (set of dense points) on that segment. Call the attractor point-set governing the actualization of an organ's actions a "part-object" — a subset of a subset of the fractal attractor of the world. If the universe is the plane of consistency of our world, then the body's plane of consistency is the Milky Way of its potential orbits and trajectories, and a part-object is a star. The body without organs is a region of the Milky Way marked by a constellation but including an infinity of background stars visible at varying degrees of intensity. As we will now see, the behavior patterns that begin to develop are the constellation as perceived from a civilization center. The glare of city lights begin to obscure all but the brightest stars in its region of the sky: in the end, only the "meaningful" ones outlining the constellation's symbolic shape remain. It is these interpreted (dedensified) attractor points that will govern the socially significant actions of the organs of the unified adult body as Big or Little Dipper into authorized surplus-value satisfactions.

The behavior patterns that begin to take hold reflect habitual patterns in the baby's surroundings. It begins to learn that a particular impulse will be followed by another with a high degree of probability. Mother bends over crib. Eyes meet. Smile-kick. The kick translates the expectation that the smile will give way to a suck, and the stomach will be happy. The connective synthesis of eye-to-eye is followed by the connective synthesis of mouth-to-breast. The smile-kick threshold state is the conjunctive synthesis of two connective syntheses. More, actually. It conjoins those two with the passive connective synthesis of back-on-bed, and if the kick swings wide, the painfully active one of toe-to-crib. The baby's conjunctions become more segregative as its disjunctions become increasingly exclusive. Who needs a toe ache? The baby tones down its vibrations, pares down its conjunctions. It focuses in on the succession from one habitual connection with the world to the next, and on the privileged organs and sensations associated with it. The smile-kick was a contraction of many levels of sensation: hunger, pressure on the back, the visual perception of the mother, a pain in the toe. Sensations inessential to the expectation of the breast are filtered out, and one sensation is focused in on above all the others. It did not even figure on the list because it is of a very different nature: joy.

To understand joy, we must understand what follows the much expected mouth-to-breast connection. The baby is burped.[47] As we have already seen, a sensation is a surplus value, an excess effect accruing to the global level of a correlated molecular population. Each of the sensations on the kick list was a surplus-value in excess of the sensations they in turn enveloped: excitations of the eye's population of rods and cones, for example, were contracted into an overall perception which had the added value of being able to interact with similar contractions by other organs (the toe's contraction of a multitude of nerve endings is one). A mass of sensations, a veritable infinity of impulses, is contracted into a restricted set of higher order sensations. That set of sensations is again contracted, along with the set of mouth-to-breast sensations, into a single retrospective sensation. The whole process is summed up in a burp. The burp marks the satiation point, alleviating the last tension associated with hunger. Sleep (happy oblivion) follows. The joy of the smile and kick is evidence of a feedback loop. Regurgitation—the all-too-human warmth of vomit on the baby's chin, the taste of the curdled milk's second coming—is utterly superfluous, a useless end effect that evaporates in a whiff of bad breath. The burp is an afterthought, an evaporative aftereffect (a consumption-consummation). But it leaves a trace. It is recorded. The vomit is the final gastrointestinal landmark before oblivion, the period at the end of a prayer of deliverance (if vomit could speak, it would praise the breast with religious fervor). The joy is the vomit fed back into the threshold smile-and-kick state that will have led to it. It is the future-past of vomit: the memory of burps past and the expectation of burps to come. The feedback level of sensation is a higher order sensation superimposed on the other sensations. Hovering over the conjunctive synthesis leading from eye-to-eye to mouth-to-breast is a recognition. A *re*cognition. An abstract thought that is in fact the afterthought of the afterthought it anticipates. Resonance has become *redundancy*. "So that's it! Again! Praise the breast!"[48]

This is the beginnings of human subjectivity. So far, there is only a "larval self."[49] It is ineffectual, fleeting, and strictly localized. It is tied to the conjunctive synthesis over which it hovers. It is actualized whenever that synthesis is actualized, in other words periodically, as the baby moves through the circuit of anticipated states its life is beginning to be. This self is not alone. There are many conjunctions of the same nature, and a similar self for every one of them. The baby is a teeming mass of larval selves, each associated with a threshold state featuring a privileged organ on the way to satisfaction through connection with another privileged organ. On the feedback level of recognition, there are always at least two organs in play, usually nominally belonging to distinct bodies: mouth and breast. But it is no exaggeration to say that on this level the breast is as much a part of the baby's body as it is of the mother's. It is infolded in the infant brain. The human body as supermolecule has no determinate boundaries. It is the in-between of biological bodies, as infolded in memory. It lies at the crossroads of two causal lines. One goes from determinacy (genetics: the biological memory constituting the in-between of bodies of different generations) to indeterminacy (a contractive threshold state culminating a social encounter across the generational divide); the other from indeterminacy (the appearance of the mother's face above the crib is uncaused as far as the baby is concerned: a gift of the gods) to determinacy (habit: lived memory, interbody action folded into the fabric of everyday life).

Although it is convenient shorthand to refer to organs as part-objects, they are in actuality only the *object* part — the presence in the actual of a virtual point set of the fractal attractor. Even this is a misleading formulation, because presubjective memory traces (of the mouth associating it with the breast and of the breast associating it with the mouth) are more directly involved in the recognition at the basis of the selves than are any organs in their physical presence. These dual connective imprints are on the order of thought (intensive rather than extensive), and are thus closer in mode of composition to the virtual attractor governing the actualization of the threshold state than the organs are (they are superposable as opposed to juxtaposable). The actual organs are indexes, twice removed, of the two-headed fractal attractor of smiling.[50]

The breast comes to overshadow the mouth. The mouth is always available for service; the breast is not. So the anticipation is breast-directed. The beselved body in fact lives more outside its literal boundary than inside it: the feedback loop of recognition tends to elide everything but the breast, which comes to epitomize the overall process of surplus value production-eruction. The fractal attractor is eclipsed by a whole attractor — the awaited breast seems to stand alone, the final cause of satisfaction, its end and origin in one, the preeminent image of a joyful future-past. The entire complex causality with all its multiple levels and vibrations and crisscrossed trajectories begins to seem like a straight, nipple-drawn line to and from the equilibrium state of gentle burping and satiation. A routine circuit develops from one satisfaction to the next. The breast, now more metaphysical image than organ, governs a tendency: a *drive* channeling the baby's actualizations of its bodily potential toward a favored satisfaction. The suckling drive is to the baby what the Second Law is to warm liquid: an exhortation to be entropically satiated.

There are any number of part-objects in a baby's life, all associated with drives of varying strengths constituting more or less habit-forming circuits of anticipation-satisfaction. Only some, like the breast, become addictive whole attractors. The body's syntheses become focus more and more on them, to the exclusion of other drives, let alone vibrations that never made it to the level of a recognized tendency. This creates a tension between all the downgraded vibrations and the privileged few imaged as whole attractors. The downgraded ones clamor against the metaphysicalized organs and strive to throw off their tyranny. The body's whole attractors and their potential circuits constitute a "limitative body without organs" (closed constellation) which enters into combat with the "nonlimitative body without organs" of the submerged fractal attractor point sets and their infinitely more varied potential paths (open constellation).[51] The nonlimitative body without organs repels the sacred organs, and the limitative body without organs attracts them back, inducing the rebel vibrations to recontract into a tame satisfaction. A new cocausal tension arises that prevents the body from sinking into entropic lethargy, maintaining it as an active dissipative structure. Active, but not as active as it could be. Over all, the body's action is limited to the kind characterized earlier as reaction: recording of memory, recognition of part-object, repetition of satisfaction, reproduction of the same circuit. The whole attractors always manage to reimpose their supremacy — with the aid of reinforcements from even more powerful reactive forces. Growing up is one long, constantly renewed becoming-reactive of active dissipative forces.

This is leading us to a whole new level, on which recognition becomes *reflection*. Some of the body's vibrations resonate with its surroundings and are amplified. Some clash with them and are muffled. Resonant vibrations are identified as belonging to the body in some more essential way clashing ones. "Good baby!" They come back amplified into virtues (the genealogy of morals). It would be interesting to calculate the percentage of what a child just learning to talk hears that is commentary on what it just did, is doing, is about to do, or should have done. "Baby just used the toilet. Good baby!" "Baby came to daddy. Good baby!" "The next time you throw your peas on the floor ..." Scratch the surface of reflective commentary and an order-word erupts in its naked form: "Never do that again . . . always do what I tell you." The sensations of the first feedback loop are bumped up a level, contracting into sensations of pride or shame or guilt. Overflying the larval selves are new fledgling selves. "That's it!" becomes "that's me!" "That was me, baby just used the toilet." "Baby just went to daddy." Recognition has become self-recognition. "I just threw my peas on the floor. Was that really me?" Objective anticipation (Will she or won't she come?) becomes moral reflection (Was that *me*? Am *I* like that?). Everything begins to happen between a "me" and the "I" doubling it (another redundancy). A proper name holds the two together. All of this constitutes the creation of an incredible new potential, but also marks an important setback: the path taken at a point of bifurcation can now be "willed," but powerful forces descend to assure that what the body wills is, on average, what "society" wills for it.

The reactive nature of the syntheses of recognition provides a hook for reactive forces from the social field to clamp into the flesh. A society is a dissipative structure with its own determining tension between a limitative body without organs and a nonlimitative one. Together, in their interaction, they are called a "socius" (the abstract machine of society). The nonlimitative body without organs of a socius is the sum total of its constituent supermolecular bodies, or individuals, from the point of view of their potential for "free" or "willful" action, in other words for the undetermined selection of singular states as a locally– globally correlated population. The limitative body without organs of a socius is a set of whole attractors proposed by a society for its individuals, the better to exploit their habit-forming potential. A grid of abstract categories systematizes images of suggested attractor states and maps the patterns of reproductive action and consumption they authorize. Husband/wife, parent/child: replicate the family and the satisfactions of conjugal life. White/Black, man/woman, heterosexual/homosexual: replicate the customary separation between the races and sexes and the satisfaction of feeling superior. Faithful/infidel: replicate traditional religion and the satisfaction of being right. Rich/poor: replicate social disparity and the satisfaction of economic exploitation. The list goes on. The grid is a proliferating series of exclusive disjunctive syntheses adding up to a system of value judgment. You are either all one or all the other, and if you're the other you're not as good. If you don't get as much out of life as I do, it's quite simply because you don't deserve it. Value judgment and distribution of value are two sides of the same coin. Surplus value's done! Come and get it! But I'm better so I get a bigger piece of the cake. As infantile as this is, it is no mere child's play. What is ultimately reproduced is society's capitalist balance of power. The whole system is an apparatus of capture of the vital potential of the many for the disproportionate and sometimes deadly satisfactions of the few.

The fledgling selves were still plural and relatively localized, vacillating between staying on their own level and stepping down to larval status. A full-fledged self only takes wing after the grid of value judgment has been successfully applied to the body, incorporeally transforming it into its assigned categories. "That's me! / Am I like that?" gives way to the smug satisfaction of "Yes indeed, that's me and I'm proud to be one." Unless of course the body happens to fall into one or more of the downgraded categories (as most do). Fewer satisfactions are offered to such lowly beings, so the tension between the limitative and the nonlimitative bodies without organs remains high and the motivation to fall in line decreases even as the dangers of not doing so increase. Order-words proliferate, whispered commands and threats passed from lip to lip. If the body doesn't say "I do," it's in trouble. Its homegrown habitual circuits rigidify even further into a set of preestablished paths ordained for it in accordance with its categories: school paths become career paths, play gives way to marriage, a new family replaces the old. Children grow up in the image of their

parents. And so the world turns. The body is led as on a leash from one
threshold in life to another. A respectable person with respectable
satisfactions is born. Praise the Lord! It's a human. Everything is now
I-to-I in civilized connections. Problem is, some eyes are higher than
others.

Vomit still clings invisibly to the grown-up baby's chin, even as its "I"
looks down at others. As it mouths its value judgments, it exhales a
smell of rot. The odor of sanctity. Larvae are teeming ever more
restlessly the more deeply they are submerged, eating away at the
body's flesh as it smugly zombifies, clamoring to get out and to release
into the world things even more subhuman than maggots.[52] Sometimes
the tension grows to the breaking point, and a crisis ensues. Recupera-
tive mechanisms usually ensure that the larval breakout is a breakdown leading back to the grid. The categories reactivate. The leash
tightens. In rare instances, breakdown veers into breakaway, a line of
escape back to the nonlimitative body without organs and the increased potential residing there. That is called "art" (whether or not a
painting or poem is ever produced). In still rarer instances, the
individual is joined in its breakaway by other individuals in its correlated population. The balance of power tips, mayhem ensues, a
societywide crisis sets in. This is called "revolution" (whether or not a
new government is created — on second thought especially when one
isn't). These are instances of a molarity becoming-supermolecular,
reactualizing its potential for expansive, inclusive syntheses in which
the population as a whole sensitizes to the singularities of its individuals, resonating with more than against them, combining potentials and
creating new ones rather than subtracting potentials already clamoring to express themselves. Supple individuals enveloped in a supple
superindividual, with possibilities for unheard-of, inhuman (superhuman?) bifurcations on both global and local levels. A rebecoming-
active of the body politic. An infusion of life. A breath of fresh air.

In our culture, such things are prevented from happening by a
process of *application* (a channelizing overlay of social categories)
centering on the family.[53] Deleuze and Guattari call that process
"Oedipus." Their analysis of it in *Anti-Oedipus* is perhaps the best-
known aspect of their work. It boils down to the process just discussed:
the reinforcement and amplification of the body's whole attractors,
conventionally expressed as authorized social categories to be in or

conjoin with (man/woman, husband/wife, boss/employee, and so on). The still relatively unpredictable part-objects are more successfully regularized by being refocused on a higher level. Their allure attaches to whole bodies identified by social category, rather than to organs on those bodies experienced as a matrixes of transformational potential. Connections are now person-to-person. The coordinates are set. Entropic equilibrium sets in.

The vomit can speak now, but the breast is no longer a mysterious entity, causing but uncaused — only a regressive plaything. The fervid praise lands elsewhere (on a divinized man, of course, the better to solidify the balance of power). The breast is doubly privatized. It belongs to a mother-substitute, and the mother-substitute is a lawfully wedded wife belonging to a pious zombie. Redundancy. Everything is private, and everything private has a double assignation (yours and mine). Our possessions are dearer to us than life itself, but we know how to share them with those we love. Love is conjugal. By definition. Everywhere, wholly attractive couples dance ritual circles around each other like Newtonian planets around an invisible sun. Everywhere, the lifeless promise of mutual possession. Bodies mouthing the same touching refrains: "I do," "I am yours," "If you touch him I'll kill you." You will see, if you turn on the TV. You will see repeats — and commercials for home goods. You will see that the future has folded into the past. All of the endless variations on what it is to be human (not to mention inhuman) that can be observed in the social field have folded into a limited grid of repetitive categories, which have folded yet again into the reproductive family unit. Reduction. Collapse of the wave-packet. The future-past as the eternal return of the same, rather than the continual creation of difference. The TV screen is only one of many mechanisms for reducing the boundaries of the universe to the dimensions of a microcosm. They make the wife the husband's mother, and the boss his daddy: everything is always already reduced to categories that are then mapped back into a whitewashed childhood home with a comforting fire crackling in the den. The fifties never stop coming back (after a fashion). The big lie, then as now: children are cute. Was it me who threw peas on the floor? Must have been somebody else. I was good as gold. Or: Remember the time I threw peas on the floor? Wasn't I a card! But: There was that mysterious big white thing with a dark spot in the middle with a darker spot in the middle of that. And it kept coming back. Was that God? Couldn't have been. It was only Mother. Then again: that spot looked an awful lot like the pupil in Christ's deeply caring big blue suffering eye. We all know that he was white.[54]

We are all under pressure to regress. When we do, the past we resurrect is a myth: a golden age of satiation free from gastrointestinal upset; a garden of Eden of home comfort the fifties never were. Everything has gotten fuzzy, indeterminate, both this and that, nipple and god. But this kind of indeterminacy is totally different from the kind we have discussed up to now. It is not an objective indeterminacy, only a retrospective, fantasied one: an imaginary confusion between the present and the past, not the real choice presented by indefinitely bifurcating becomings. It is not an impingement of chance. It is highly determined—overdetermined. The "this and that" that everything is tend to be the same "this" and the same "that," over and over again, like a broken record. It's a trap. The whole thing is an optical illusion produced by overcoding. It is an objective illusion, a real imaginary capture that exploits a reactive streak in every body to trap them in the same fantasies, in identical suburban homes, in predictable careers, in adorable hobbies that offer controlled reconnection with subhuman part-objects as long as they don't get out of hand. Have you seen my rock collection?

The only easy way out of stereotyped regression is stereotyped breakdown: I see it now, it's all a lie . . . I wasn't good and I wasn't cute . . . that dark spot was between my mother's legs . . . but she belonged to him . . . I wanted to fuck my mother and kill my father. Or was it the other way around? I've got it: I didn't have a prick to do it with so I had to learn to love my father and be my own mother, but she was already herself and I hated her for that . . . Wait a minute, Am I a boy or a girl? Am I gay or straight? Am I me or somebody else? Am I alive or dead? Did I kill God or am I God? *Or, or, or.* The *and* of the indeterminate "this *and* that" was just a way of getting in a good *or* or two. We've heard it all a million times before. Luckily, there is psychoanalysis to teach us how to keep swallowing our childhood vomit with all-too-human dignity. It keeps things discreet, behind closed doors. Too bad it costs so much to get across that threshold (to each his private surplus value). For those who don't pay, there are more archaic alternatives. The current sheriff of Phoenix is named Dick Godbehere. Divine election.

Vote for Dick! If you wander from the straight and narrow path, He will flash his big blue eyes and even bigger gun, and shepherd you into His home.[55]

A quick glance around the social field reveals that many bodies are neither normally familialized nor stereotypically infantilized, and that they sometimes do things most law-abiding folks wouldn't even dream of. This suggests that trap of molar personhood only has a limited hold after all. There is noise in the person-to-person communication. The whisperings accompanying the transmission of order-words sometimes blurs into distant echoes of rebellion, like a faraway conversation in a foreign tongue invading the phone line. The fact that many people, more and more it seems, consider those who amplify the noise into action to be deviant and disgusting is evidence that metastable molar personhood will nevertheless be with us for a very long time to come. They are right on one count. Such people *are* deviant. Gloriously so. Which is more disgusting (or pathetic): to throw a rock through a courthouse window or to collect and label it? To break out in larvae or to pin an insect?

Pause

A quick sketch of how this differs from some common psychological and psychoanalytic conceptions:

1. There is no interiority in the sense of a closed, self-reflective system. There is only multileveled infolding of an aleatory outside, with which the infolding remains in contact (as a dissipative structure). Reactive forces do impose "self"-reflection on the infolding at a certain level. On that level, a more rigid boundary takes shape between "self" and "other," but the cordoning off is never complete. The self remains susceptible to identity crises brought on by confusions between "inside" and "outside." A membranous porosity subsists, muted, on other levels and always threatens to break through. Subjectification is the constitution, through interlocking passive and active syntheses on every stratum, of infoldings of varying porosity.

2. "Human" subjectivity in the sense of personal thought or feeling is a special case existing only on one level of a dissipated human body system: the bounded, dominated level of the body as subjected group.

A human subject in the broad sense is a superindividual composed of a multitude of subindividuals comparable to muck and sedimentary rock, but doubled by surplus-value layers of larval and fledgling selves. These grow intrinsically from the contractive syntheses (impersonal perceptions-sensations) of their infoldings. As in the case of muck, an overcoding mechanism exists (Oedipus). It does not create a self, but acts on already-constituted surplus-value selves to extract a categorical person (stereotyped, familialized, pious reproductive system). The person always has the potential to reconnect with its impersonality to become a subject-group: singular, orphan, atheist, inhuman. Since a person is only as stable as its constituent contractions — that is, metastable — it can be precipitated into a crisis state despite its best intentions.

3. In other words, there is no self-sufficient agency that can qualify as intentional. There are varying degrees of choice at successive threshold states. The "will" to change or to stay the same is not an act of determination on the part of a unified subject in simple response to self-reflection or an internal impulse. It is a state of self-organized indeterminacy in response to complex causal constraints. It constitutes a real degree of freedom, but the choice belongs to the overall dissipative system with its plurality of selves, and not to the person; it is objectively cocaused at the crossroads of chance and determinacy. It is an objective illusion of the molar person to perceive the physical reality of free action as a metaphysical freedom or "human right" exercised by a unified, self-directing, full causal agent.

4. The family is not a closed microcosm, even if it is represented and represents itself as one. It opens directly onto the social field. A body does not grow up sheltered from society, enclosed in the family that feeds it. Rather, the family opens the body to society's feeding itself off it. The family is a device for the capture of body potential (channelization) by social forces of domination dedicated to the vampiric extraction of surplus value and the cyclic resupply of the bodies from which this surplus value is sucked. What the family reproduces is more fundamentally collective value relations than discrete physical bodies. The family is a microcosm of society only to the extent that Oedipal processes at work throughout the social field collapse categories belonging to other levels of organization into family

categories (equating for example, foreman with father, treating one as the signifier of the other) — in other words, to the extent that overcoding mechanisms select the family as the target for a multiple overlay creating a closed set of Imaginary–Symbolic relays (Oedipus again).

5. *Desire* is not desire for an object, except to the extent that whole attractors (represented by anything from an organ to a god) are imposed on the body by reactive forces. It is not a drive in the Freudian sense, and it is not a structure in the sense that language is a structure in the Saussurian model adopted by Lacanians. It can be made to be these things on one of its levels. That level is more the straitjacketing of desire (desire turned resentfully against itself). Desire is the production of singular states of intensity by the repulsion-attraction of limitative bodies without organs (governed by deterministic whole attractors) and nonlimitative bodies without organs (governed by chance-ridden fractal attractors). In its widest connotation, it is the plane of consistency as multiple cocausal becoming (interactions between any number of fractal and whole attractors on many levels; nothing less than the abstract machine). On the human level, it is never a strictly personal affair, but a tension between sub- and superpersonal tendencies that intersect in the person as empty category. In an ethical context, it is the tendency of one of the states created by the interplay of bodies without organs to remain in existence or return to existence, not for merely reproductive ends, but in order to actualize its potential to increasingly higher degrees: Spinoza's *conatus*. It is the relative advantage of the nonlimitative body without organs over the limitative one, the relative strength of inclusive disjunction over exclusive disjunction (the superposition of states, the adding together of potentials from normally segregated states): Nietzsche's will to power. In *Anti-Oedipus*, a tendency of this kind was called a "desiring-machine." Due to persistent subjectivist misunderstandings, in *A Thousand Plateaus* the word was changed to the more neutral "assemblage."[56]

6. The unconscious is not fundamentally a repository of submerged feelings and images as in the vulgar Freudian model. Neither is it fundamentally a Lacanian dialectic between the Imaginary (dyadic confusion, especially between self and other) and the Symbolic (as structured by the sacred trinity of the father-phallic "signifier of signifiers," the son the sacrificed signified, and the holy ghost metaphor

and metonymy). It can be made to be these things, on two of its levels. More broadly, though, the unconscious is everything that is left behind in a contraction of selection or sensation that moves from one level of organization to another: It is the structurations and selections of nature as contracted into human DNA. It is the multitude of excitations of rods and cones and nerve cells as contracted into a perception of the human body. It is the perceptions of the human body as contracted into larval selves. It is the larval selves as contracted into fledgling selves. It is the fledgling selves as contracted into the overself of the person. It is an interlocking of syntheses, natural and cultural, passive and active: productions of production, productions of recording, productions of consumption. Production. Becoming. It is continually changing as all of those levels are superposed and actualized to different degrees as the body jumps from one more or less indeterminate threshold state to the next. The only things the unconscious is not are present perception and reflection (personalized redundancy).

7. The subject is effectively split, as Lacanians describe it to be. But the split between self and other is only a recapitulation on the Oedipal level of more fundamental bifurcations. Clearly, there can only be an "other" to confuse "one"'s self with if there is first a "one" to have a self: in other words, if subjectivity functions as a closed system. One must come before two in order for two to be a doubling in which there is no three. Theories of subjectivity as a constitutive splitting arising from an imaginary dialectic of presence and absence, fusion and fragmentation, beg the question. They assume what they end up denying: "oneness" (enough to give presence and absence, fusion or fragmentation, a modicum of meaning). The added third term, the almighty triangulating phallus, only abstracts the assumed unity into a mysterious whole object — which must itself split if it is to cause a splitting in what it endows with fractured identity (its unity consists in always being absent to itself). The Lacanian theory of splitting spirals into increasingly metaphysical speculation that only reduplicates at ever-higher levels of abstraction that which it fails to explain (a confusion between one and two). The proliferating metaphysical splits between otherness and identity, Imaginary and Symbolic, signified and signifier, subject of the enunciation and subject of the statement, translate a real bodily bifurcation: between the human person and its subhuman individuals, the limitative and the nonlimitative body without organs,

reflection and the unconscious as defined above. The fractal gap between the person and its individuals is translated by Oedipal mechanisms onto a level at which it can be interiorized in a personality structure. Transposed onto that level, it appears as the distance separating the self from its reflection (the "Was that me?" of the mirror stage). Lacanian splitting is a retrospective projection of distinctions belonging to the personal level of the constituted subjected group onto the entire dissipative system of the body: the multitude of individuals that contract to produce the person is reduced to the one-two-(three) of self-other-(phallus), distinctions which can exist only on the second-order level of identity and identity loss.[57] Identity and identity loss correspond to being in or slipping out of one's assigned category and the paths through the social field associated with it; they are the end effects, not the foundation, of the process of individuation. Lacanians need to learn how to count: three, four, five come before one, two, three. What is founding is the objective indeterminacy of the body's nonidentical threshold states. Their complication (the multiplicity of noncompossible choices they envelop) is represented by the Lacanian model as an imaginary undifferentiation. Their superposition with identity appears as an irresolvable dialectic. The singular future-past of the threshold becomes a revolving door: a single past that returns in the future (repetition-compulsion). The jagged line of becoming buckles into a circle. What is left out is precisely the reality of the unconscious ("the real is impossible"). Desire, the plane of consistency, is short-circuited by an infinite feedback loop of metaphysical redundancy.[58] At the center of the feedback loop, a private sun that is and isn't there. An ever-present absent object of overpowering attraction inspires an impossible ritual quest for fulfillment. Not incidentally, this is good for business. The Commodity is the capitalist incarnation of the phallus as Master Attractor. Love may be the light of one's life, but a toaster is an acceptable substitute. "When the going gets tough, the tough go shopping," to quote a popular suburban bumper sticker. To quote Barbara Kruger: "I shop therefore I am."

8. A corollary to the status of the split subject as a derived, second-order formation: the body without organs is *not the "fragmented body"* of psychoanalysis. A frequent critique of Deleuze and Guattari casts them as toddler visionaries in men's clothes preaching a return to the

maternal body. From within a psychoanalytic framework, those are the only terms in which their calls for a "return" to the body without organs can be understood: as a regression to the "pre-Oedipal" body, a denial of the "fact" of castration. Outside the Oedipally organized Symbolic order there is said to exist only an undifferentiated infant body (the OwB: organs without a body) laboring in a prelinguistic state of imaginary confusion between (fusion with) self and mOther.[59] The only alternative to resigning oneself to the adult "reality" of desire-as-lack is to exult in an imaginary union with a long-dead ghost from an incestuous past. This precludes lucidity of thought in academics and strategic action in politics: anarchism as an infantile disorder.[60]

This line of reasoning reflects a refusal to accept—or an inability to understand—the point just made: for Deleuze and Guattari the Oedipal alternatives of phallus-castration, plenitude-lack, identity-undifferentiation are retrospective illusions projected onto the infantile body. They are the normalized *adult* perspective on it. The so-called fragmentation exhibited by the "pre-Oedipal" body is in fact the fractality of part-objects as defined earlier—not the debilitating lack of an old unity but a real capacity for new connection. It is not a negativity in contrast to which a plenitude might be desired. It is a positive *faculty* for the production of connective syntheses involving a clear perception of "necessity" and an experimental assessment of chance (the chances of exploiting the margin of error in the artificially closed system of personhood in order to break out of its deterministic confines). What lies outside Oedipal subjectivity (actually, beside it: it is always contemporaneous with identity even if it is submerged by it[61]) is an effective superposition of an unaccustomed range of pragmatic potentials, not a protometaphysical "confusion." A return *to* the body without organs is actually a return *of* fractality, a resurfacing of the virtual. Not regression: invention. The body regains the self-transformative "freedom" accompanying the hyperdifferentiation of the dissipative structure at a point of bifurcation. Supermolecularity. Individuation at its most intense. As always, it involves an increase in "sensitivity" (lucidity), and a multiplication of strategic options. As well as a raising of the stakes. The degree of danger increases apace with the degree of freedom. There is no invention without a commensurate dose of instability. All the more reason to make the escape with utmost sobriety.[62]

9. A more sophisticated psychoanalytically oriented critique of Deleuze and Guattari's notion of the body without organs than the caricature just addressed has been developed by certain feminist authors.[63] These critiques, however, still accept a basic equivalence between the fragmented body and the body without organs. Given that equivalence, Deleuze and Guattari's exhortation for men to "become-woman" on their path of escape from molar manhood can only be seen as a denial of difference and thus a short-circuiting of gender politics. The added exhortation for women to lead the way by first "becoming-woman" themselves has the ring of the all-too-familiar gesture of abstracting an essence of "femininity" and exalting it as a state of grace that all women should occupy, in blatant disregard of the real conditions under which women actually live.[64]

Deleuze and Guattari do not deny the reality of sexual difference. They simply argue that it does not lie at the foundation of subjectivity. In their view, the binary couple Man / Woman is one of the interlocking sets of coordinates on the categorical grid defining the person. They correspond to Nobody (*Personne*). They are empty categories. "Woman" is simply the oppositional term without which "Man" would have no meaning. It is simply that in contrast to which what is designated "Man" is deemed superior. It is a patriarchal construct. "Man" is the Standard: the socially established measure of humanity against which individuals are judged and hierarchically valued. "Woman" is the sub-Standard: the sidekick necessary to give "Man" something to be superior to, an "Other" in contrast to which He can be all the Samer. "Woman" as an accessory "Man" is etymologically embedded in the English language. In Old English, the word meant wife-Man. "Man" and "wo-Man" belong to the same level and the same system of categorical judgment. They designate two poles of the same exclusive disjunctive synthesis.[65]

No real body ever entirely coincides with either category. A body only approaches its assigned category as a limit: it becomes more or less "feminine" or more or less "masculine" depending on the degree to which it conforms to the connections and trajectories laid out for it by society according to which coordinate in gender grid it is judged to coincide with. "Man" and "Woman" as such have no reality other than that of logical abstractions. What they are abstractions of are not the human bodies to which they are applied, but habit-forming whole attractors to which society expects it bodies to become addicted (love, school, family, church, career: artificially closed energetic systems revolving around subtypes of each gender category). "Man" and "Woman" and their many subcategories designate stereotyped sets of object choices and life paths (stable equilibriums) promoted by society. They are clichés that bodies are coerced into incarnating as best they can. No body *is* "masculine" or "feminine." One can only *come to* one's assigned cliché, like metal to a magnet that recedes farther into the distance the closer one draws, in an endless deflection from invention. The only end is death. Gender is a fatal detour from desire-in-deviation (every body's secret potential and birthright). It is akin to a mineralogical typecast; it is a reactive overlay, a molar overcoding (*re*production). A body does not *have* a gender: it is gender*ed*. Gender is done unto it by the socius. What is engendered is a social brick, a building block used to construct not the walls of a courthouse but of another factory of guilt: the family fortress. Gender is a form of imprisonment, a socially functional limitation of a body's connective and transformational capacity. Although thoroughly social, gender is not of course arbitrary in the sense that bodies are assigned categories at random. Gendering is the process by which a body is socially determined to be determined by biology: social channelization cast as destiny by being pinned to anatomical difference.

The feminine gender stereotype involves greater indeterminacy ("fickle") and movement ("flighty") and has been burdened by the patriarchal tradition with a disproportionate load of paradox (virgin/whore, mother/lover). Since supermolecularity involves a capacity to superpose states that are "normally" mutually exclusive, Deleuze and Guattari hold that the feminine cliché offers a better departure point than masculinity for a rebecoming-supermolecular of the personified individual. They therefore recommend what they call "becoming-woman" for bodies of either biological sex. Becoming-woman involves carrying the indeterminacy, movement, and paradox of the female stereotype past the point at which it is recuperable by the socius as it presently functions, over the limit beyond which lack of definition becomes the positive power to select a trajectory (the leap from the realm of possibility into the virtual—breaking away). This necessarily involves a redefinition of the category by and for those it traditionally targets: "fickleness" translated into a political refusal on the part of women to remain fixed within the confines of the home or other constrictive arenas of work (the feminist project of breaking down the barriers of traditional marriage, uncompensated domestic labor, and "women's work" generally); "flightiness" made to soar to heights of versatility in artistic creation (the invention of a women's writing). From a dismissive category to increased degrees of collective freedom; from value judgment to revaluation. Strategies of category alteration other than revaluation also have a place. The feminine cliché can be strategically misapplied: for example, it can be assumed by a man wishing to escape his socially assigned orbit of affects and actions (in any number of ways, from having a sex-change operation, to being the "passive" partner in a gay relation, to living as a "female-identified" heterosexual). Or it can be taken to such an extreme by a target body, played with such skill by a woman, that the tables turn and men are caught in their own identity trap ("feminine masquerade").[66]

As long as there is familial overcoding, there will be a need for gender politics to defend and empower those disfavored by the exercise in containment that is molar Man. Action in the conventional political arena aimed at elevating the status of individuals relegated to sub-Standard conditions by social overcoding is an indispensable aspect of becoming: women, gays, and other sexual minorities coming more fully into their collective potential by asserting their "equality." But revaluing a category, or even inventing new categories, is not enough in itself. Asserting the equality of "Woman" to "Man," or of any category to any other, only establishes an equal right to the privileges — and limitations — of molarity. It is the system of molarity itself that needs to be dismantled before human bodies will be able to fully reclaim their potential. Breaking into the existing order is a necessity, but not an end in itself. It is fundamentally a becoming-the-same — molarized. It is ultimately self-defeating unless it is used as a protective mechanism, a political shield for becomings-other. Breaking in is an enabling strategy for breaking away.

The ultimate goal, for Deleuze and Guattari, is neither to redefine, misapply, or strategically exaggerate a category, nor even to invent a new identity. Their aim is to destroy categorical gridding altogether, to push the apparatus of identity beyond the threshold of sameness, into singularity. It is to lift the body from the constraints of reciprocal difference in a system of approximate closure (variation within external limits set by an overcoding differential grid imposing a segregative binary logic) and catapult it into the absolute difference of dissipation (a bodily state so differentiated that it differs even from itself, holding its past together with its many futures in each of its undecidable presents; the body itself as a nonbinary, material differential in an irreversibly open system enjoying infinite degrees of freedom; life in the vortex; intensity). The end of gender politics, for Deleuze and Guattari, is the destruction of gender (of the molar organization of the sexes under patriarchy) — just as in their view the end of class politics is the destruction of class (of the molar organization of work under capitalism).[67] The goal would be for every body to ungender itself, creating a nonmolarizing socius that fosters carnal invention rather than containing it, however evenhandedly: from difference to hyperdifferentiation, in a locally–globally correlated cascade of supermolecular self-inventions.

Deleuze and Guattari's formulation of the concept of "becoming-woman" is indeed sexist. The burden of change is placed on women, since it is their cliché that is singled out. They do not dwell on the possibility of a similarly revolutionary becoming-man that would push the masculine stereotype beyond *its* threshold of recuperation (following, for example, strategies of the kind employed by some segments of the gay and lesbian S/M communities who theatricalize "masculinity" in order to take it to a deconstructive extreme).[68] It would be impossible for a straight man to become-man in this way, since in doing so he would not be becoming other than he already is but rather staying the same, only more so. Becoming is not immediately an option for heterosexual men. The Standard Man-form with which their bodies and desires are in near-total symbiosis is the personification of anti-becoming. Molarity is by nature unbecoming. It is "real" men, molar men, who should consent to "go first." I.e., self-destruct. De-form themselves. Dissociate their bodies and desires from the apparatus of overcoding that has up to now defined them, and forced complementary definitions on others in their name. It is only when they cease to be that they will be able to become. Given the privileges the existing social order accords them, it is unlikely that molar men will embrace this mission of self-excision with immediate enthusiasm. Their suicide may have to be assisted. Women and sexual minorities "should" not go first — but neither should they wait.[69]

10. It should be abundantly clear by now that a call for an end to binary systems of difference is not a call for undifferentiation or sameness. Oppositional difference *is* the same, it is the form of the Same: it is the most abstract form of expression of society's homogenizing tendencies. Saussure, the godfather of the diacritical thinking so prevalent in cultural analysis today, is quite explicit about this. He says, first, that meaning (linguistic value) "is a system of equivalence between things (signifieds and signifiers) belonging to different orders," and second, that signs only have value by virtue of their reciprocal difference, and have no positivity.[70] How can language be a system of equivalence, yet be made up entirely of difference? Only if difference amounts to the Same.

Saussure openly describes language as a reductive mechanism. "Language is a *self-contained whole* and a principle of *classification*." What it classifies is the "confusing mass" of things we experience in the world, what he disdainfully calls the "heteroclite." Language in its Saussurian functioning provides a unity ("whole") for that which by nature has no unity, and in relation to which unity must always stand apart ("self-contained"). The unity of language exists on a level of pure abstraction ("language is a form, not a substance") at which there is only negative difference: a sign is understandable only in opposition to what it is not. "Man" is "not-Woman," "Woman" is "not-Man," "Adult" is "not-Child". . . . None of these terms have positive content. They are empty categories forming an oppositional grid cleansed of the heteroclite. For Saussure, language is still referential, if arbitrarily so. A category conventionally designates a thing (the celebrated tree diagrams). In a Deleuze–Guattarian framework, one would be tempted to reverse that formulation and say that bodies (as defined above: as indeterminate energetic matrixes) *are designated for* the categories, and in the process are constituted as things (determinate, socially manipulable objects) — that language is prescriptive rather than referential. "It's a boy!" Determination. Prescriptive equivalence. "We'll make a man of him, even if it kills him": it is hereby ordained that the body before us shall, with all due haste, leave one order, the "heteroclite," to join another, deemed "difference." Oppositional difference. The body is negativized as the price of its entry into an officially recognized system of meaning. It gains "value" (both in the linguistic sense and in the sense of utility or prestige in the dominant cultural order), but loses, from society's determining perspective, the particularity of its time and of its space; what is unreproducible in it. These fall away in favor of what it has in common with other similarly prescribed bodies: membership in a class. An equivalence is imposed between two orders that lifts a body out of its uniqueness and places it in a system of "difference" ("not that") in which it is reduced to the Same (one in a class of "not that"s). This process of linguistic perception (in our strong sense as a material grasping) is *identification* (a body's advent to personhood through incorporeal transformation; in the "private" sphere, a body's negative difference, or social value, is called "personality"). Identification is arbitrary in the sense that there is no "natural" connection between a body and its category, but necessary in the sense that society nevertheless demands that the link be made (on the basis of anatomy).[71]

For Deleuze and Guattari, the singular, the "heteroclite," is not "confused" and unanalyzable. It simply obeys other, far more complex, rules of formation. It is "undifferentiated" only from the point of view of a system of "difference" predicated on equivalence and yielding sameness. "Undifferentiation" is the flipside of this "difference."[72] It is that in contrast to which negative difference (identity) has value. It is not outside but rather integral to the system of identification. The "heteroclite," rather than being undifferentiated, is hyperdifferentiated. It is the realm of supermolecular individuality. The operative distinctions made by its rules of formation are too fine to be caught in the mesh of binary abstraction: they are "indeterminate" by its measures.

The real distinction between orders is not "identity versus undifferentiation," but *"identity-undifferentiation versus hyperdifferentiation."*[73] Identity-undifferentiation is a system for the determination (reduction) of potential (value). Value in this context *is* a positivity, but not in the sense that it has "presence" (simple being; identity by the traditional definition of self-sameness). Here, value is the dynamic interplay, at a given point in space-time, of material tensions enveloping potential paths of becoming. Hyperdifferentiation is conceptually indeterminate from the point of view of oppositional difference. But it is materially indeterminate in "itself"—which is a teeming void (as opposed to a diacritical emptiness). In other words, it is seething with fractal future-pasts (singularities; dense points). The kind of positivity it has is the pragmatic copresence of unactualized potentials (complication).[74]

Operating within the framework "identity (negative difference) versus undifferentiation (confusion)" leaves a body three options. Becoming the person it is said to be: the slow death of stable equilibrium. Opting out of that path, into its opposite: neurosis and eventual breakdown. Or shopping-to-be: Not exactly mental stability, but not quite breakdown either.[75] The frenzy of the purchasable—potential experienced as infinite choice between havings rather than becomings. Stealing away from the shopping mall on an exorbital path tangent to identity *and* undifferentiation is called "schizophrenia."[76] Schizophrenia is a breakaway into the unstable equilibrium of continuing self-invention.

normality is the degree zero of

MONSTROSITY[1]

Becoming-Other

A man complains of being hungry. All the time. Dogs, it seems, are never hungry. So the man decides to become a dog. To be a dog, one must walk on all fours. The hero decides to wear shoes on his hands, only to discover that there is no hand left to tie the laces on the fourth shoe. What does a shoe-shod dog tie laces with? Its mouth. Organ by organ, the man becomes a dog.[2]

He is not imitating a dog; he is "diagramming." He analyzes step-by-step the qualities of two molar species, resolving them into constellations of abstract relations of movement and rest. In other words, he gradually extracts from each body a set of affects: ways in which the body can connect with itself and with the world. He is exploring the bodies' "mode of composition" or dynamic range. At each point in the progression, he combines a certain number of affects from each abstract body in a singular way and incarnates them in his allegedly human matter. He resolves the bodies into two bundles of virtual affects, or bodies without organs, and then actualizes a selective combination of them. What he comes up with is neither a molar dog nor a molar man, but a monster, a freak. A dog with shoes. He has selectively conjoined two molarities. The selection was determined, on the conscious level, by the perception of a molar constraint: hunger. It does not matter whether that constraint or dogs' exemption from it is "objectively true." The constraint was effectively perceived and led to action. The process is real, if not entirely rational. The premises' lack of truth value is a direct result of the nature of the constraint. The outcome of the process reveals what it was.

The man's becoming-dog fails. He reinvents Man and Dog organ by organ, but he hits a snag. The tail defies transformation. Rather than freakishly combining with its human analog, it stubbornly remains just what it is—in order for its analog to stay the way it is. The process stops, and childhood family memories pour in. The analog of the tail, of course, is the penis. It is now clear what constraint was being escaped: Oedipus, phallocentrism, molar personhood itself. The man's anti-Oedipal desire was not strong enough, or his powers of analysis not refined enough, to pull the linchpin.

The escape attempt was not rational because the constraint is not rational. Molarity is a mode of desire, as is any move away from it. Oedipus has no truth value. It is a matter of force: it is a categorical overlay, an overpowering imposition of regularized affects. Because it constricts actions into a limited dynamic range, it is inevitable that it will be experienced by the overcoded body as a physical constraint. Becoming begins as a desire to escape bodily limitation. Whether the constraint in question is generally characterized as a "natural" or "cultural" necessity makes little difference (all constraints are both simultaneously: "real" hunger is as much an economic reality as a digestive fact. Conversely, as Foucault has shown, "cultural" limitations are effective only to the extent to which they insinuate themselves into the flesh.) What matters is that the constraint is there, and that there is a counterdesire to leave it behind.

Becoming is a tension between two modes of desire—molarity and supermolecularity, being and becoming, sameness-difference and hyperdifferentiation. The point of departure is inevitably a molarized situation within the confines of which alternatives tend to present themselves as choices between molar beings. A molarity other than that normally assigned to the body in escape from constraint suggests itself as an image of "freedom." Although the choice may be couched in molar terms, the process set in motion is not itself molar. It carries both of the molar normalities involved out of themselves into the realm of the monstrous. Becoming, in its simplest expression, is a tension between modes of desire plotting a vector of transformation between two molar coordinates. A new dynamic range outlines itself in the in-between: a fusion of potential relations of movement and rest mapping a mutant trajectory never before travelled by Man or Dog. The categories taken as starting points are images of the attractor state of stable equilibrium typical of molarity: Man as Oedipalized animal, Dog as tail-wagging pet sharing human hearth and home. Domesticity and calm. But something happens, as if the perception of the constraint set up affective interference patterns perturbing the shape of contentment, forcing each contained and self-satisfied identity to be grasped outside its habitual patterns of action, from the point of view of its potential, as what it is not, and has never been, rather than what it has come to be. Becoming is an equilibrium-seeking system at a crisis point where it suddenly perceives a deterministic constraint, becomes "sensitive" to it, and is catapulted into a highly unstable supermolecular state enveloping a bifurcating future. The man, having superposed human and canine affects, faces a choice: fall back into one or the other molar coordinate, or keep on moving toward the great dissipative outside stretching uncertainly on the wild side of the welcome mat. He may either revert to his normal self or suffer a breakdown (identity confusion between Man and Man's Best Friend); or he may decide not to look back and set out instead on a singular path of freakish becoming leading over undreamed-of quadrupedal horizons. What the next mode of locomotion would be is any body's guess. In this story, however, the man opts against living dangerously. He turns his back on the high-energy equilibrium of hyperdifferentiation, preferring to plod home, mesmerized by snapshots, to reclaim his old familial self.

Although the indeterminacy of the supermolecular state invites the use of such words as "choice" and "freedom," it is not a question of a consciously willed personal decision. Becoming is directional rather than intentional. The direction it moves in may appear "unmotivated," "irrational," or "arbitrary" from the point of view of molarity; but becoming is no more deserving of these epithets than molarity itself. Both are modes of desire. Neither is "free" in the sense of being untouched by deterministic constraints. Molarity and supermolecularity are different ways of responding to constraint: actualizing it in the body, or "*counteractualizing*" it by removing the body from its normal habitat.[3] Supermolecularity or "becoming-other" necessarily begins with molarized bodies, but it does not actualize them. It counteractualizes them, in an alteration of their perception of constraint. The man does not literally become a dog; but neither is dogdom unscathed. Both are affectively redefined. The movement is a double translation, of Man into something with canine affects, and of Dog into something more human than science would allow. The process of translation begins at a *sub*personal level. The perception of the constraint of hunger seems to come out of nowhere. It imposes itself on the man as a fact of life that has suddenly leapt into his consciousness and can no longer be ignored. Where the process leads is toward a *supra*personal level, into a beyond of mutation and monstrosity. Personhood is in the middle: preperception and postbecoming, it is the empty equilibrium state. The place where nothing happens.

Becoming-other is not imitation. Imitation respects the boundaries between molar wholes, setting up comparisons between bodies considered separately, as entities unto themselves. It conceives of the body as a structural whole with determinate parts in stable interaction with one another. The model is the organism: a body is made up of parts (organs) with identifiable characteristics, supposedly intrinsic qualities, which predispose the whole they compose to certain habitual patterns of action. In other words, the body is defined by that which in or of it remains the same. It is abstracted from the singular flow of its movements through the world and the succession of often chance alterations it undergoes in the course of its life's path. The body is defined by its similarity to itself across its variations: self-identity. Other bodies may have more or less the same intrinsic qualities and habitual actions, and thus share the body's self-identity. These bodies are considered particular instances of a type. In this mode of thought, bodies are reduced to what they have in common, with themselves and with others of their species. They are grasped solely from the point of view of their generality. They are subsumed by a general idea, or norm, formed by a double system of similarity (intrinsic and extrinsic: of the organism to itself, and to others). Deviations from the norm are disregarded within certain limits.

The similarities defining one body can be contrasted to those of another body belonging to a different type. To each organ in the first body corresponds a functionally equivalent part in the other. But this time the comparison body has intrinsic qualities and habitual circuits of action exhibiting a level of deviation from the norm that cannot be disregarded. Paw versus hand. Similar, but different. There are degrees of sameness. To each its general idea. A man makes his hand move "like" a paw, and presto, he's "done" a dog imitation. He has made one representative part of one body-type coincide with a habitual action proper to a corresponding part of another species. The general idea "Dog" temporarily superimposes itself onto a body belonging to the general idea "Man." After the imitation, both bodies revert. Nothing has changed. Nothing was translated. Nothing mutated. No new perception came. No body escaped. Nothing really moved. Everything took place on the level of the person.

The mode of thought characteristic of imitation is "common sense": the abstract overlay of one predefined, self-identical whole on another, playing on degrees of similarity ("differences") between their parts. Analogical thought—the Empire of "Like." "I was just 'like' you when I was your age," the sage father says to his son (read: "Be me when you grow up"). "It's just 'like' her to do that. People never change" (read: "If you change, I'll lose my hate, and then what would I have to live for?"). "Politicians are 'like' that—all crooked. Nothing ever changes" (read: "I refuse to think the world can change so I myself won't have to"). Like, habit, reaction: same difference. Imitation of life.

Scientific and philosophical "good sense" operates in essentially the same way as common sense: isolation of the typical individual (considered outside the real flow of its actions; as essentially dead); decomposition into parts and determination of intrinsic qualities (dissection); logical recomposition into an organic whole exhibiting signs of "life" (artificial resuscitation); extrinsic comparison between wholes (analogy).

Common sense and good sense share an image of thought that assigns the development of a "general idea" as its goal (categorical thinking: Man and Dog as classes).[4] To the extent that they reach this goal, they coincide with neurosis. The analogical correspondences established by good/common sense delineate a system of potential symbolic relays from one organic (molar) whole to another. The singularity of each individual (its "minority") is eclipsed in the play of similarity-difference. The social contract of molar coexistence has been sealed: "Shake!" (paw = hand). Resemblance dominates, boundaries blur, metaphors proliferate and identity confusion looms. We are back in the Oedipal logic discussed in the previous chapter. Puppies are cute and cuddly (just "like" a baby! Both have to be toilet trained). Soon, they learn to wait whining at the door for the return of their master (whose voice of authority they always recognize, "like" a good wife). Love and regression in a fur coat. It is often remarked how dogs and their owners grow to resemble one another. Becoming-the-same.[5]

Becoming-other is a different animal altogether. It does not proceed analogically. It ends where analogy begins. Nor does it activate metaphor: rather than establishing equivalences between organic wholes, it diagrams differences in potential associated with bodily parts as such (the organs "hand" and "paw" as part-objects governed by a fractal attractor). What thought-in-becoming investigates is first and foremost realms of action—what paw and hand can do, where bodies can go, not on average, but in the extreme: their range of affect, or "latitude."[6] Rather than decomposing a typical individual into intrinsic qualities, it unfolds potentials enveloped in a singular individual at a crossroads of mutation. Rather than cleaving to resemblances, it exploits a difference in nature in order to compose another, taking two latitudes that do not coincide and yielding a third that coincides with neither. Thought-in-becoming is more abstract than analogical thinking, since it bears primarily on what may or may not come to pass, rather than on what "is" by general consensus. At the same time, it aims lower and stays more concrete. The goal is not to develop a general idea (model) that would stand out and above (transcend) the bodies it subsumes; it is to create a new body at ground level. In spite of its emphasis on the nonexistent, the procedure of becoming is entirely immanent. In other words, it operates on the same plane as its "objects." Thought-in-becoming starts in the middle, at the point of intersection of two realms of action (bodies without organs), in the milieu common to two bodily dynamisms (in the Man-Dog case, the domestic environment).[7] The interiority of the bodies involved does not concern it. It lodges itself instead in the distance separating them, in their space of interaction, the field of their exteriority to one another. It is that plane of coexistence, or consistency, that is the ultimate object of the process. To become a new body, an old body needs a new milieu through which to move. Becoming-other orchestrates an encounter between bodies, considered from the point of view of their virtuality, in order to catapult one or all onto a new plane of consistency, in the kind of leap in place characteristic of incorporeal transformation.

Analogical thought starts from an isolated individual considered to be typical, and ends in a category coherent enough to take its rightful place in a preexisting system of good/common sense. Thought-in-becoming takes that end point as its beginning, counteractualizing the entire system of analogy, metaphor, and Oedipality:[8] it moves in the inverse direction, from the general (the categorical or stereotypical) to the individual. With the individual understood differently—as unique, not as typical. It strives to invent the singular animal that could walk away from Oedipus.

Becoming is bodily thought, beyond the realm of possibility, in the world of the virtual. At once superabstract and infraconcrete, it grasps the environment of molarity common to different bodies from the perspective of the potential curtailed. Thought is an unhinging of habit. As a body matures, it develops a repertory of stimulus–response circuits. The regularity of the normalized situations within which the body is placed is inscribed in it in the form of autonomic reactions. Same input, same output. Same stimulus, same response. On schedule. The circularity of the everyday. Training. "Growing up." Reactivity. But something happens when habits of speech and action start to accumulate. Each scheduled stimulus takes its place in a growing constellation of others "like" it, to which there is a correspondingly increased constellation of "like" responses. The task of training is to ensure that the "appropriate" response will be matched to the stimulus more often than not. This requires good/common sense: analytical thinking capable of discerning the degree of similarity-difference of the stimulus presented to those in its constellation, and of selecting the fitting response. But for each stimulus, there is now a host of analogous responses that might be substituted for the "right" one. If the body selects one of those responses, its habitual course through the common environment of molarity may be ever so slightly deflected. A crack has opened in habit, a "zone of indeterminacy" is glimpsed in the hyphen between the stimulus and the response. Thought consists in widening that gap, filling it fuller and fuller with potential responses, to the point that, confronted with a particular stimulus, the body's reaction cannot be predicted.[9]

Thought-in-becoming is less a willful act than an undoing: the nonaction of suspending established stimulus–response circuits to create a zone where chance and change may intervene. It does not close the door on analogy and analytical thinking, but rather pulls it open, suspending analysis just long enough to carry it over the threshold of habit. Thought-in-becoming expands the selective capability of good/common sense to the point at which it becomes other than it is: a momentary stall instead of an automatic response, then a spring into a new, synthetic, mode of operation.[10] "Rational" thinking is not overturned, nor the ego dissolved. They are set ajar, opened onto a space of invention — raised, in fact, to a higher power as their hitherto canned responses take on flexibility to the measure of the moment. Becoming is a mode of synthetic thought whose relation to analytical thinking and the ego is less a countering than a counteractualization — a change in mode striking habit, molarity, even reactivity itself.

Thought-in-becoming is the process of a body's rebecoming-supermolecular. The body regains the "spontaneity" characteristic of the undomesticated body, becoming an untrained animal again, or a child, or anything else it chooses. But always with a difference. For the response selection must be informed by the peculiarities of the shared environment, to avoid precipitating a crushing reaction from the molarizing forces that delimit and police the common space within and around coexisting bodies. It must also take into account the quirks of the mutating body, to avoid hitting a snag that will make the process crash under its own weight (something as small as an insufficiently de-analogized tail is all it takes). Becoming is supremely pragmatic, or it fails.

Becoming-other is an exponential expansion of a body's repertory of responses. Not only does each stimulus evoke an indeterminate number of pragmatic responses, but there is a change in the body's mode of response. The body is *capable of* selecting any one of these responses, but it does not *have to*. It envelops a growing number of bifurcating futures in each of its presents, but none is preordained. Its responses are no longer autonomic. Increasing complication. A fractal abyss has reopened where there was only a hyphen between stimulus and response, cue and canned reaction. The body's zone of indeterminacy, though confined to its synapses, has widened beyond measure. Autonomic responses have been counteractualized as *autonomous*. This increase in the body's degrees of freedom is called "imagination." Imagination is rational thought brought back to the body. It is a pragmatic, synthetic mode of thought which takes the body not as an "object" but as a realm of virtuality, not as a site for the application of an abstract model or prefabricated general idea but as a site for superabstract invention. It bears directly on the body's *affects* — its capacity to affect and be affected, to act and to perceive, unleashed.

Imagination, like habit, is a circuit — less between regularized stimuli and acquired responses in the actual world than between the actual and the virtual as such.[11] Thought-as-imagination departs from the actual, dips into the fractal abyss, then actualizes something new. It short-circuits molarity, passing directly from a particular state of things to a singular response. The generality of molar existence is present only to the extent that the selection of the response is still informed, as a pragmatic precaution, by the system of similarities dictated by molarity.[12]

The fact that becoming-other takes analogy, metaphor, and molarity as its point of departure and moves from the general to the individual means that it is social through and through. It is a collective undertaking, even if only a single body mutates. Its point of departure is not the *general in general*, but *this* generality ("my" Home), the categorical level of *this* body (Man or Dog?), in *this* situation (Oedipal or not?). Becoming starts from the general as operative in a particular situation: in other words, *as instituted*. There is no other way. Generality has no existence outside of its application to actual bodies. It is an overcoding that exists only as imposed and reimposed, habitually, in an endless being-made-what-one-is-a-priori (generally the same). It is no less a process than becoming, it just moves in a different direction and frequents different circles. Even if a body becomes in the privacy of its own home, with no one else around, not even the dog, it is still committing a social act. Becoming performs an operation on collectively elaborated, socially selected, mutually accepted, and group-policed categories of thought and action. It opens a space in the grid of identities those categories delineate, inventing new trajectories, new circuits of response, unheard-of futures and possible bodies such as have never been seen before. It maps out a whole new virtual landscape featuring otherworldly affects.[13] Other bodies may slip into that zone of indeterminacy, or autonomous zone, creating the conditions for a contagion of becoming-other—a process as fragile as it is infectious. When supermolecularity succeeds, the forces of molarity must accommodate or kill it. Accommodating a supermolecule means adapting the grid of molar identities to it. A new category is added to the recognized list, and procedures are established to ensure that the integration of the new kind of body into the shared environment does not upset the general equilibrium. A life-space opens, but it is no sooner surveyed than institutionalized, or captured: molarity is an apparatus of capture of energies that escape it.[14] If the bodies that come to inhabit the newly recognized (remolarized) space of affect simply move in without reproblematizing it, they are merely finding new accommodations for their own curtailment: adopt-a-sameness. For the becoming-other to continue, the bodies-come-lately must submit the new invention to the same treatment to which it submitted the molarities of it took as its point of departure. Becoming must keep on becoming, in an indefinite movement of invention opening wider and wider zones of autonomy populated by more and more singularities. Becoming-other begins by differentiating one molecular body from two molar categories, then slides into a cascade of differentiations, creating a volatile situation, with bodies moving in all directions at cross-purposes, in maneuvers of capture and escape that only increase the chances of collision and mutation. Successful becoming-other concerns the entire body politic, precipitating a hyperdifferentiation that exponentially multiplies the potential bodily states and possible identities it envelops. Becoming bears on a population, even when it is initiated by a single body: even one body alone is collective in its conditions of emergence as well as in its future tendency.[15]

Becoming is an escape, but it is not for that reason negative or necessarily oppositional. The body-in-becoming does not simply react to a set of constraints. Instead, it develops a new sensitivity to them, one subtle enough to convert them into opportunities — and to translate the body into an autonomous zone effectively enveloping infinite degrees of freedom. The body is abstracted, not in the sense that it is made to coincide with a general idea, but in a way that makes it a singularity, so monstrously hyperdifferentiated that it holds within its virtual geography an entire population of a kind unknown in the actual world. It is probable, but not a foregone conclusion, that the body-in-becoming and its cohort will be reduced to the confines of a category — the world may just have to expand to fit them. Becoming-other is the counteractualization of necessity.

The image of a body at home alone is misleading. It rarely happens that a becoming-other pivots on a single body. Most becoming-others are initiated by preexisting populations who develop a collective sensitivity to the molar constraints applied to them and join to counter-actualize them. Becoming can only proliferate with carefully formu-lated group strategies (whether the group is yet to come or already here — and it is preferably both). Becoming-other is thoroughly political. The social movements of Blacks, aboriginals, feminists, gays and lesbians — of groups relegated to sub-Standard conditions — provide far better frames of reference than Standard Man alone at home with his dog, em-barking on an anti-Oedipal adventure. The becomings of typically individualist Standard Man (usually -animal or -woman) are almost always destined to fail, because they do not draw on the power of an actual population.[16] Any population, no matter how oppressed (molarly compressed), envelops more affects or potential actions than the most ingenious individual body. Solo becomings are constitutionally limited — leaving home on all fours is not likely to solve the problem of world hunger.

Becoming-other is directional (away from molarity), but not directed (no one body or will can pilot it). It leaves a specific orbit but has no predesignated end point. For that reason, it cannot be exhaustively described. If it could, it would already be what it is becoming, in which case it wouldn't be becoming at all, being instead the same. Again. A snapshot of the past. Utopian thinking that would assign a shape to the supermolecularity-to-come is a function of molarity, it belongs more to the constrictions of the past than to any expansive future. It is an apparatus for the capture of synthetic thinking and the desire for a new world that animates it. There are, of course, harsher containments. Utopia is the gentle death of revolution.

The most that can or should be done is to enumerate ways in which becoming might be mapped without being immobilized. "Strategies" is the best word for ways of becoming: they are less theories about becoming than pragmatic guidelines serving as landmarks to future movement. They have no value unless they are immanent to their "object": they must be verified by the collectivity concerned, in other words submitted to experimental evaluation and remapped as needed. Some suggestions:

1. *Stop the world.* Becoming is about movement, but it begins with an inhibition. At least some of the automatic circuits between regularized stimuli and habitual responses must be disconnected, as if a crowbar had been inserted into the interlocking network of standardized actions and trajectories constituting the World As We Know It. The resulting zone of indeterminacy is a tear in the fabric of good / common sense. Society's molar equilibrium is breached by a fractal void into which freakish thought-bodies rush as if sucked into a creative vacuum,

and out of which more mutant becomings come pouring. Stopping the World As We Know It, at at least one of its spatiotemporal coordinates, is a prerequisite for setting up the kind of actual–virtual circuit crucial to the political imagination. Tactical sabotage of the existing order is a necessity of becoming, but for survival's sake it is just as necessary to improve the existing order, to fight for integration into it on its terms. These are two sides of the same coin, and they should be practiced in such a way as to reinforce rather than mutually exclude one another. Neither is an end in itself. Their combined goal is a redefinition of the conditions of existence laid down by the molar order: their conversion into conditions of becoming. The end is for there to be no end, to turn collective existence into a repeatedly self-applied series of incorporeal transformations. This state of supermolecular hyperdifferentiation might be called "permanent revolution," provided that it is understood that the revolution has many rhythms, it can be instantaneous or spread over ages. Its pace will depend on historical conditions, and the collective desires embodied in them. Becoming concerns speed, but speed is relative. The velocity of becoming must only be different from the reflex speed of the existing apparatuses of molar capture. Bodies-in-becoming have no future if the perceptual capabilities of molarizing forces are enough in synch with them to grasp them for what they are not (*yet*). Sometimes extreme slowness passes more easily unnoticed.[17]

2. *Cherish derelict spaces.* They are holes in habit, what cracks in the existing order appear to be from the molar perspective. The site of a breach in the World As We Know It is dysfunctional for molar purposes, and is therefore perceived by good/common sense as a simple negative: a lack of functioning, a wasteland. It is seen for what it is not (without the *yet*). Its danger as a site of political invention goes unnoticed. The derelict space is a zone of indeterminacy that bodies-in-becoming may make their own. Autonomous zones[18] of this kind come in many guises. They may be geographical: an "underdeveloped" area in the capitalist economy, or a "Third World," which may in fact occur within the borders of the "First World" (the "ghetto"). Or they may be widely scattered through the social field, physically separated from one another so that even though they are geographically im-planted they do not define a continuous territory. For example, a sexual minority may turn the privacy of the home or a semiprivate club into an autonomous zone in which experimentation may be under-

taken in relative safety. Or they may be entirely deterritorialized. Daydreaming is an autonomous zone for the "delinquent" in school.[19] Religion is one for latter-day "pagans" fleeing organized (molarized) belief (the Church). Politics is one for "dissidents" fleeing standardized (molarized) collective action (Ideology). Even though autonomous zones are derelict spaces that become sites of escape, they should not be thought of as "outside" the existing structures in any straightforward sense. Escape always takes place *in* the World As We Know It. Autonomous zones are interstitial, they inhabit the in-between of socially significant constellations, they are where bodies in the world but between identities go: liminal sites of syncretic unorthodoxy. The "outside" of autonomous zones is not the relative outside of topography, but an absolute outside that is ever and already in this world, contiguous to every one of its spatial coordinates. Autonomous zones are irruptions in the actual world of that other dimension of reality — the virtual (bodies' plane of coexistence, or field of mutual exteriority). Bodies in flight do not leave the world behind. If the circumstances are right, they take the world with them — into the future. "A structure is defined by what escapes it." Autonomous zones may be thought of in temporal terms, as shreds of futurity. Like "outside," "future" is only an approximation: there are any number of potential futures in the cracks of the present order, but only a few will actually unfold. Think of autonomous zones in terms of time, but tenseless: time out of joint, in an immanent outside (Nietzsche's untimely).[20]

3. *Study camouflage.* Something new, "in order to become apparent, is forced to simulate structural states and to slip into states of forces that serve it as masks."[21] To succeed at the reform side of the coin, to work within the existing order to ensure the survival of oneself and one's group, requires the ability to "pass" on the "inside." This is *seeming to be what you are* (by molar definition).[22] Bodies-in-becoming must be passing-persons capable of simulating the molar being assigned to them by the grid of political value judgment. This is a delicate operation, fraught with the danger that a group gaining representation in such apparatuses of capture as government and media will be trapped into operating entirely on their terms. It is all too easy to become what you are, and thus unwittingly condemn your supermolecule to a molar death ("recuperation").

4. *Sidle and straddle*. Reform politics favoring gradual change runs the risk of slow death by creeping molarity. Oppositional politics intent on head-on confrontation at all costs carries other dangers: sudden death on an ill-prepared battleground, or through instantaneous molarization. The latter is brought on by the common expedient of a would-be body-in-becoming defining itself solely as the inverse of what it desires to escape, in a kind of mirror stage of politics in which one becomes what one hates (the "microfascism" that often infects oppositional groupuscules).[23] When in doubt, sidestep. In establishing actual–virtual circuits, an effectively revolutionary movement establishes many other circuits: reform–confrontation, molarity–minority, being–becoming, camouflage–showing oneself, rationality–imagination, and many permutations of these. Becoming is always marginal, a simultaneous coming and going in a borderland zone between modes of action. The place of invention is a space of transformational encounter, a dynamic in-between. To get there, one must move sideways, through cracks in accepted spatial and temporal divisions. Charging straight ahead may be necessary and effective at times, but as a general principle it is as self-defeating as uncritical acceptance of reform. Revolutionary sidestepping is called "transversality."[24]

5. *Come out*. Throw off your camouflage as soon as you can and still survive. What one comes out of is identity. What one comes into is greater transformational potential. To achieve the goal that has no end means ceasing to seem to be what your are in order to *become what you cannot be*: supermolecular forever. The goal is a limit approached, never reached. Coming out is never complete. What is important is the p ocess: desire for the future.

These stra egies, taken together, with others like them, constitute *resistance*: friciion in the molar machine.

The Revenge of the Same

Molarity presents itself as stasis, but like becoming-other it is in reality a productive process: a making-the-same. Stasis, or entropic equilibrium, exists only under special conditions, in an artificially closed system. It is constructed, and its preservation requires a certain level of energy expenditure. Although the system of the Same stands for stasis, it is surreptitiously active. Molarity is productive activity kept to the minimum necessary to guarantee relative closure. It tends toward entropy, but entropic equilibrium, again like its supermolecular nemesis, is a limit never reached.

The synthetic mode of thought proper to becoming-other is imagination. Since its only "object" is paradox (strategic indeterminacy), contradiction holds no sway over it. Molarity, on the other hand, knows *only* contradiction: binary distinction is the element of its analytical thinking. The oppositional categories it deals in are by definition general ideas which no particular body can ever fully embody. While becoming-other is rife with endless complications, becoming-the-same is haunted by an irresolvable contradiction written into its very mode of operation: its objects can never be what it makes them.

Becoming-other is problematic.[25] Happily so. Its problem is complication, which is also its measure of success. The contradictions of becoming-the-same are nagging reminders of irresolution, the threat of eventual catastrophe. When molarity is not morose, it is apocalyptic. That is *its* problem.

The productive processes of becoming-other and becoming-the-same follow very different paths. Becoming-other goes from the general to the singular, returning thought to the body grasped from the point of view of its transformational potential—monstrosity. Becoming-the-same moves to avoid that same potential, going from the typical to the general, from the individual grasped from the point of view of its predictability to the Standard of that normality. When becoming-other starts to succeed, it carries its operations to a higher power, aiming all the more intensely for the connective freedom of fractality. By contrast, it is when becoming-the-same begins to falter that it carries its process to a higher power. When it does, what it aims for is not the superabstraction of immanence. It contents itself with abstraction plain and simple. It takes the divide-and-conquer approach of rational analysis to the extreme, carrying thought ever farther from the body and the quantum world it inhabits. Rather than taking the materials at hand and synthesizing, it strives to make the ultimate separation, and to make it binding: the separation of thought from the body (transcendence). This escalation of segregation is called "morality": the move from general ideas to the Idea as guarantor of the

"Good."[26] Becoming-other is the madness of the imagination. It is eminently ethical, in Spinoza's sense of tending toward an augmentation of the power to live in this world. Morality (molarity) is the delirium of Reason. It sets its sights on paradise (glorified generality). Since becoming-other concerns this world, and revels in its "thisness," we are always already where it wants to take us.[27] To qualify for it, all one must do is to be alive. To succeed at it, one need only live more fully: dissipate (expend energy at a state far from equilibrium). To qualify for molar paradise, on the other hand, it is necessary to pass a test. The select achieve death (maximum entropy).

A silent film by Louis Feuillade gives some concrete indications on the workings of this molar machine: *Vendémiaire*. In the final days of World War I, members of a well-to-do-family from the north of France who are either too young, too old, or too female to be war heroes flee to unoccupied territory in the south to work on the wine harvest. There they meet one daughter's husband-to-be and a sinister pair of German prisoners of war passing themselves off as Allies until they get enough money to flee to Spain. The Germans' plan is to rob the vineyard owners and frame a gypsy coworker. One of them, about to be found out, hides in an empty grape storage tank, and dies from toxic gases produced by grapes fermenting nearby. His corpse is found still clutching the loot, the gypsy woman is saved, and the dead man's lonely comrade betrays himself by drunkenly speaking in German.

The film is bracketed by grapes. Not only does the grape harvest motivate the plot, but the grapes themselves, rather than any human hero (they are all at the front), also resolve the dilemma. Every crucial moment in the film is expressed in terms of wine: love is expressed by the scintillating image of the faraway wife dancing in the husband's army-supply wine cup; the German menace in its highest expression is one of the escapees stomping on the grape vine; heroism is exemplified by an altruistic trooper who braves death to bring wine back to the trenches to give his comrades a taste of the homeland that will revive their will to victory; when victory does come, it is toasted with wine, and the movie ends with a sentimental tableau of the vines and a final intertitle saying that from these vineyards a new nation will be reborn. An abstract flow of wine infuses a glorified national body with intimations of rebirth, arrogating to itself the powers of love and virtue. It is a seminal flow presenting itself as first and final cause.

The image of the wine contracts into itself the sensations attached to everything valued in the film. But does not merely establish a monopoly on surplus value. It presents itself as the producer of all value. The war, we are led to believe, was won with wine. It expresses love, and thereby motivates the man to be a good husband and give sons to the nation rising; it expresses patriotism, and thereby spurs the soldiers to victory. The film abstracts from the bodies and things of postwar Europe a transcendent plane of ideal identities: spouse, family, nation, traitor. Then it fills the "good" with glory by filling them with a miraculous liquid: glorious Husband, glorious Wife, glorious Family, glorious growing Nation. The potion works its magic before our very eyes. Thanks to it, a new France will rise. Praise the wine!

That the wine's miraculous powers lead to a *re*birth (Vendémiaire is the first month of the French Revolutionary calendar) is a tacit acknowledgment that its productivity is parasitic of productions taking place on other levels. Its causality is an optical illusion. It is not an image of active production: it is an image of reaction. The entire plot revolves around *re*cognizing the Germans' line of escape and *re*acting to it in time to block it. An incidental effect of the wine's unmasking of the scheming Germans is that the gypsy proves to be a dependable, hard-working woman in spite of her heathen blood. The wine operates exclusive disjunctive syntheses: it is evaluative and distributive. It shows the ideal bodies of the film for what they're worth, and gives generous portions of glory to the deserving ones. Germans don't make it. Gypsies do, more or less. Less than more: the gypsy's role is a minor one. She is forgotten by the time the final encomium to wine comes on.

Vendémiaire was made in 1919, in the aftermath of World War I. Every great war has a powerful deterritorializing effect: the mobilization of troops and supplies, families broken, entire regions leveled. The film presents an image of society apparently meant to insert itself into that disjointed situation to help induce a unifying reterritorialization in a new moral order. The gypsy's role has to be downplayed because she belongs to a wandering race that does not respect territorial boundaries even when it is accepted into them. But her role is nevertheless an important one: she gives the wine an opportunity to demonstrate its Christlike generosity. It absolves her of her sin of being born an infidel. Perhaps she will be the exception to the rule and embrace the French faith. Everyone left alive will be invited to communion.

In the film, wine instantaneously and incorporeally transformed the bodies to which the categories were applied into a strong and ordered nation mirroring the prewar period as the film wishfully remembers it. The social fluidity of the off-screen situation after the war is not in fact unique to that period. It can even be seen as an accelerated, nightmarish vision of changes inherent to industrialization: the uprooting of individuals from their ancestral homelands, the blurring of territorial, racial and ethnic boundaries, the break-up of the traditional family structure. The mechanisms of selective evaluation the film sets in motion could just as easily be applied to social movement associated with forces other than war. The concern of the film is less a particular instance of social dislocation than the dangers posed by social fluidity per se. The film translates that perceived threat into its own terms. The real alternative between potentially creative chaos and reproductive order is transposed into a moral distinction between valued terms on the identity grid and devalued ones: honest French and conniving Germans, good self and evil other. This is exactly the kind of move we defined in the last section as an Oedipal mechanism. The distinction between the sameness of order and the indeterminacy of hyper-differentiation is transposed into a distinction between identity and undifferentiation: some bodies are what they are and are good; others are not what they seem to be and are bad. Bad bodies combine two identities that should be mutually exclusive. They imitate a valued identity in an attempt to mask the devalued one that is rightfully theirs. Indeterminacy is presented as a criminal juxtaposition of two already-defined molar identities in a rigidly bounded body (as opposed to a superposition of any number of real but undefinable supermolecular potentials in a fluid body). A true identity and a false one: them or us, ally or enemy, lying thief or patriot. Before the bad body has been put to the test, it is impossible for the good guys to tell which side it is on. It passes in one identity, but under the surface continues to function in the other. It embodies a contradiction in terms. The problem is to resolve the contradiction, to determine which of the possible identity categories a given body should be confined to. Social fluidity—the hyperdifferentiated outside of every image—is "recognized" in the film as a masked Other that is in fact a devalued same: a bad identity. Fluidity is displaced onto a supernatural agent of selective evaluation that afffixes a category to a body by the way in which it pools (for example, into the standard-issue wine cups of the battlefield heroes) or wafts (poison gas) in its vicinity. This agency makes it possible in principle to determine which category a given body truly belongs to. In practice, outside the theater, the situation is less clear; it is not at all certain that a substitute for filmic grape juice will step in to save the day.

In the image, the outside of the image is *identified* as Other.[28] The identification is retrospective: the film not only transposes its outside into an internal contradiction, it projects it back in time to a point before the war was won, before the issue of what form a national rebirth should take could even be raised. The complicated, future-looking "elsewhere" of the autonomous zone has become a neutralized "other" relegated to the past tense.

Mechanisms of capture and containment like the one charted in *Vendémiaire* induct the outside into a system of interiority. That system consists in a grid of identities abstracted from actually existing bodies and transposed onto another dimension: from the here and now into the great beyond.

Molarization involves the creation of a "plane of transcendence."[29] In one aspect, the plane of transcendence is an image of the glory beyond (in this case, a utopian future France); in another, it is the identity grid coextensive with that image; in yet another, the medium that brings the image to light (the apparatus by means of which the identity grid is reapplied to and evaluates some of the bodies from which it was abstracted). The plane of transcendence, however, is best understood not in terms of the content of any particular image, or even in terms of a medium, but as the process presiding over the creation of a certain kind of image (general images: those constituting categories, identities, good/commonsensical ideas)[30] and certain media functions (reductions: from the multidimensionality of life in the flesh to the two-dimensional flatness of the silver screen and the lives of those who are identified with its images).

A plane of transcendence is a movement of abstraction, but at the same time of embodiment. It moves in two contradictory directions simultaneously: toward a beyond, and back to our world. Abstraction and reconcretization (application). For an image of generality can only exist concretely, on the screen or in a photograph; an Idea has nowhere to be, if not in a book or on our lips or in a brain. Applied abstraction is the only kind there is. Transcendence, despite its best efforts, is a mode of becoming immanent. This is its sadness: its very existence is a contradiction in terms. Molarization is the in-itself of contradiction. The abundance of oppositional images and binary distinctions it produces express its own impossibility. Its problem is always to take a *both/and* and make it an *either/or*, to reduce the complexity of pragmatic ethical choice to the black or white of Good or Bad, to reduce the complications of desire as becoming to the simplicity of mind or body, Heaven or Hell. The world rarely obliges.

The double movement of the plane of transcendence, abstraction-application, is transformational but in a different mode than becoming-other. Rather than plunging into the fractality of the living body, it tries with utmost dogmatism to elevate bodies to its own level of perceived stasis and putative wholeness. The plane of transcendence lifts bodies out of the uniqueness of the spatiotemporal coordinates through which they move. It abstracts them, extracts from them a system of identity. That identity grid is actualized in images, in an instantaneous redescent of the plane of transcendence toward the flesh, via a technical and social apparatus or medium.[31] In descent mode, the plane of transcendence reconnects to the bodies from which it rose, but in a way that imposes upon them conformity to its system, demands that they live up to its abstraction, embody its glory. It disregards what is most intimate to bodies, their singular way of decaying, their tendency to escape not only from molar constraint but from themselves (illness and death, not to mention becoming). Bodies that fall prey to transcendence are reduced to what seems to persist across their alterations. Their very corporeality is stripped from them, in favor of a supposed substrate — soul, subjectivity, personality, identity — which in fact is no foundation at all, but an end effect, the infolding of a forcibly regularized outside. Transcendence is the glorification of habit.

Vendémiaire portrays the saving agent of molarization, the active principle of the plane of transcendence, as a superhuman substance responsible for the creation of all value. Wine is the soul of the film. Every molar organization produces an image of transcendent agency of this kind.[32] For the State, it is often the blood of the race or the flag; for Christianity, the blood of Christ; for the Family, the phallus and semen. The categorical grids policed by these images of agency are analogs. Because every term on one identity grid corresponds to a functional equivalent on each of the others, it is possible to circulate among them with metaphoric–metonymic ease. What some Marxists call a society's "dominant ideology" is its system of authorized symbolic relays between various planes of transcendence. However, to attribute anything approaching full causal power to a "dominant ideology," as if it were the soul or subjective essence of a society, is to fall into a molar trap. It is to accept the plane of transcendence too much on its own terms. Lending credence to the miraculous powers of images of agency plays into the hands of molar–moral containment.

Wine cannot capture a criminal, any more than a nonexistent God can punish one, or a flag defend freedom. This is not to say that these images lack all causal force. Molar images of agency are "quasicauses."[33] If their causal force is "quasi," it is not because they produce effects only on the conceptual level (by influencing belief) or on the linguistic level (through a semiotic constitution of the subject). If the account of thought and language presented in the first chapter has any validity, there can be no direct causal link from one expression to the next. An expression must be *converted* into a cause (it is a surplus value): it must leap the fractal gap into content, alienate itself in the dominated force field it expresses but with which it can have no common form or correspondence. The identity grid created and conveyed by the plane of transcendence is a code, as defined earlier: an order and organization of functions. In itself, it is empty and inert. To act, it must step down to a lower dimension.[34] By "lower" is meant "higher": "enveloping a greater heterogeneity of formations and therefore a correspondingly wider range of potentials," "more inclusive." The plane of transcendence, in order to accomplish its mission of containment, must swoop back down on bodies, dirty itself with their decay and impermanence. It cannot do that by itself. Before a category will take, its code must be applied, the target body must be prepared, made receptive to overcoding. Openings must be cut into its perception to provide entryways for generality; it must be coaxed into acquiescence or punished into docility, to give it habits of thought and behavior in consonance with society's overall autonomic desire for stable equilibrium; it must be kneaded into shape, to make it physically able to fulfill the productive, reproductive, and destructive duties it will be assigned in the central molar domains of Work, Family, War; its desire must be turned to glory; it must be marked (Hard-hat, suit, or uniform? Dress or pants?).

The power of the plane of transcendence depends on its becoming immanent to the social field to which it applies. It is only effective to the extent that it alienates itself in its content, is actualized by disciplinary institutions (such as cinema or school) that operate on levels of reality other than its own, which is that of evaporative meaning effects (images, words, thoughts). Disciplinary institutions do the dirty work of transcendence. Their function is to see that a body is channeled into the constellations of affect and orbits of movement set out for it by its assigned category. That category is a map of habit, a coded image enveloping a life's path, a blueprint for how a body it will be cut, cajoled, kneaded, tortured in return for what is considered just compensation (a share of society's surplus value).[35] By the time a body claims its due, it is likely to reproduce in its own imagings the codes it has forcibly absorbed.

The life cycle of a plane of transcendence: 1) production of a coded image, 2) application of the code to bodies / infolding into habit, 3) unfolding into life's paths, 4) reproduction of the code in new images (most likely with defects or selective modifications). A plane of transcendence is a cycle of becoming-transcendent, becoming-immanent, and rebecoming-transcendent: A special kind of virtual–actual circuit. One designed to finish each cycle having lessened the gap between between the inducted bodies and their Ideas (their assigned "personal" images; their identity and the general ideas "appropriate" to it).[36]

An image belonging to a plane of transcendence is a cocause in the sense that it participates in one line of causality among many, none of which taken separately is a sufficient cause for anything, all of which have power only by virtue of their interaction and ability to alienate themselves in each other. But it is a special kind of cocause—a quasicause—to the extent that it denies its own insufficiency and alienation, glorifying itself as the ideal of agency. It is part of the functioning of a plane of transcendence to obscure the fact that molarization, like molecularization, is a virtual–actual circuit between thought and states of things. But its amplitude is narrower. Its outside limits fall shy of superabstraction on the virtual side and of hyperdifferentiation the actual side, swinging no further than analytic abstraction and identity confusion. Haunted as it is by contradiction, driven as it is by the impossible desire to make corporeality disappear into ideality, the plane of transcendence as quasicause tends to turn its circuit into a vicious circle.

It is imperialist by nature. A system of interiority, the plane of transcendence has no mechanisms by which to interact with the outside as outside, no terms with which to understand it in its own right. It can only deal with an unidentified body by putting it to the test, either assigning it an acceptable category and taking into the fold, or assigning it a bad category and attacking it. Incorporate or annihilate. Anything perceptible to the forces of molarity, but resistant to selective evaluation, is reacted to as a potential threat to the purity of the plane of transcendence and the stasis it polices. Molarity cannot tolerate anything remaining outside its purview, it must constantly expand its domain in an outward drive of conquest of the "Other," identified as *Enemy*. That becomes the catch-all category, *the* operative category. If bodies can be duplicitous, passing as one identity while continuing to incarnate another, every body is a potential enemy. Any body might prove to be an intruder threatening the beloved identity with masked subversion and contamination by foreign matter. Molarization is as paranoid as it is imperialist. Any suspicious movement, even on the part of a duly identified body—particularly one assigned a devalued identity—lands it in the enemy camp, an internal enemy answering to the enemy from without: a potential defector from habit, a subversive and degenerate. A new front of domestic conquest widens the war for molarity. Institutional regularization becomes ever-more severe (discipline), and selective evaluation increasingly vigilant (surveillance). Discipline requires rigid segregation of bodies according to category, in order to prevent unseemly mixing and the identity blurring it may lead to. Surveillance requires a carefully maintained hierarchy, a pyramid of supervisory and command positions.

Molarity's plane of transcendence promises two things: oneness (unity in identity) and rest (heaven). The promised oneness tends to translate as extreme compartmentalization; the longed-for rest, as an anxiety-ridden war on two fronts. The attempt to reduce the distance between the plane of transcendence and the states of things to which it is applied only widens the gap (the Good is no closer). The goal of making the plane of transcendence coextensive with the plane of immanence on which it depends for its effectiveness is farther than ever from realization (the quasicause has not been converted into a full cause). The closer molarization comes to success, the worse it fails. The more vigorously it inducts bodies and internalizes its outside, the more bodies seem to elude definitive capture. Heaven has turned into Hell on earth. Even harsher measures are taken against the ever-present specter of the ubiquitous Enemy.[37]

Molarization is another word for "fascism."[38] Fascism is a manic attack by the body politic against itself, in the interests of its own salvation. More precisely, it is an attack by the "whole" of society, its image of unity or plane of transcendence, against its "parts," its bodies or plane of immanence. It is desire turned against itself.

Fascism can be defined as the incorporeal transformation of a system operating under two deterministic constraints and tending toward stable equilibrium into a highly unstable, frenetically dissipative structure. The constraints are oneness—maximum order—and rest—maximum entropy. Together they define the fascist attractor—becoming-the-same. But by thermodynamic definition they are a contradiction in terms. Maximum entropy (rest) means maximum molecular chaos (disunity). Order, or the maintenance of correlations at a distance (unity in movement; oneness), requires infusions of energy and is thus negentropic. The constraints of entropy and order can be synthesized into a stable equilibrium only in a closed system. No system is closed. The outside always seeps in, if only because the energy infusions necessary for the molar synthesis require an opening onto an aleatory outside. This entails the perception of another attractor—the unpredictability of becoming-other. That attractor is defined by two constraints as well: disorder and differentiation. Since it is of the outside, becoming-other is naturally the more inclusive process. The constraint of differentiation is in fact the entire system of stable order. Becoming-other encompasses becoming-the-same: it takes a stable equilibrium, welcomes a measure of instability (chance), and incorporeally transforms the system into an active order that counteractualizes oneness and rest into a line of perpetual self-escape. Becoming-other is "anarchy." Since it undermines identity, its process can be considered schizophrenic.[39]

Every society responds to both attractors. A social formation is defined by its particular mix of becoming-other and becoming-the-same, schizophrenia and paranoia, fascism and anarchy.[40] The attractors are limit-states, unreachable extremes lying at opposite ends of a continuum of potential syntheses of interiority and the outside, closure and open-endedness. Social and political systems can be tracked along the continuum according to which extreme they are approaching, in other words their preferred impossibility: the pure immanence of continual social self-invention (permanent revolution) or the pure transcendence of perfect and enduring order (paradise) — an unviably superabstract line of escape, or the viciously abstract circle of domestic peace through violence.

Because the attractor components of anarchy-schizophrenia are not a contradiction in terms, it constitutes the more powerful pole of attraction. Disorder can be entropic (molecular chaos) or negentropic (intrusion; infusion of energy). Differentiation can be less active and more stable, or less stable and more active (metastability: order within wider or narrower margins of error, with greater or lesser chances of enduring). Its terms are asymmetrical, each containing a range of variation. They are in tension, but their tension takes the form of a highly complicated set of differentials mapping a matrix of virtual potentials (as opposed to a grid of possible identities). A tension of this kind is called a "value" (in Nietzsche's sense, not an economic or moral sense).[41]

Since anarchy-schizophrenia welcomes chance, a society tending in its direction possesses a nearly infinite degrees of freedom. Its terms are not mutually exclusive in principle: the potentials they define can accommodate *both* molecularity *and* molarity, chaos and order, intrusion and closure, and each of these *both* in the form of virtual superposition *and* as actual coexistence. The attractors of fascism-paranoia, on the other hand, are oppositional terms in irresolvable contradiction which nevertheless attempt to impose themselves on the social body as a necessity. They define a field of death. A social formation taking fascism-paranoia to the extreme does not so much self-transform as self-destruct. A fascist state is a suicide state.[42] Between the disciplinary mechanisms providing its point of departure and the death frenzy of its end there is less a difference in kind than a difference in degree. There is nothing extraordinary about fascism. It is normality to the extreme, an exacerbation of the constituent tension of identity, an acceleration of the vicious actual–virtual circuit peculiar to the process of social induction. Fascism is social Reason, and Reason is its own revenge.

Although fascism-paranoia and anarchy-schizophrenia can be conceived as two poles at either end of a continuum of variation, they are not symmetrical. This asymmetry is underlined by the fact that anarchy-schizophrenia effectively encompasses fascism-paranoia. Theirs is not a formal distinction between two binary opposites, but a real distinction between modes of dynamic interaction and directions of movement. The two poles are virtual modes of composition or consistency extrapolatable into diverging vectors. They may be actualized in "collective" bodies (States; institutions; modes of production), "individual" bodies (human beings; animals; minerals), or sub-bodies (thoughts; desires; perceptions-sensations), and all three simultaneously to varying degrees. In every case, they comprise a heterogeneity of levels and a multiplicity of constituents. A formation actualizing one pole more strongly than another will display a tendency to follow a different path through the world than a formation piloted more often than not by the other pole. Fascism-paranoia and anarchy-schizophrenia are transpersonal drives in reciprocal presupposition.[43] The former can only indirectly acknowledge its reciprocal presupposition with the later: fascism-paranoia merely implies anarchy-schizophrenia in its segregative reactions to indistinct perceptions of chaotic incursions and supermolecular activity. Fascist-paranoid bodies are autonomic, never autonomous.[44]

The distinction between the two virtual poles, or drives, can be conceived as a battle between a limitative body without organs or plane of consistency and a nonlimitative one. Both are selective, but in different modes. Fascism-paranoia is segregative (tends toward exclusive disjunctive synthesis and the creation of rigidly bounded compartmentalizations: ghettoes); anarchy-schizophrenia is expansive (tends toward inclusive conjunctive synthesis and the mixing of bodies and desires: miscegenation). Fascism spreads death (strives for stasis), anarchy stretches the limits of life (fosters mutation). A molar identity category is an image of fascism-paranoia's whole attractor. It is a coding of affects (ways of affecting and being affected) applied to a body in such a way as to modify its interaction with other bodies, moving both the individual (overcoded as a person) and its assigned collectivity (overcoded as a class) closer to the attractor state of would-be stable equilibrium. The application of the category is an attribution of the supposed wholeness characterizing the attractor state to the target body. In the process, the target body's sub-bodies are incorpo-really transformed into what are in principle smoothly functioning parts of an organic whole that corresponds part for part to similar wholes on other levels (forced analogy; the body as a microcosm of the "body politic," with the leader as "head" of state and his ceremonial sword a symbol of the phallus said to constitute collective desire). "Part-objects" are translated into "organs," each of which functions, by metaphoric transference, as a whole attractor in its own right.[45] The result is an infinite microcosmic regress of representations of the unrepresentable — of the impossible attractor state of oneness and rest (an endlessly boring proliferation of analogical images of pretended unity: institution as organ of the State, person as organ of the institu-tion, body-parts as organs of the individual, the cells as organ of the body-part. . . . all, of course, work in perfect harmony for the common good: the Russian dolls of morality).[46]

This imposition of whole attractors on the body is the operation called Oedipus in the last chapter. In its broadest definition, it is the process of molarization as such. Fascism-paranoia, the molar-moral drive of Oedipal desire, works to fashion society into samenesses of varying scales — a *mise en abyme* of homologous organic structures (normality as the embodiment of analogy; being as self-similarity). Fascism-paranoia is the condition known as being in the molar–moral "majority." The image of the cell fits best: its lethal, imperialist process resembles nothing more than a metastasizing cancer.[47] Anarchy-schizophrenia is anoedipal desire that respects the partiality of bodies (their polymorphous connective potential; their "perversity"; their difference). It induces them to follow the fractal attractor of the world as infinitely open system. Its constituents are not discrete if interlock-ing organs or cells (abstract models of wholeness; points describing ideal geometrical figures; images of being as a closed structure). They are superposable "dense points" (essentially imageless shreds of vir-tual space-time; dynamic coordinates of becoming in a superabstract, non-Euclidean, post-Einsteinian space). Anarchy-schizophrenia is "becoming-minor."[48] Since its process is mutational, it can be likened to a virus (it hijacks and scrambles life codes, rather than replicating them wholesale).[49] A society (socius) — any formation, for that mat-ter — is an endless tug-of-war between the cancerous limitative body without organs of fascism-paranoia and the viral nonlimitative body without organs of anarchy-schizophrenia, as cosmic principles.[50] The two virtual poles together constitute Desire.

More of the Same

Few societies ever approach either limit-state. Hitler's Germany and Cambodia under the Khmer Rouge are examples of murderous fascist-paranoid attack taken to suicidal extremes. Grouping together such ideologically divergent formations—one "far right," the other "far left"—is in no way meant to minimize the very real differences between them. The distinction between fascism-paranoia and anarchy-schizophrenia advanced above is a dynamic distinction between virtual tendencies, *not* a typological one between actual formations. Typologies of actual molar organizations can be derived from it, but their categories neither coincide with nor contradict traditional demarcations based on ideology or mode of production[51] ("fascism-paranoia" is not a terminological substitute for "fascism" proper). The analysis focuses less on a formation's present state conceived as a synchronic structure than on the vectors of potential transformation it envelops. But the approach is not by that token diachronic: it is unconcerned with plotting a line of descent from the past to a more or less deterministic future, and implies no evolutionary or teleological framework. A typology based on virtual tendencies charts a superlinear network of possible futures and indicates actual points of intervention likely to influence which future is selected. It assesses direction and quality of movement (mode of composition) and maps pressure points (opportunities for resistance). Functioning only within a pragmatic horizon, it claims no scientific status. It must be continually rethought, as happily proven wrong as right.[52]

Social formations approaching the supermolecular extreme are harder to locate than fascist-paranoid ones. They neither take a Statist form nor revert to so-called primitive social structures, and thus slip through existing categories of political organization. In addition, they elicit a ferociously repressive reaction from molar forces, and rarely last long enough to be perceived by history in any other than negative terms, as the opposite of order—"anarchy" as a pejorative epithet. Social breakdowns such as May 1968 in France and the initial phases of most modern revolutions (anywhere the cry for "direct democracy" is heard) can be considered supermolecular becomings-other to the extreme. But becoming-other may also take the shape of more diffuse and longer-lived "movements" which—in the judgment of both those in power and already-established opposition forces—are of indefinite and highly suspect ideological character: examples from sixties include the Situationists in France, the Provos and Kabouters of the Netherlands, the Yippies and their allies in the U.S.; in the seventies, the Italian autonomists; in the eighties, the convergence of squatters, associated marginals, and extraparliamentary Greens in Northern Europe; and in general, the "radical" wings of feminist and other minority movements. One of the few examples of a possibly supermolecular formation holding a territorial base over a significant stretch of time is the Catalonian anarchists during the Spanish Civil War.[53]

Most actual social formations fall midrange between the extremes and display complex tendencies moving in both directions simultaneously. For most of the twentieth century in the West, the ideological category corresponding most closely to the dominant middle-range formation is the liberal or social-democratic nation-state.[54] This formation departs from the fascist-paranoid dynamic most significantly in its response to pressures from the outside, from the field of exteriority without which no structure of interiority—no molar apparatus of capture—can survive. When it perceives an "Other," or ubiquitous Enemy, its reflex action is more modulated than the draconian "be one or die" of fascism. It insists on molarization as the prerequisite to a recognized right to exist, but rather than forcing the perceived intruder into a preexisting identity category, it gives it the latitude to redefine one, or even fight for a new one all its own. Adaptive enough to adjust its identity grid when required, it avoids a continual state of war against the foreign bodies that crop up even in the most obsessively cleansed social field. It manages to be at least grudgingly dialogical and integrative. Molarity with a human face.

The identities open to redefinition are, of course, sub-Standard ones. Their status is upgraded, but at a price. Groups working to revalue them must agree to operate within the established limits of individual and collective action. They must behave, act like "responsible" citizens. They must measure up to Molar Man. Labor, women, Blacks, and at times sexual minorities, may be admitted into positions of power, but only to the extent that they become, for all practical purposes, capitalist, male, white, and straight—honorary members of the majority. The "Other" (the outside) is interiorized by being identified, and all identification is against the Standard of the European White Male Heterosexual as the Western embodiment of good/common sense, in politics as in personal conduct. Minorities are expected to become equal-in-theory but in practice less powerful versions of the Same: children of Molar Man. *Neonormalities*. The divide-and-conquer approach of fascism-paranoia is toned down to a paternalistic recognize-and-subdue.

In the economic domain, this "corporatism" (molar incorporation; "integration") takes the form of a Keynesian alliance between capital and labor, laying the foundations for a welfare state.[55] In the political domain in the U.S., it takes the form of an electoral system monopolized by two parties which, though often hard to distinguish, preserve a residual asymmetry. The Democratic Party serves as a holding pen for identified others, helping minorities win limited institutional participation—thereby translating their volatile movements of resistance into a predictable dialectic of opposition, presiding over their accession to the political mirror stage. The Democratic Party tilts ever so slightly toward the anarchist-schizophrenic pole, the Republican Party toward the fascist-paranoid. The tension between the limitative and nonlimitative bodies without organs that constitutes the social field is recapitulated by representational politics as a rivalry between Parties that are roughly homologous—similar enough to operate within the same ground rules, different enough that their gentleman's agreement to takes turns in office yields a degree of continuing systemic self-adjustment. The staying power of the liberal nation-state rests on its adaptive ability to *represent* the "Other"/the outside—but only represent it. Stirrings at ground level in the social field, embryonic escapes into hyperdifferentiation, are translated into a circle of mirror-image rivalry—others as alter-Sames vying for a "piece of the pie." The rivalry is not, as a rule, allowed to turn vicious. The outside is perceived, but neither as the inventive movement of desire that it is, nor fundamentally as the ubiquitous Enemy of fascism-paranoia. It is perceived as a representable reserve of rivals and potential partners, a collection of molarizable interest groups. The existence of others is acknowledged, but is in the same stroke transposed onto a different level of collective existence, a system of party politics open only indirectly to "grass roots" social agents through their "representatives." Social agents of desire are allowed to act, literally. They are given power on condition that they delegate their transformational potential to "actors" on the "political stage." The real movement of desire is channeled into a level at which it can be watched and contained, becoming a "forced movement," a parody.[56] The mass media are a specialized perceptive apparatus charged with aiding in this parodic translation of difference into more of the same. The liberal nation-state is not repressive as such. It is "democratic." It makes the "right" to vote "universal"—in other words, it gives every body the "free" choice to abdicate power.

The electoral system as it functions in a "democracy" creates a separate political domain that seems to stand apart from society. Party politics translates dispersed movements occurring ground-level throughout the social field in a manner that selectively contracts them into a smaller space. It provides them with a second arena, a representative space apart governed by its own procedural rules, with its own perceptual apparatuses and forms of expression. This translative separation may be experienced by the bodies whose power is abdicated in it as a simple "alienation." But it is much more than that: it is a process of transformation, as was the plane of transcendence, though in a different way. The space apart does not stand above bodies and try to force them to coincide with it, to elevate their mundane world to its heavenly level. Quite the opposite, this "separate" sphere is entirely at home among bodies whose movements it translates. It transposes movements into its particular arena and then retransmits them laterally to their source, in modified form. "Democratic" government is a force converter (as opposed to a categorical model). It gathers up movements of desire, rephases them, then changes their direction, sending them back to propagate at ground-level in waves of gentle ordering. It is less godly than cerebral, serving as a kind of central nervous system for a brain damaged society. It is not moral, just managerial. What it demands of its bodies is a practical acceptance of certain parameters of action, rather than a principled conformity to an absolute ideal.

"Democracy" embraces the becoming-immanent fascism fears most, but cannot exorcize. The singularity that prevents a body from coinciding entirely with its identity category can be made a strength. If it is amplified enough to win recognition on the level of representation, it is allowed under certain circumstances to modify the category, a variant of which can then be reimplanted in society with the help of institutions designed to service the new identity (unions, caucuses within parties, lobbies, etc.). In other words, a body has the option of generalizing its deviancy. It can pool its force of singularity with that of others considered similar to it, translate it into a general movement (parody it), and insert that movement into an identity category (custom-made quasicause) whose new meaning (modified code of actions) is then reapplied to the social field. In this way, a body can join with others deemed to be of its kind in carving out a customized social space for itself. It need not accept an identity category as is—but it must accept identification. It need not accept a particular general idea—but it must accept the idea of the general in general. The only condition is that the body molarize.

"Democratic" government, situated as it is on the same level as the bodies and institutions it manages, is subject to its own laws. It is not above but between the molar formations it governs. It serves as a medium conveying a molarizing force. It does not itself act in a molar fashion overall. Molarity is overcoding, the imposition of a plane of transcendence or absolute identity grid, whereas "democracy" is *recoding*. Government regulates more than reigns. It arbitrates between old and new molar formations and adjusts them to one another. "Democratic" government places all collective formations in a space of coexistence of which itself is a part—even though it is a part that recapitulates the whole ("represents" it). The whole is now relatively open-ended, but still bounded by administrative borders; the governed space of controlled self-transformation does not qualify as a pure field of exteriority. "Democracy" is limited becoming-supermolecular contained by a loosely bounded field of exteriority or immanence.

Fascist-paranoid quasicauses and institutions devoted to their actualization abound in a "democracy," in spite of the relative openness of its mode of composition. Or rather, because of it: they proliferate precisely because they too take their place in a field of immanence. No single quasicause can claim a monopoly on governance or coincide completely with the territory (as does the blood of the god-king in an absolute monarchy, the blood of the race in a fascist state, the spirit of

God in a theocracy, or the toil of the workers in the state capitalism of the old-style Eastern European "Communist" regimes). The becoming-immanent of the administration of the territory disjoins the actual, everyday machinery of government from miraculous, overarching powers of unity. One quasicause, however, remains more equal than the others, and special title to it is claimed by the central government: the general idea "democracy" itself. Only mildly fascist-paranoid, it presents itself as fallibly godlike (Greek), and although it is the fundamental quasicause of the liberal nation-state it in fact overflows State borders, carried abroad by the neocolonial expansionism of the late capitalist economy. In a "democracy," everyone hates the government but loves the political-economic "system," vaunted as the nation's most valuable export. There is a certain disjunction not only between the "grass roots" and the central government, but also between the central government and its fragile unity (the "system"), and between that unity and the territory. The gaps between these levels allow more forcefully fascist-paranoid quasicauses to operate locally within the State, with a broad array of fascist-paranoid, or despotic, institutions serving to apply them. But only in miniature. What the "democratic" government arbitrates between and mutually adjusts are *minidespotisms*: school, office, church, family, police, and a growing number of variations on each.

This expands the definition of "democracy": every body's "free choice" to delegate its becoming in return for living out its "productive life" in the despotism it most desires. Choose your quasicause. "Democracy" is the quasicause representing the choice of quasicauses: equal opportunity despotism.

Most of the minidespotisms that proliferate under "democracy" are more normalizing than outright disciplinary. They often allow several quasicauses to function simultaneously, and apply them almost haphazardly. Bodies are not required to conform in their life's path to a rigidly defined code of actions and expressions enveloped in a particular quasicause. Neither total conformity nor sincere belief is necessarily called for. All that is required is that their *form* be respected. Once again, that the body be molar; that it be generalizable; that its trajectory through the world be more or less predictable; that it work and ideally reproduce itself, and in the process reproduce the social order (with slight generational variations).

In other words, the only minidespotism to which every body is required to submit without exception is its Self. The only universally applied quasicause is the soul, or a suitable substitute (a conscience will do, or simply a phallus). Molarity is reduced to the most miniaturized and generalizable form humanly possible: supposedly self-directing subjectivity operating within the limits of good / common sense as socially defined (individual life confined to an artificially closed system ruled by the whole attractor of stable equilibrium, also known as the "American Dream"). Molarity molds itself to the human shape, in a personalization of the plane of transcendence. Every body becomes a "legislating subject," at least in the privacy of its own home. In a "democracy," the kingdom of Oedipus, a man's home is his castle. Thus even in a liberal nation-state where neonormality reigns supreme, the form that every body must respect is still fundamentally a State-form. The State itself can afford to depart from that form, because it has seen to it that its citizens will take up where it leaves off.[57]

Stringently disciplinary mechanisms are not dismantled, however. In fact, they experience the same multiplication and dispersion as other molar institutions. When bodies refuse molarity or simply overstep the limits of molar sense, they are abandoned to unabashedly disciplinary minidespotisms (prison, reform school, and so on). In a liberal nation-state, these are the exceptions that prove the rule. Frankly fascist institutions are also tolerated, and proliferate up to a point (the Ku Klux Klan and its neo-Nazi offspring). But they are only tolerated at an even more local level, as grass-roots associations without a recognized right to participate openly in the government or express themselves broadly in the media.[58] Fascism proper has been relegated to the pores of society (survivalism), but fascism-paranoia is everywhere.[59]

Still More

Every formation is defined by thresholds of movement beyond which its mode of composition changes in nature and it ceases to be itself. The liberal nation-state has two such limits: molar humanity, and the capitalist relation.

The liberal nation-state's ability to find an integrative response to perceptions of the outside is stretched to limit when confronted by sexual minorities. This is because a successful becoming-woman,

becoming-lesbian or -gay, becoming-sadomasochist, or becoming–
boy lover, directly challenges the universal form of molarity under
"democracy": Oedipal personhood itself.[60] Molarity is the bottom line,
and true sexual becomings endeavor to erase it: to the extent that they
are antiphallocentric and play on the fractality of the part-object, they
attack the only fascist-paranoid quasicause that paternalist democracy
cannot do without. In principle, there is nothing that prevents these
becomings from being re-Oedipalized or corporatized. This happens
up to a point. But once unleashed, pressures toward hyperdifferentiation
build exponentially. A given liberal government can integrate some,
but never all, of the sexual minorities its population invents. It must
redraw the line somewhere, but is restrained by its own ideology of
"civil liberties."

The task of resetting limits falls to the minidespotic groupings closest
the fascist-paranoid pole. The rise of the New Right in North America
in the late seventies is an indication that the threshold state was being
reached. It is no accident that the issues it chose to do battle on were
those the Old Left considered secondary "lifestyle" or "cultural"
questions. The New Right, for all its apparent archaism, has been far
more attuned than the traditional Left to the actual lines of force in late
capitalist society. It perceived that the most volatile pressure points
have shifted from class conflicts to subjectivity battles. The antiabortion
movement that has been so central in rallying the Right is just one front
in a continuing campaign in defense of Molar Man (and God—the
concept that abortion is murder assumes a soul present from conception). The defense of the family against feminists and assorted "devi-
ants" is an attempt to shore up the system of oppositional difference as
embodied by gender. The antiobscenity and antipornography movements police the part-objectification of desire. The "drug war" and
anti–drunken driving campaigns are a reimposition of good / common
sense as applied to the body, and dovetail with the health craze that is
repropagating the general idea of the body-as-organism. The assault
on affirmative action and on the inclusion of non-Western cultural
content in the curriculum rehabilitate white European privilege
(faciality). Cultural-political issues such as these are fundamental.
Their importance should not be underestimated. They are used as
angles of insertion into the social field for minidespotisms of properly
fascist cast which, unlike their rivals on the survivalist fringe, are

patently Statist in orientation. When a social formation reaches one of its thresholds, it starts to supermolecularize in spite of itself, facing a network of bifurcating choices leading to any one of a number of modes of composition and alternate futures — including alternate fascisms.

So far, Western societies in general and the U.S. in particular have not turned fascist. On the contrary, their overall mode of composition has passed the threshold of molarity, crossing the limits of the liberal nation-state to enter a new realm: neoconservatism. The neoconservative transnation-state corresponds to what is called "postmodernism" on the cultural level, and in political economy "postindustrial society" or "late capitalism." It is characterized by a breakdown of the Keynesian alliance and a renewed war by management against labor, accompanied by a dismantling of the welfare state. In spite of this, society's pressure points do not revert to sites of class conflict, but remain in the "cultural" domain of "lifestyle" issues and forms of expression. This is because when the threshold of molarity is passed mechanisms kick in to prevent new modes of extramolarity from overflowing the other threshold of modern "democracy" — the capitalist relation.

Capital is a quasicause, but of a very different kind than the ones we have seen up to now. The grid of capital is simple. Its categorical distinctions are two in number: worker/capitalist and commodity/consumer. Although they receive endless ideological expression, they are not ideological by nature. The categories do not have to be perceived by the body they apply to, or even be clearly conceived of by it — let alone believed in — in order to be activated. They are automatically in operation in any state of things touched by capital. They are *operative categories*. Capital itself is not an image of social agency operating on other levels, as are "God," "democracy," "soul," or "wine." It *is* a social agency, one of the most powerful that has ever existed. Capital functions directly through incorporeal transformation, without having to step down or up to another level. It *can* jump levels. A general idea of it can be produced and function in conjunction with a plane of transcendence. But this kind of "ideological" application of the Idea of capital is supplemental. Capital is often given a fascist-paranoid image, but it does not have to have one. Pull out a hundred-dollar bill, and whatever object is before you, even a human body, has been given a price. You have been incorporeally transformed into a consumer, and the other object or body has been transformed into a commodity.

Regardless of whether you "believe" in capitalism. The hundred-dollar bill is an image of capital as means of payment. This kind of working image of capital functions differently from the fascist-paranoid images that may also be provided for it. It is a vehicle of concretization rather than a tool of abstraction. Capital can be given an image—in fact it *must* have one in order to act—but it is imageless as such. It is a body without organs. In other words, a network of virtual relations, a selection of which is immediately actualized at ground level wherever one of capitalism's working images (organs) goes. These images are conveyances (components of passage). They bring to designated bodies at each spatiotemporal coordinate through which they circulate a relation that fundamentally changes those bodies' social and physical reality. That relation *is* capital as an immanent social agency.

Money incorporeally transforms the relationship obtaining between bodies into a potential exchange. The body designated as the commodity is given an abstract value. This abstraction has nothing to do with moral–molar ideas. It is numerical, quantitative rather than qualitative. A commodity-body is generalized in a way that not only disregards minor deviations from a norm but is basically disinterested in the body's intrinsic qualities and their similarity-difference to those of other bodies. The commodity-body is reduced to a pure equivalence. It is generalized in the sense that any number of other bodies carry the same numerical value, and could be substituted for it, exchanged in its stead. The actualization of the capitalist relation transforms a body's degrees of freedom into a bifurcating network, not of virtual futures for the body to become, but of possible objects a consumer might own—any consumer. The other body is generalized as well. Becoming has been translated, but not into a molarized being—as was the case with fascist-paranoid quasicauses—but into a having.

The equivalence that is set up is entirely unequal if judged by any other criteria than numerical. It equates elements that are obviously heterogeneous—a desired body (which is perhaps even desired for its unique intrinsic qualities) and a piece of paper bearing a recognized denomination. Apples and oranges. The exchange is just as unequal: also active in the consumer–commodity encounter is a third heterogeneous term, which may be a single human body or (more often) a collective apparatus, and is rarely physically present at the buying site. It is not assigned a numerical value, it simply collects—surplus value.

A portion of the money that changes hands is deflected from the circuit of commodity/consumer encounters into a space formally different from the consumer space but on the same plane as it. The path of deflection runs transversally from the space of purchase into an associated space where a different mode of relation dominates: a bank, for example. Money accumulating in the bank assumes heightened powers — en masse, it can step out of its role as a means of payment to become a means of investment. Capital, with a capital C: money begetting more money, accumulating interest, building factories. . . . A series of investment encounters is always implicated in the series of purchase encounters.

This is where the second axis on the capitalist grid comes in: worker/ capitalist. The heterogeneous third term, always involved even if physically absent, is of course the capitalist. Bodies that collect surplus value and control money as means of investment are capitalists; bodies with only enough money to use it as a means of payment are workers. Workers are human bodies that have been converted into commodities for purchase by capitalists. Although it is against the principles of "democracy" for human bodies to be bought outright like objects, they are nonetheless given a numerical value, called a wage. What is bought is less the bodies than aspects of their life: a quantity of their time (the workday), the physical and intellectual activity they can perform in that time (labor), and the concentration and attitude of cooperation necessary to perform that activity (docility). Yet another unequal exchange: the capitalist must give none of those things in the same quantity, or at least in the same way, in order to collect the transversal flow of value the wage relation produces.

The capitalist relation is a nexus between two modes of relation in reciprocal presupposition: the commodity relation and the wage relation.

This is a quite basic restatement of the Marxist theory of the "formal subsumption" of labor by capital. By that phrase is meant that wherever a recognized image of capital is found (whether gold, paper currency, stock, whatever), there is a potential site for the actualization of a commodity relation or a wage relation and their interconnection. What is important for present purposes is that: capital is a quasicause with tremendous transformational potential; that it functions immanently, in a field of exteriority constituted by the dynamic in-between of bodies; that it has images but is imageless as such; that it is capable of transforming states of things without the intermediate step of the application of a plane of transcendence; and that it grasps the bodies it transforms from a very particular angle, in other words partially. It has all the characteristics of desire as earlier defined. Capital is an unmediated desire, or abstract machine. A society actualizing that desire can be conceptualized as a particular mix between fascism-paranoia and anarchy-schizophrenia (tending strongly toward the latter). However, capital's mode of operation is unique enough to justify considering it a virtual pole in its own right. It can be analyzed as a virtual mode of composition that is perceived as such only when the constraints of molar personhood start to falter.

Neoconservatism is the clear perception by a liberal nation-state of the capitalist attractor in all its purity, as a virtual pole of existence. It is the coming out of capital, a new golden age of greed that dares to say its name. Without a wince. Capitalism no longer has to justify itself. It no longer has to hide behind fascist-paranoid quasicauses and argue that it serves the common good. It can dispense with belief and good sense, because it is now stronger than molarity, and stronger than the ideologies that help to reproduce it. The men who personify it—the Donald Trumps and Michael Milkens of the world—do not so much represent an ideological cause as embody a desire. An abstract desire, a mania for accumulating numerical quantities. Possessing things is understandable from the moral–molar point of view, as is wanting to accumulate capital for what it can buy in the way of time, things, and activities. But to accumulate more than anyone could ever spend? And then keep on accumulating greater and greater sums, with no other interest or aim in life? That is beyond good and evil. The neoconservative capitalist is defined less by what he possesses than by what possesses him. He is the personification of a mode of irrationality. In itself, the agency of that irrationality is not abstract like the quantities it begets and induces these post-human bodies to accumulate. It is superabstract.

"Partiality" is a key word for understanding capital's basic mode of operation. The capitalist relation grasps the body not as a putative whole, but partially, from two precise angles: its potential to buy or sell a commodity, and its potential to sell its time and activities or to buy those of others. The quasicause of capital resolves the body into a set of privileged affects enveloping certain paths of movement and circuits of unequal exchange. The capitalist relation is abstract in the sense that it is indifferent to its content: it doesn't matter *what* a body buys or *what* activities it sells, only *that* it buys, and if doesn't happen to be a capitalist, gets a wage-earning job. But it is ultimately superabstract because its terms are fundamentally imageless operative categories immanent to society, rather than categorical images standing as wholes apart from the population they purport to unify. The capitalist relation consists of four dense points — commodity/consumer, worker/capitalist — which in neoconservative society are effectively superposed in every body in every spacetime coordinate. When capital comes out, it surfaces as a fractal attractor whose operational arena is immediately coextensive with the social field.

That is the meaning of the "real subsumption" of society by the capitalist relation.[61] Under formal subsumption, the four dense points of the capitalist relation are not yet immanent to all of society's spacetime coordinates. There are still domains it has not fully penetrated: leisure time, belief, family relations — anything defined as "private." That is the meaning of "privacy" in the liberal-democracy: less a reserve free of governmental intervention (which on the contrary makes leaps and bounds as "social welfare" and "protective" services proliferate) than an oasis not yet fully exploitable by capital. Other undercapitalized domains persist on the periphery, in the "Third World." Real subsumption involves a two-pronged expansion of the capitalist relation. First, an *extensive expansion*, whereby capitalism pushes its geographical boundaries to the point that it encompasses the globe (before launching into space aboard commercial satellites). This a neocolonialist movement imposing the capitalist relation of unequal exchange on all the nations of the world (the creation of a foreign debt is the point of entry for management of national economies by international investment brokers acting collectively through the International Monetary Fund and the World Bank).[62] Capitalism becomes a transnational machine that swallows weak nation-states whole and can no longer be completely controlled by even the strongest (the much lamented "decline" of the U.S.). Second, an *intensive expansion*, whereby the last oases of domestic space are invaded by the four irrepressible dense points. This is "endocolonization."[63]

As powerful as the capitalist quasicause is, it remains a quasicause. It can only move into a prepared medium. It still relies on an army of despotic, disciplinary and liberal institutions to open bodies to it, to make them susceptible to its magic (armies, schools, churches, malls, . . .). These institutions concretize the capitalist relation. They determine that *this* purchase is made rather than another, that *this* activity or quantity of time is bought rather than another. They determine the particular forms of content taken by the capitalist relation, as superabstract form of expression. They select one exchange *here and now* from a countless number of theoretically possible "equivalent" exchanges (that is, involving the same abstract quantity of monetary value). The quasicause of capital evaluates the mode of relation obtaining between the bodies involved in its actualization (consumer or commodity? capitalist or worker?). A whole constellation of interlocking institutions selects the content of that encounter. The evaluative quasicause is a "collective assemblage of enunciation." The selective constellation of institutions is a "machinic assemblage." The two together constitute the abstract machine of selective evaluation that is capitalism. Capitalism is the cofunctioning in the same field of immanence of processes of extreme abstraction and utter concretization. The system of regularities that determines how superabstraction is embodied in particular situations is the capitalist "axiomatic" (as distinct from despotic overcoding and liberal recoding). An axiomatic functions by inclusive conjunctive synthesis.[64]

When capital comes out under neoconservatism and real subsumption is a fait accompli, the choices offered by the axiomatic become effectively infinite (for those with adequate cash flow). "Postmodernity" is the presence of the consumer/commodity axis of the capitalist relation in every point of social space-time: endocolonization accomplished. Everything can be bought, even life itself. There is a patent out on the human genome. A new mouse was just copyrighted. Whole species are now being bought and sold. Life forms are not simply captured by an external mechanism and put up for sale (as in the fur industry or trade in wild animals for pets); the very form of a life that has never existed in nature is commercialized at its point of emergence. It is captured from its future. The capitalist machine has developed perceptual abilities that enable it to penetrate life and direct its unfolding. It can go straight to the code of its molarity, resolve it into its constituent part-objects (in this case genes), recombine them to yield a special-order product (adult individuals), and market the final product—or the transformational *process* itself, at any one of its steps. Capital never operates *as* a code. It operates *on* codes. As embodied in the liberal nation-state, it recodes relatively static forms of content and expression on the molar level. Freed by the neoconservative transnation-state to follow its fractal attractor to the limit, it operates a fission and reconstitution of transformational matrixes on the molecular level (its axiomatic regularizes *decodings*). Capitalism is now more processual than it is productive, more fundamentally energetic than object-oriented, quantum rather than quantitative or qualitative. It has developed its transformational powers to such a degree that it can grasp matter at its point of emergence from the virtual.

"Postmodern" neoconservatism is much more than the miniaturization and dissemination of mutually adjustable codes, a definition more suited to Western society's previous mode of composition. "Postmodernity" is the conjunction of superabstraction and extreme powers of concretization at every point in a social field saturated by the capitalist relation. What can be bought or brought forth with money is effectively infinite. It is not only white mice whose molecular makeup has been capitalized. Human identity has undergone the same treatment.

Media, marketing, and advertising are mechanisms for abstracting and commercializing codes of human identity and their molecular components (in this case, the subcodes in question are affects). It is often remarked that "postmodernity" is associated with an information-based economy in which images as such (in the everyday usage) become the basic commodity. The subject of a despotic State must assume its assigned identity category and unfold its life along the lines laid down by the code enveloped in its images. The citizen of the liberal nation-state is given the latitude to recode an existing code, to redefine a category. The denizen of the neoconservative transnation-state can *invent* new codes by mixing and matching images. Gender becomes increasingly negotiable, as new sexualities come onto the market. A body may be "transsexual," "bisexual," "asexual," "sex addicted," "sadomasochistic," or many other things. A whole service industry exists for each. Race sells (this season, wannabe rappers abound in white suburbia). It used to be that assuming or redefining an identity took a lifetime. Now it can be done in as long as it takes to shop for an image. What used to be mutually exclusive identities or behaviors can now overlap quite comfortably in the same body, which may run through an endless series of self-transformations (serialized inclusive conjunctive synthesis). The unchallenged reign of Molar Man has ended. Often, all that remains of Oedipality is a caricature: a person will get "flaky," or pass from one whole-hearted "complex" to another with amazing rapidity. Life as a succession of soap operas. Postnormality.

The "lack of affect" in "postmodern" culture that some commentators find so disturbing is in fact a surfeit.[65] Affect has been deterritorialized, uprooted from the spatiotemporal coordinates in which it "naturally" occurs and allowed to circulate. Gender, race, ethnicity, religious practices, belief systems, beauty, health, leisure — and every other aspect of molar human existence — has been resolved into component parts: images that may be purchased by a body and self-applied as desired. The old territorialities (habitual constellations of affect and patterns of movement) are divided into image-borne packets which are reimplanted in social field, either separately or in free combination, and allowed to proliferate. The affect packets are actualized in a new substance at an unfamiliar location, the shreds of patterning they envelop left to unfold in chance directions, at an adjusted (usually accelerated) rate. Affect has not become "flat." Human existence has not been made unidimensional. It has simply been grasped from another dimension by the social machine. Traditionally, images enveloped molar codes. They were images of whole attractors — and only indirectly of the dominated part-objects composing those attractors. With "postmodernity's" deterritorialization of affect, images envelop what were formerly subcodes of molarity: they now attach directly to part-objects, and function in much the same way as the working images of capital itself. Subjectivity is becoming isomorphic to capital — an axiomatic governed by a fractal attractor. It is being disengaged from the plane of transcendence of "human" being, becoming an immanent abstract machine of mutation (with the mass media serving as its collective assemblage of enunciation, and a range of apparatuses from television studios to fashion shows to health clubs combining to form its machinic assemblage). Society now grasps "human" existence in its virtual dimension, or from the angle of its mutational aptitude. The images so ubiquitous in the urban landscape are nothing less than commodified transformational matrices in an escape run from molarity.[66]

The body is now allowed to exercise its partiality more fully. The self is allowed to relarvalize. This post-human condition is not fundamentally a regressive state (although it can easily turn into one: re-Oedipalization). It is perfectly functional (it involves shopping). Neither is it in any way revolutionary. If it is a becoming, it is fundamentally a becoming-consumer. The body's realm of possibility has expanded beyond anything anyone could have imagined even a generation ago. But that extramolar transformational potential tends to be restricted to image-consumption and -production. Even when it isn't, it is everywhere reined in by the one remaining deterministic constraint: the double axis of the capitalist relation. You can go anywhere your fancy takes you and be anyone you want to be—as long as your credit is good, and you show for work the next day.

The expansion of potential in "postmodernity" goes hand in hand with the real subsumption by capital not only of society, but of all of existence. This creates a situation of structural *cynicism* (as opposed to personal hypocrisy). Hypocrisy—thinking or feeling one thing while saying or doing another—implies a molar framework of human being that defines the noncoincidence of thought-feeling and speech-action as a problem. This assumes a more or less bounded interiority that has intrinsic qualities (thought patterns; personality traits), can express them in words and gestures, and remains identical to itself across the variations of its sayings and doings. The demolarization of humanity has destroyed the conditions for this kind of self-similarity. Verisimilitude has been replaced by simulation as the explicit operating principle of individual existence. You no longer have to believe in the legal system to be lawyer, or in the government to be a civil servant or politician. A businessman doesn't have to believe, even pretend to believe, that capitalism is a force for human betterment. All a body need do is desire—and subordinate its desiring to earning and consuming. Society no longer requires a true correlation between interiority and its external manifestations, or a more or less accurate correspondence of a body to its model (its official, now residual, identity category). The only correlation it demands of everyone is between buying power and image consumption. The only correspondence it requires is with the credit card company.

"Postmodernity" is not nothing; it constitutes a limited becoming-supermolecular that can increase some bodies' degrees of freedom beyond anything seen before. The fact that society has reached the point that it can forego both interiority and belief and embrace creation is not to be lamented. A real cause for concern is that it has done so in a framework that restricts mutation. The forced movement of liberal "democracy" (parodic verisimilitude) has re-become real movement (simulation),[67] but within limits: a body's transformational potential is indexed to its buying power. This means that the privilege of self-invention will never extend to every body. Not only do most bodies *not* have infinite degrees of freedom, alarming and increasing numbers are starving or malnourished. Mere survival is a privilege in the brave new neoconservative world. Capitalism's endocolonial expansion has made the law of unequal exchange that is written into its axiomatic an inescapable and lethal fact of life. Its outward surge of expansion has nearly exhausted the earth, threatening to destroy the environment on which all life depends. Capitalism has not ushered in an age of universal wealth and well-being and never will. All it can do is displace its own limits.[68] The limits of capitalism used to be external boundaries falling between its formations and non- or precapitalist ones: between molarity and molecularity, the capitalist class and the proletariat, the "First World" and the "Third World," resource depletion and techno-logical progress. These boundaries were overtaken by capitalism as it grew to saturate its field of exteriority: Molarity/molecularity has been counteractualized as a distinction between commercialized codes and equally commercialized subcodes (the identification of the "Other" replaced by trafficking in affects for use in becoming-other). Some proletarians have been integrated as corporatist workers who are both commodities on the "job market" and consumers (Fordism), while growing numbers have been relegated to a "permanent underclass" locked out of steady employment and thus restricted to participating in the economy as consumers—of the inadequate social services still available after the gutting of the welfare state.[69] The inclusion of all nations in the international debt economy and the creation of "periph-eral" areas of underdevelopment in the very heart of the Western world's largest capitals have blurred the boundaries between the "First" and "Third" Worlds. The first three limits have been internal-ized by capitalism, in the sense of being subsumed by its axiomatic. The last limit, between resource depletion and technological "progress," not only remains but has become absolute—the death of the planet.

This limit cannot be internalized by capital (although the nuclear arms race of the Cold War period that transformed the "advanced" nations into permanent war economies based on postponed conflagration was a delirious attempt to do just that). It can, however, be crossed. It is capitalism's destiny to cross it. For although capitalism has turned quantum in its mode of operation, it has done so in the service of quantity: consumption and accumulation are, have been, and will always be its reason for being. Capitalism's strength, and its fatal weakness, is to have elevated consumption and accumulation to the level of a principle marshaling superhuman forces of invention—and destruction. The abstract machine of consumption-accumulation has risen, Trump-like in all its inhuman glory. Its fall will be a great deal harder.

What the final deterministic constraint that is the capitalist relation ultimately determines is global death. The virtual pole of capitalism turns out to be no less suicidal than fascism-paranoia, though in a very different way—by virtue of its success, not because of an irresolvable contradiction endemic to its dynamic. Capitalism is not defined by its contradictions.[70] It is the social tendency to overcome contradiction. The four fundamental dense points of its axiomatic grid constitute a creative tension, a real differential, the unmediated operation of a mode of transpersonal desire. Fascism-paranoia is a desire for unity that is applied to a body by an interceding agency whose operation consists in carrying a body outside of itself in order to find its identity. It is also a transpersonal desire, or abstract machine, but one that is mediated by a detour through molarity. The logical contradictions haunting fascist-paranoid formations are indirect expressions of a forcibly personalized desire to transcend matter. Capitalism's limits are a direct result of its more successful desire to make itself immanent to matter (in the process of which, as a side effect, it frees some bodies to transcend forced personification).

The culture of "postmodernism" is incapable of rising to the challenge of disarming the final constraint of capitalism. The two strictly coincide. "Postmodernity" as we know it is the cultural condition accompanying the coming out of the capitalist quasicause from under the yoke of the fascist-paranoid ones that have traditionally curtailed it. In spite of that, it is as ill-equipped to avert a swing back toward the fascist-paranoid pole (a reconversion of society into a more limited mode of capitalism) or an outbreak of fascism proper as it is of forging ahead into full hyperdifferentiation. A swing back to the fascist-paranoid pole could easily be brought on by a self-preservative response to the threat of extinction on the part of the many minidespotisms still operating in the capitalist field of exteriority, and an outbreak of fascism by an attack response by those same minidespotisms against the real movements of supermolecularization that the volatility of the present situation occasionally allows to slip out of the confines of relative becoming (becoming relative to commodification). Disciplinary and even outright fascist minidespotisms are not merely archaic holdovers. They are *neoarchaisms* with a perfectly contemporary function: putting the brakes on capitalism.[71]

The reason that "postmodern" culture is powerless to respond to these threats is that even though the human body is no longer necessarily grasped as a molar whole and even though the concretizations of the desire possessing it may be partial or even perverse, it is still subsumed by a superabstract relation that pertains to a single human body considered separately. You cannot be a part-consumer or a fraction of a worker. Either you consume or you don't, either you work or you don't: this last remaining exclusive disjunctive synthesis short-circuits the contagious potential of becoming-other. The capitalist axiomatic ensures that no virtual-actual circuit other than its own will reach full amplitude, simply by requiring that every body considered to be of any worth, regardless of who or what it is and how it desires, have its own bank account. Every body must buy. The vast majority must work. We all stand naked and alone before the capitalist relation that has come to encompass existence. "Private" interest, defined in monetary terms, will almost always win out over other forms of desire. You cannot be a "functioning member" of capitalist society if you do not retain the good/common sense to realize that the literal bottom line is the bottom line. "Private" is in quotation marks because what is being described is a thoroughly social mechanism. "Private" interest applies to a body taken separately; but as an operative rule written into the capitalist axiomatic, if it applies to one body it applies to them all. Capitalism dispenses with the need for its subjects to accept ideological or moral justifications of its (or their) existence. But when it does produce precepts, one is heard with overwhelming regularity: the idea that a body can serve the interests of society by serving itself (not only "can": can *only*). "Self-interest" is the basic capitalist expression of the Common Good. That is to say, it is the most direct expression of the capitalist quasicause's impersonal "conatus"—the tendency of a system, once actualized, to persist and expand. A tendency of this kind was defined earlier as "ethics." Capitalism is the ethic of greed.

Faced with such a compelling adversary, it is not surprising that most becomings-other fall short. A body may cross the threshold of molar individuality with relative ease. But few are they who find their collectivity. The hyperdifferentiated futures a body-in-becoming holds in virtuality rarely come to pass. Becomings are everywhere in capitalism, but they are always separated from their full potential, from the thing they need most to run their course: a population free for the mutating.

To Be Continued

If there is a way out of this impasse, it will not lie in turning back. There is nothing to be gained by taking an oppositional stance toward "postmodernity"—as if it were a topological space it was possible to demarcate and step out of, a surpassable historical period uncontaminated by formations belonging to other "ages" or a subjective stance an individual could adequately define and choose to eschew. "Postmodernity" as we know it is one aspect of a broader dynamic that covers the face of the earth and actualizes both our subjective and objective conditions of existence, no matter who or where we are, whether we like it or not, and whether or not we like to believe it. There is no getting outside it. Lamenting the loss of such "traditional values" as belief and sincerity and reverting to moralism, or mourning the "death of the subject" and reverting to molarism, will only take us a step back in capitalism, or on to something worse.

If there is a way out, it is right where we are: in the final constraint. We must reclaim molecularity as a limit. The absolute limit of capitalism must be shifted back from planetary death to becoming-other. The extramolarity (relative molecularity) we are now allowed must be pushed beyond the pale of self-interest. The last bastion of good/common sense must come down. The way lies ahead, in taking the inventive potential released by capitalism so far that we become so other as to no longer act in the perceived "private" interests of a separate Self that we have in any case already ceased to be (if we ever were it). We must embrace our collectivity. This requires a global perception of the capitalist relation as the constraint that it is, the development of a systemic sensitivity to its axiomatic, and shared strategies of resistance to it and its symbiotic despotisms, in a world-wide resonation of desires. The aim would be less to overthrow neoconservatism than to counteractualize its residually molar individuals as a local–global correlation of becomings-other. We are in this together, and the only way out is together, into a supermolecularity where no quasicause can follow: a collective ethics beyond good and evil. But most of all, beyond greed.

The equilibrium of the physical environment must be reestablished, so that cultures may go on living and learn to live more intensely, at a state far from equilibrium. Depletion must end, that we may devote ourselves to our true destiny: dissipation.

If this sounds vague, it is. It is one body's desire for a future it cannot envision, for the very good reason that in that future there would be no place for it—having finally become what it cannot be.

Notes

First references to central works for which a serviceable translation exists (see *Pleasures of Philosophy*, note 10, and *Force*, note 69) give two sets of page numbers: the first (in Roman) to the translation, the second (in italics) to the original French. References to works that have not been translated or for which the translation is of questionable quality give only the French pagination (in Roman).

Pleasures

1. SHADOW OF THE DESPOT: Gilles Deleuze, "Nomad Thought," p. 148 [*173*].

2. Deleuze and Parnet, *Dialogues*, p. 20 [*13*] (translation modified). On the relationship between PHILOSOPHY and the STATE, see also *A Thousand Plateaus*, pp. 374–80 [*464–70*]. Deleuze develops an extended critique of RATIONALIST PHILOSOPHY in *Différence et répétition*: see esp. "L'Image de la pensée," pp. 169–217.

3. MONSTROUS OFFSPRING: Deleuze, "I Have Nothing to Admit," p. 12 (translation modified); *Pourparlers*, p. 13.

4. HEGEL: "What I detested more than anything else was Hegelianism and the Dialectic" (ibid.). KANT as "enemy," ibid. The study alluded to is Deleuze, *Kant's Critical Philosophy*.

5. A SECRET LINK: Ibid.

6. INTELLECTUALS IN SOCIETY: See Deleuze's discussion with Michel Foucault, "Intellectuals and Power," pp. 205–17 [*3–10*].

7. ACADEMIC APPARATUS: Deleuze, "I Have Nothing to Admit," p. 113 [*14*].

8. BRING OUT MADNESS: Félix Guattari, "Sur les rapports infirmiers-médecins" (1955), in *Psychanalyse et transversalité*, p. 11.

9. INSTITUTIONAL PSYCHOTHERAPY: Guattari, *Psychanalyse et transversalité*, pp. 40, 173n, 288–89. The journal *Recherches*, of which Guattari was an editor, was the mouthpiece of the institutional analysis movement. Number 21 (March–April 1976) of *Recherches* is a collectively written history of La Borde.

10. ANTIPSYCHIATRY: Relations were strained because Guattari believed that Laing's communitarian solution reconstituted an extended Oedipal family (Guattari, "Mary Barnes, or Oedipus in Anti-Psychiatry," *Molecular Revolution*, pp. 56–58 [*La Révolution moléculaire* (1977), pp. 132–34]) and because he was critical of Basaglia's assimilation of mental illness and social alienation and his rejection of any kind of institutions for the insane (*Psychanalyse et transversalité*, p. 264). (Readers should be wary of the translation of *The Molecular Revolution*: Guattari's specialized terminology is inconsistently translated or simply glossed over.)

11. GAY-RIGHTS MOVEMENT: In 1973, Guattari was tried and fined for committing an "outrage to public decency" by publishing an issue of *Recherches* (no. 12) on homosexuality. All copies were ordered destroyed (*La Révolution moléculaire*, p. 110n), but the volume was later reprinted under the title *Trois milliards de pervers*.

12. LEFTIST BUREAUCRACY OF REASON: *La Révolution moléculaire* (Recherches), p. 144. The disintegration of the left into dogmatic "groupuscules" and the amoebalike proliferation of Lacanian schools based on personality cults confirmed the charge of bureaucratism but belied the potency of the mix. Guattari himself began his political life in the early fifties with stormy attempts at membership in two Trotskyist splinter parties (*Psychanalyse et transversalité*, pp. 268–71).

13. STATE PHILOSOPHY: *Différence et répétition*, pp. 49–55, 337–49.

14. LEGITIMATED SUBJECT: Lyotard, *The Postmodern Condition*, pp. 32–33.

15. PRUSSIAN MIND-MELD: Jürgen Habermas's notion of "consensus" may be seen as the updated, late-modern version.

16. CIRCUMSTANCES: Deleuze, *Pourparlers*, pp. 39–40.

17. OUTSIDE THOUGHT: See Foucault's essay on Blanchot, often quoted by Deleuze: "The Thought from Outside."

18. The terms SMOOTH SPACE and STRIATED SPACE were in fact coined by Pierre Boulez: see *A Thousand Plateaus*, pp. 477–78 [596–97].

19. LISTEN TO A RECORD: *Dialogues*, p. 3 [*10*].

20. OPEN SYSTEM: Deleuze, *Pourparlers*, p. 48.

21. PLATEAU: See *A Thousand Plateaus*, p. 158 [*196*].

22. On STYLE in literature, see Deleuze, *Proust and Signs*, pp. 142–50 [*193–203*].

23. TOOL BOX: Deleuze and Foucault, "Intellectuals and Power," p. 208 [*5*].

24. On the creation of the world, see *Habit*, note 44, below. Also: Deleuze's image of philosophy as approaching an author from behind to produce a MONSTROUS OFFSPRING is *antiphallic* in spite of its manifest content: it expresses a desire, on the part of a physiological male, to wrest writing away from the State-form of phallogocentric identity. The aim is not to impose one's Self on the "object" of one's attention (the sadism of patriarchal judgment). Nor is it to re-produce an author's identity as one's own, in the expectation that newcomers will re-reproduce it as their own (the boring Oedipal normality of discipleship as sequential adoptive parentage: becoming the mentor's son in order to have sons by him; the male mothering of metaphysical brotherhood). The approach is antigenerational and anti–male bonding. The idea is to avoid the officially approved face-to-face of the intellectual missionary position in favor of an encounter between primary and secondary author in which both disappear as identified individuals—and as an academic species. The goal is to abolish One and Two, One and the Other—the form of identity itself—in a process of mutual mutation. It is a refusal to exercise the patriarchal prerogative of imposing self-likeness, an attempt, by bodies sexed masculine, to cut the *pro* off male *creation*, to destroy the centrality of the phallus. The phallus can no longer fulfill its "natural" function of guarantor of male identity if, when men meet, they beget monstrosity. Deleuze's image expresses a desire to *pervert* the phallic function, in the literal sense of "turning away from" (away from the "royal road" of the unconscious, as Freud dubbed the Oedipal complex). It expresses a desire to bypass that crossroads (the alternative between the castration of sadistic revolt and conformist reproduction), and veer off on less traveled paths—including but emphatically not limited to regions for which a patriarchal map is normally drawn. The "anti-Oedipus" is an "unnatural" desire to reclaim pleasure for invention, polymorphously.

FORCE

1. EXISTING FORCE: Deleuze, *Nietzsche and Philosophy*, p. 3 [*3*].

2. WOOD: This example is mentioned in passing by Deleuze in *Proust and Signs*, p. 4 [*10*], and again in *A Thousand Plateaus*, p. 409 [*509*].

3. On QUALITIES and SIGNS, see Deleuze, *Différence et répétition*, p. 314, and *A Thousand Plateaus*, p. 317 [*390*].

4. AS MANY MEANINGS AS FORCES: *Nietzsche and Philosophy*, p. 4 [*5*] (translation modified).

5. AFFINITY WITH A FORCE: *Nietzsche and Philosophy*, p. 4 [*5*] (translation modified).

6. VALUE IS THE HIERARCHY OF FORCES: Ibid., p. 8 [*9*] (translation modified).

7. On RECIPROCAL PRESUPPOSITION, see *A Thousand Plateaus*, pp. 44–45, 145–46 [*59–60, 181–82*], and Deleuze, *Foucault* (1986), pp. 40–41, 68, 74–75, 88–89 (for comments on the English translation of this work, see note 69 below).

8. HAND-TO-HAND COMBAT OF ENERGIES is a phrase from Proust ("un corps-à-corps d'énergies"). See *A Thousand Plateaus*, pp. 321 (and note 19), 338–39 [*59–60, 181–82*]. On the "battle" between form and content, see also Deleuze, *Foucault*, p. 119.

9. The terms FORM OF CONTENT and FORM OF EXPRESSION derive from the work of linguist Louis Hjelmslev. For Deleuze and Guattari's development of the concepts of form, content, expression, form of content, and form of expression (as well as the related distinction between matter and substance discussed below), see *A Thousand Plateaus*, pp. 40–41, 43–45, 66–67, 89, 142–43 [*55, 58–60, 86, 113, 178*] and *Foucault* (1986), pp. 39–42.

10. On REAL versus LOGICAL ("modal") DISTINCTION, see *A Thousand Plateaus*, pp. 44, 57, 58, 64, 72 [*59, 75, 76, 83, 92*].

11. On the DIAGRAM, see *A Thousand Plateaus*, pp. 141–43, 146, 537n16 [*176–79, 183, 265n16*] and *Foucault* (1986), pp. 42–44, 79–80, 90–91, 95. In the vocabulary of *The Logic of Sense* and *Foucault* (used sporadically in *Différence et répétition* and in all other works), the abstract points of the diagram are called SINGULARITIES. The term "diagram" is borrowed from C. S. Peirce; see Guattari, *Les années d'hiver. 1980–1985*, pp. 290–91.

12. Deleuze and Guattari do not themselves use the term TRANSLATION in this general sense. In their vocabulary, translation is a specific mode of dynamic transfer among others ("induction," "transduction," "transcoding"). See *A Thousand Plateaus*, pp. 60, 62 [*78, 81*]. For a Deleuzian usage of the concept of translation similar to the one developed here, see José Gil, *Métamorphoses du corps*, pp. 122–26. For thought reproducing the dynamism of the apprehended object (MIMICKING it), see *Logic of Sense*, pp. 147, 161, 282–87 [*173, 188, 327–32*]. On REDUNDANCY, see *A Thousand Plateaus*, pp. 79, 84 [*100, 106*], and *Logic of Sense*, pp. 31–33, 125–26, 146–47 [*44–47, 151, 172–73*] (meaning as double; the word translated as "division" on page 31 of the English is "*dédoublement*"). "It is not enough to say that consciousness is consciousness of something; it is the DOUBLE of something, and everything is consciousness because it has a double, however far away and estranged from it" (*Différence et répétition*, p. 284).

13. NO CONFORMITY, COMMON FORM, OR CORRESPONDENCE: *Foucault* (1986), pp. 41, 71.

14. THE BEING OF A NONRELATION: Ibid., pp. 69–72, 86, 88, 119.

15. DOUBLE DYNAMISM: "It is accurate to speak of a double series of events unfolding on two planes, echoing each other without resemblance, one series real . . . the other ideal" (*Différence et répétition*, p. 244).

16. On MIND-BODY PARALLELISM, see *Spinoza: Practical Philosophy*, pp. 18, 86–91 [*28, 92–98*].

17. On the relation between words and states of things as a NONRELATION, see *Foucault* (1986), pp. 69–72, 86, 88, 119. On a similar nonrelation in perception between things and images, see Deleuze, *Bergsonism*, pp. 24, 25, 53, 107, 109–11 ("interval") [*14, 16, 112, 114–17* ("*écart*")]; in behavior between action and reaction, *Cinema I*, pp. 61–66 ("interval") [*90–97* ("*intervalle*")]; in human life between conscious thought and the real becoming at its basis (thought in the widest sense, as the abstract machine), *Logic of Sense*, pp. 321–33 ("crack") [*373–86* ("*fêlure*")], and *A Thousand Plateaus*, pp. 198–200 ("crack") [*242–45* ("*fêlure*")]. On the necessity for philosophical thought to "burst things asunder" ("*fendre les choses*") in order to see beyond their apparent unity and conformity to words and grasp their conditions of existence, *Foucault* (1986), pp. 59–60. This fissuring in all its forms is the SCHIZ of "schizoanalysis" (the name Deleuze and Guattari give the form of philosophy advanced in

Capitalism and Schizophrenia). It is instructive to compare the various uses of the word "schiz" in *Anti-Oedipus*: see, for example, pp. 39–40, 131, 132, 230–31, 241, 244, 287, 315, 351, 378 [*47, 55, 158, 273–74, 286, 290, 341, 376, 410, 453*]. The "*point aléatoire*" discussed at length throughout *Logic of Sense* is another word for the cutting edge of fracturing. To the nonrelations listed above, Derrida would add another: between speech and writing.

18. *The Logic of Sense* is an extended meditation on the SEPARATION-CONNECTION of "being" (states of things), thought, and language. In it, Deleuze repeatedly expresses the autonomy of these "parallelisms" and their simultaneous imbrication. What was said previously of the relation between content and expression could be said of things, thought, and language (and will be said in what follows for other formations): they are really distinct but in reciprocal presupposition. As the following discussion will illustrate, they are overlapping moments of becoming that can be placed in continuity or disjunction, depending on the point of view. Meaning is the "articulation of their difference" (*Logic of Sense*, p. 24 [*37*]). The articulated differentiations constitutive of meaning can be multiplied indefinitely. "Language" is divisible into the autonomous planes of speech and writing, and each of these is divisible in turn into distinct modes of discourse. Conversely, the planes can be telescoped, for example by bringing words into collision with things and letting thought fall. In the present discussion, the important point is not the particular way in which any of these planes is defined, but rather the principle of their structuring as variations on one another and the pragmatic possibility of tailoring the analysis of their structuring to a concrete task at hand.

19. On the ABSTRACT MACHINE, see *A Thousand Plateaus*, pp. 70–71, 141–42, 223–24, 510–12 [*90–91, 175–78, 272–73, 636–38*] and passim, and *Foucault* (1986), p. 44.

20. On anti-Platonic ESSENCE, see *Proust and Signs*, passim; *Différence et répétition*, p. 239; *Logic of Sense*, pp. 34–35, 214 [*48, 250*]; and *Bergsonism*, pp. 32–33, 34 [*23–24, 27*]. (In numerous passages in many of his works, Deleuze rejects the term "essence" because of its Platonic overtones, preferring such terms as "event," "problem," "Aion," or "Idea.") On the EVENT, see *Logic of Sense*, pp. 148–53 [*174–79*] and passim. In *A Thousand Plateaus*, the event is called an "incorporeal transformation" (see note 40, below).

21. DIAGRAMS: See *A Thousand Plateaus*, pp. 135, 146, 183, 218, 544, 545 [*169–70, 182, 225–26, 266, 359, 362*].

22. On the ATTRIBUTE and the EXPRESSED as the two faces of meaning, see *Logic of Sense*, pp. 20–21, 166, 182 [*32–33, 195–96, 213*], and *A Thousand Plateaus*, pp. 86–87 [*110*].

23. LANGUAGE, FORCE, POWER: "Language sets limits (for example, the point at which *too much* is reached), but it also goes beyond limits, restoring them to the infinite equivalence of an unlimited becoming": *Logic of Sense*, p. 2 [*11*] (translation modified).

24. TO CUT, TO DIE: *Logic of Sense*, pp. 5, 63, 151–54 [*14, 80, 177–80*].

25. On the FUTURE-PAST, see *Logic of Sense*, pp. 5, 77, 150 [*14, 95, 176*].

26. On the "sterility" of meaning, see *Logic of Sense*, pp. 31–32, 95 [*44–45, 116*] (in the present work "sterile" will usually be replaced by EVAPORATIVE to avoid any phallic connotations).

27. ONE UNIFIED FIELD: Chapter 3 of *A Thousand Plateaus*, "The Geology of Morals," charts the vicissitudes of content and expression on the physical, geological, biological and cultural "strata." On MONISM, see *Bergsonism*, pp. 92–93 [*94–95*], and passim; *Spinoza: Practical Philosophy*, pp. 92–93 [*120–21*] ("Nature"); *Logic of Sense*, pp. 103 ("the potential energy of the pure event"), 177–80 ("univocity") [*125, 208–211*]; and *A Thousand Plateaus*, pp. 20–21, 153 ("matter equals energy"), 254, 266, and passim (the "plane of consistency" or "plane of immanence") [*31, 190–91, 311, 326*].

28. On EFFECT, see *Logic of Sense*, pp. 4–11 [*13–21*] and passim.

29. José Gil, who bases his project of an "anthropology of force" on Deleuze and Guattari's Nietzschean-derived theories of meaning, also emphasizes that the emergence of the sign or diagram corresponds to a MOMENTARY SUSPENSION OF BECOMING: "There is an entropy proper to sign systems that diminishes their capacity to signify. When two opposed forces enter into relation, the force that takes the upper hand in the combat leaves a remainder. This remainder, which measures the relation between the forces, or the gap between them, is also a measure of the power one force has over the other. However, the remainder is no longer a force signifying itself for another force, for the action of the operator [Gil's term for the abstract machine] has ceased; part of the remainder may form a precipitate constituting a sign, in residual form.

Thus the sign emerges from the absence of the operator, as a distant residue of force; it is at once the memory of the operator's activity and the result of its cessation. As long as the forces are at work, no sign emerges; there is but the pure activity of the operators, producing things (which of course become signs for other forces). We see that the meaning of the sign has to do with a differential gap resulting from the relation between forces" (*Métamorphoses du corps*, p. 20). The moment of suspension corresponds to the interruption of desire constitutive of the BODY WITHOUT ORGANS (defined in *Habit*, "Burp") as described in *Anti-Oedipus* (see esp. pp. 1–16, 36–37 [*1–22, 43–45*]).

30. FRACTALS: For an illustration of the basic procedure behind the Koch curve, see *A Thousand Plateaus*, p. 487 [*608*]; for a full illustration of the snowflake effect, see Gleick, *Chaos: Making a New Science*, p. 99; on a randomized Koch curve forming a coastline with islands, see Mandelbrot, *Fractals: Form, Chance, and Dimension*, p. 85; on the "random walk" as a "space-filling" (or "plane-filling") fractal, see Mandelbrot, *Fractals*, p. 92; also on "space-filling" fractals, see Orbach, "Dynamics of Fractal Networks," pp. 814–19 ("The structure ceases to be fractal at very [large] scales, where it appears homogeneous or continuous," p. 814); on the solidity of nature concealing fractal porosity, see Gleick, *Chaos*, pp. 105–106, and Stewart, *Does God Play Dice?*, p. 229 (the universe as a "multi-fractal"); on fractal geometry and computer graphics, see Jeffrey, "Mimicking Mountains," pp. 337–344; on MEANING AS OPTICAL EFFECT, see *Logic of Sense*, pp. 7, 70 [*17, 88*], and *Différence et répétition*, p. 119. The concept of the fractal, explicitly mentioned only once in passing in *A Thousand Plateaus*, has become increasingly important in Guattari's writing: a prime example is "Cracks in the Street," trans. Anne Gibault and John Johnston, a paper on Balthus delivered at the Modern Language Association convention in New York, December 28, 1986 (as yet unpublished). [Since this writing, "Cracks in the Street" has appeared in French: Guattari, *Cartographies schizoanalytiques* (Paris: Galilée, 1989), pp. 319–31. The same book develops the philosophy of the fracture at great length, and in directions strikingly similar to those of the present exposition. The fracture at the basis of meaning is explicitly related the concept of the fractal (for example, pp. 142, 173, 218–24), which is in turn connected to the concept of the synapse (pp. 89–92, 199–205). Both are discussed as processes of "possibilization."]

31. Dionysus was dismembered after his first birth. On the LAUGHTER of Dionysus-Zarathustra, see *Nietzsche and Philosophy*, pp. 193–94 [*222*]; and the preceding pages on JOY as the affirmation (willing) of the eternal return (repetition-translation) of difference (multiplicity and fissure). For more on the ETERNAL RETURN, see *Différence et répétition*, pp. 59–60, 311–14, 379–85; on the AFFIRMATION of the eternal return as Mallarmé's dice-throw, see *Nietzsche and Philosophy*, pp. 25–27, 197 [*29–31, 225*], and *Logic of Sense*, pp. 58–65 [*74–82*] ("Of the Ideal Game"); on the "cosmos" (or CHAOSMOS) as the unity of nature and culture, see *A Thousand Plateaus*, p. 337 [*416*] and the references for "monism" in note 27 above; on the uncaused cause ("IMMANENT CAUSE"), see *Spinoza*, pp. 53–54 [*78–79*], and *Foucault* (1986), p. 44. On the FOUNDATIONLESSNESS of the foundation of be(com)ing, see *Différence et répétition*, pp. 123, 151, 164, 296, 352–53.

32. DIFFERENT SEMIOTIC ORGANIZATIONS: Deleuze, *Proust and Signs*, pp. 5–12, 84–88 [*12–20, 103–109*], and the glossary to *Cinema I*, pp. 217–18 [*291–93*]; see also *A Thousand Plateaus*, "On Several Regimes of Signs," pp. 111–48 [*140–84*].

33. DELEUZE VERSUS GUATTARI: Guattari, for example, is fascinated with phenomena of subjective redundancy (resonance, refrain, black hole), whereas Deleuze prefers to emphasize "lines of escape" from subjectivity. Deleuze comments on this temperamental complementarity in *Dialogues*, pp. 17–18 [*24*]. As can be seen by the references above, many of the properly philosophical concepts were originated by Deleuze. On the other hand, many key semiotic concepts used in *A Thousand Plateaus* are of Guattari's devising, and were first worked out in *La Révolution moléculaire* (1977), pp. 297–376 (some of these essays are translated in "Towards a New Vocabulary," *Molecular Revolution*, pp. 111–72), and in *L'Inconscient machinique*, esp. ch. 3, pp. 43–73. Guattari also contributed some of the most effectively political concepts of *Capitalism and Schizophrenia*: territorialization-deterritorialization, transversality, group subjectivity, desiring-machine, war machine, molar-molecular, micropolitics (some are discussed below).

34. HIGH SCHOOL: Deleuze and Guattari, following Foucault, use the example of the prison; see *A Thousand Plateaus*, pp. 66–67 [*86*], and *Foucault* (1986), pp. 31–35.

35. On SUBSTANCE versus MATTER, see *L'Inconscient machinique*, p. 41, *A Thousand Plateaus*, pp. 43, 340 [*58, 419*], and *Foucault* (1986), pp. 41–42. Deleuze and Guattari depart from Spinoza's views on substance on one crucial point: for Spinoza, there is only one substance, and only two ATTRIBUTES of that substance are knowable to human beings (thought and extension). Deleuze and Guattari redefine attribute under the influence of the Stoics. For Deleuze and Guattari, each attribute coincides with a substance, and the number of both substances and knowable attributes is infinite. Substances can be organized into general types according to their mode of composition, the prime examples again being thought and extension. Compare *Spinoza: Practical Philosophy*, pp. 51–52, 108–109 [*72–74, 147–48*] with *A Thousand Plateaus*, pp. 86, 153, 157 [*110, 190, 195*]. Deleuze develops his reading of Spinoza at great length in *Expressionism in Philosophy: Spinoza*.

36. A rule-of-thumb overview of the semiotic framework: CONTENT is what is overpowered, EXPRESSION what overpowers. Both content and expression are substance–form complexes. Content considered outside its encounter with expression, therefore as having neither form nor substance, is MATTER OF CONTENT (the overpowered thing as a bundle of potential affects, in other words, abilities to affect or be affected). Expression considered outside its encounter with content, as having therefore neither substance nor form, is MATTER OF EXPRESSION (the overpowering thing as a bundle of potential functions). The FORM OF CONTENT, or content abstracted from its substance but in the context of its encounter with expression, is an order of qualities (a sequence of actualization of selected affects), or, at one remove from the substance of content, a literal form of containment (such as a school or prison) within which affects are actualized. The FORM OF EXPRESSION is an order of functions (a sequence of actualization of selected functions). A SUBSTANCE OF CONTENT is an overpowered thing as a qualified object (that is, as exhibiting its assigned qualities). A SUBSTANCE OF EXPRESSION is what embodies an overpowering function. The interface between content and expression is meaning or interpretation as a process of becoming (essence), expressible as a dynamic DIAGRAM or infinitive. What places the two in relation is the ABSTRACT MACHINE.

37. On the MACHINIC ASSEMBLAGE and the COLLECTIVE ASSEMBLAGE OF ENUNCIATION, see *A Thousand Plateaus*, p. 88 [*112*]; on the DOUBLE ARTICULATION (a term borrowed from the linguist André Martinet), see ibid., pp. 40–41, 44, 57 [*54–55, 58–59, 75*].

38. I DO: See Thomas Pynchon, *Vineland*, p. 97.

39. On COMPONENTS OF PASSAGE, see *A Thousand Plateaus*, pp. 312, 325 [*384, 399*] (the context is animal behavior: the component of passage, like content and expression, is a general semiotic concept applicable to nonlinguistic systems). I use CONNECTOR in a different sense than Deleuze and Guattari in *Kafka*, pp. 63–71 [*115–30*]. A "connector" in *Kafka* is the same as a "component of passage" in *A Thousand Plateaus*.

40. On the event as INCORPOREAL TRANSFORMATION, see *A Thousand Plateaus*, pp. 80–83, 85–88, 107–109 [*102–106, 109–112, 136–38*].

41. On the STATEMENT (*énoncé*) see *A Thousand Plateaus*, pp. 140, 147 [*174, 184*], and *Foucault* (1986), passim, esp. pp. 16, 27, 85.

42. The PERFORMATIVE: See J. L. Austin, *How To Do Things with Words*, pp. 133, 147. Austin comes close, in one footnote, to asserting a theory of incorporeal transformation the consequences of which, if fully elaborated, would have led him far from the analytical philosophy of his origins: "the sense in which saying something produces effects on other persons, or *causes* things, is a fundamentally different sense of cause from that used in physical causation by pressure, etc. . . . It is probably the original sense of 'cause'" (p. 113n). On the same page, he states that the action of this nonphysical causality is marked by a "break in the chain" of statements: in other words, its line of causality is discontinuous. He omits that the line of causality of sayings is discontinuous because it is punctuated by doings. Change brought about through the nonphysical causality is attributed to things, even though it is enacted in words. It intervenes in the line of physical causality—which is therefore also discontinuous. The chain of body-to-body relations is broken by a break in statement-to-statement causality. One can easy read this in Deleuze–Guattarian terms as the mutual intervention (reciprocal presupposition) of asymptotic lines of causality: lines that follow different trajectories (body-to-body versus statement-to-statement) and even belong to different orders of reality (matter and ideality), but nevertheless meet at a given point—that point being the "break" (fractal abyss) marking the operation of the

abstract machine. Deleuze develops the notion of DOUBLE CAUSALITY at great length in *Logic of Sense* (see esp. pp. 23–27, 94–99 [*36–40, 115–21*]; for Deleuze and Guattari on Austin, the performative and the illocutionary, see *A Thousand Plateaus*, pp. 77–78 [*98–99*].

43. On IMPLICIT PRESUPPOSITIONS, see *A Thousand Plateaus*, p. 77 [*98*], and Oswald Ducrot, *Dire et ne pas dire*, passim (the example developed here is on pp. 22–24).

44. IDEOLOGY: "To presuppose a certain content is to make the acceptance of that content a precondition for further dialogue.... This is not a causal transformation tied to the fact that any enunciation influences the beliefs, desires, and interests of the listener. On the contrary, it is a juridical or institutional transformation" (Ducrot, *Dire et ne pas dire*, p. 91).

45. IDEOLOGY: Deleuze and Guattari reject ideological conceptions of the link between power and language. They cite Bakhtin as saying that language is the form of ideology, but that the form of ideology is not itself ideological (*A Thousand Plateaus*, p. 525n21 [*113n17*]). This is a way of saying that language is the form of expression of power relations in society, but that as a form of expression it is nothing outside of the "forms of content" (vertical and horizontal) with which it is in reciprocal presupposition. Forms of content and forms of expression have substance, and they and their substances arise in a cocausal "combat of energies." Semiotic formations are awash in extralinguistic, pre-ideational—and therefore pre-ideological—fields of force. Power can be conceived as language-driven but not language-based. Its functioning cannot fully be explained by recourse to a concept of ideology as formative agent of speech and belief. Ideologies do exist, but their rules of formation are not coextensive with those of language or power: they are end results of processes at work on other levels, structures of meaning in the sense of evaporative end effect. An ideological statement is more a precipitate than a precipitator. What distinguishes an ideological meaning from any other evaporative effect is only the regularity with which a society produces it. That regularity is the work of a double-sided abstract machine—of power *and* of linguistic expression (simultaneously a "machinic assemblage" and a "collective assemblage of enunciation"). For more detail on regularizing processes of semiotic formation, see *Habit*, passim, on the three syntheses.

The way in which a statement envelops a literal meaning and a logical presupposition should not be confused with what Roland Barthes calls CONNOTATION and defines as the form of ideology. Connotation is the embedding of an implicit Expression/Content relation in an explicit or denotative one. If the formula for denotation, or literal referential meaning, is E/C, then connotation would be E(E/C)/C (*S/Z*, pp. 6–11). For example, a photograph of a flag: the denotative relation would be photo/cloth, and the connotative, photo(flag/patriotism)/cloth. "Patriotism" would be an implicitly conveyed content. Despite his use of Hjelmslev's vocabulary, Barthes's orientation is entirely different from Deleuze and Guattari's. His connotative content is a "signified": the process of connotation is purely linguistic, and produces its effect in the first and last instance on the level of ideas. In other words, Barthes's form of ideology *is* ideological. His formulas leave no room for the nondiscursive dimension Deleuze and Guattari insist on (again, in common with Bakhtin, whose concept of meaning as an evaluative "theme" that has a unique and unreproducible directional effect in a concrete situation can be compared to the order-word's "unity-in-movement" as described above; see V. N. Volosinov [Bakhtin], *Marxism and the Philosophy of Language*, pp. 94–105). What falls out of Barthes's equation is precisely the immediately transformational, extralinguistic *act* enveloped in the statement. Emile Benveniste makes an analogous move in relation to Austin when he argues that performative utterances are purely self-referential and that the act they perform is nothing other than the constitution of the speaking subject in discourse (see "Subjectivity in Language," in *Problems in General Linguistics*, pp. 223–31; for Ducrot's critique of Benveniste, see *Dire et ne pas dire*, pp. 70–75). Many semiotics-influenced theories of ideology combine Barthes's internalization of power in linguistic structure and Benveniste's linguistification of subjectivity (typically with varying doses of Althusser and Lacan thrown in, depending on whether the focus is the "social" or the "individual"; a useful example is Kaja Silverman, *The Subject of Semiotics*). In so doing, they doubly exclude what they set out to explain: relations of force between bodies. Because they place the functioning of power primarily on a dematerialized linguistic or subjective plane they end up doing little more than idealizing the formations of power they set out to critique.

46. On the ORDER-WORD, see *A Thousand Plateaus*, 75–89, 106–110 [*95–113, 135–39*].

47. Austin speaks at length of the conventional or RITUAL aspects of PERFORMATIVES, but he avoids the obvious political conclusions by never linking them to mechanisms of social control: see, for example, *How To Do Things with Words*, pp. 18–19. Foucault is less restrained. On education (and by extension all institutionalized speech—and all speech to the extent that it is institutional [Ducrot, note 42 above]) as ritual, see *L'Ordre du discours*, pp. 46–47.

48. On what is taught in the schools as conveying ORDER-WORDS, see *A Thousand Plateaus*, p. 75 [*95*].

49. On the ANONYMOUS MURMUR (a phrase of Foucault's), see Deleuze, *Foucault* (1986), pp. 26, 62.

50. On THE "I" as the marker of a social function, see Michel Foucault, *The Archaeology of Knowledge*, p. 95.

51. On FREE INDIRECT DISCOURSE (or "quasi-indirect discourse"), see *A Thou-sand Plateaus*, pp. 80, 84, 106 [*101, 107–108, 134*]. The concept is borrowed from Volosinov (Bakhtin), *Marxism and the Philosophy of Language*, pp. 141–59.

52. The ELEMENTARY UNIT OF LANGUAGE: *A Thousand Plateaus*, p. 76 [*95*].

53. The concept of the VIRTUAL comes most directly from Bergson, and is assimilated by Deleuze to Spinoza's *potentia*, or "power." See *Bergsonism*, esp. pp. 42–43, 55–62, 100–101 [*36–37, 50–57, 103–105*]; *Cinema II*, pp. 68–83 [*92–111*]; and *Spinoza: Practical Philosophy*, pp. 97–104 [*134–43*]; see also *Différence et répétition*, pp. 266–67, 269, 274, 357–58, and *Proust and Signs*, pp. 57–60 [*73–74*]. On the virtual in relation to Leibniz (the inherence of all monads in each), see *Logic of Sense*, pp. 110–111 [*134–35*], *Différence et répétition*, p. 23n, and *Le Pli*, pp. 31, 69, 108–109, 140–41.

54. For Nietzsche on PERSPECTIVE as an interaction of real selective forces, see *The Will to Power*, secs. 481, 490, 493–507, 518, 556, 568–69, 636 (pp. 257, 270–71, 272–76, 281, 301, 306–307, 339–40). An objective perspective is also called an OBJECTIVE ILLUSION or "objective dissimulation": see *Anti-Oedipus*, p. 373 [*448*], and Deleuze, *Cinema II*, p. 69 [*94*].

55. In *Anti-Oedipus*, Deleuze and Guattari rename the "part-objects" of psychoanalysis PARTIAL OBJECTS. A partial object is a libidinally in-

vested objective perspective of one body on another (or of one part of a body on another part, which may be on that same body or a different one). "Libidinally invested" means prone to be repeated. A partial object is the site of what I called a "REPETITION-IMPULSION." It is a private order-word, the juncture at which power and language meet on and for an individual body. The prelinguistic signs which give it expression are in a language that has only one speaker (more a jargon than a language). The repetition-impulsion is not to be confused with Freud's "repetition-compulsion," which is the tendency of a trauma-tized body to reduce its libidinal events as much as possible to one of their three simultaneous moments or dimensions (the past). For more on part-objects, see *Habit*, "Burp." On jargon and prelinguistic or "ASIGNIFYING" SIGNS of desire, see *Anti-Oedipus*, pp. 38, 289 [*46, 343*].

56. The DEPTHS OF MATTER: Deleuze and Guattari (following both Spinoza and Leibniz) do indeed assert that PERCEPTION AND THOUGHT HAVE SUBSTANCE. (Today, one might invoke the involutions of brain matter, or better, the quantum waves crossing the brain's synaptic fissures.) The assertion of substance allows Deleuze and Guattari to maintain that the proposition that thought-perception is always real and of the outside applies even to fantasy: if a fantasy has substance, it is a body, and its apprehension by another thought-body is as real as the perception of an object, or body with extension (thought and perception have only "intension," or virtual reality; they are real but not objective). See the definition of "mode" in *Spinoza: Practical Philoso-phy*, pp. 91–92 [*118–120*]: "effects [thoughts or perceptions] are indeed things, in other words real beings with an essence and existence of their own." On thought and extension as different substances, ibid., p. 52 [*73*]; on perception as having the same substance as thought, ibid., p. 104 [*142*]; on a thought as a body, *A Thousand Plateaus*, p. 86 [*110*]; on thought as OUTSIDE, *Foucault* (1986), pp. 51, 92–93, 95, 120, 126–27, and Foucault, "The Thought from Outside," *Foucault/Blanchot*; on the outside of thought as atmospheric, *Foucault* (1986), p. 129. Deleuze's essay "Klossowski or Bodies-Language" (*Logic of Sense*, pp. 280–301 [*325–50*]) covers many of these issues: see esp. pp. 327–32 on thought carrying a thing outside itself by reproducing its essential dynamism in its own substance. In this essay Deleuze calls the object's constitu-tional openness to grasping and manipulation by thought FLECTION (the process of its reproduction in thought is, of course, REFLECTION).

57. On the UNTIMELY, see *A Thousand Plateaus*, p. 296 [*363*]. On SUBSISTENCE (also called "insistence"), see *Différence et répétition*, pp. 111, 202, and *Logic of Sense*, pp. 5, 110, 180 [*13, 134, 211*] (on page 5 of the English, "*insister*" is translated as "inhere").

58. On COMPLICATION versus IMPLICATION, see *Différence et répétition*, pp. 161–62, 359, and *Logic of Sense*, p. 297 [*345*].

59. On the ORDER-WORD AS DEATH SENTENCE, see *A Thousand Plateaus*, pp. 107–108 [*135–36*]. On DEATH AS COEXTENSIVE WITH LIFE, see *Foucault* (1986), pp. 102, 115, 129; *Anti-Oedipus*, pp. 330–31 [*394–96*]; and *Différence et répétition*, pp. 148–49, 152.

60. It is possible for every "I do" to be unique, yet actualize "roughly" the same interrelation of relations, because "I do," if properly understood, expresses the realm of possibility of marriage. Every variation falling between the two relative thresholds of a meaning can be subsumed in a single diagram or statement. Such a diagram is not exact, since it does not explicitly account for each potential actualization. But, if carefully used, neither is it inexact, because it does not overstep the limits beyond which an essentially different event transpires. It is calculated to be *anexact*, to precisely span a range of virtuality. The concept of anexactitude allows one's analysis to function at a certain level of generality without losing sight of the multiplicity immanent to each unique speech act. Every essence is in any case anexact by nature because the actualizations it envelops are in principle infinite. The infinitive ("to marry") is the most economical way of expressing an essence because it connotes rigor but by its very name conveys limitlessness. A fuller expression would develop the series of actualizations implicit in the infinitive into a continuum of variation (for example, in the form of an ordered array of literal diagrams, or more adequately, as an equation or set of English instructions for the generation of any number of gradated diagrams). On ANEXACTITUDE and "VAGUE" ESSENCE (a term coined by Husserl), see *Logic of Sense*, pp. 114–15 [*139–40*], and (in relation to the Kantian "schema"), *A Thousand Plateaus*, 367, 407–408 [*454–55, 507–508*]. For more on Kant's schema, see Deleuze, *Kant's Critical Philosophy*, p. 18 [*28–29*].

61. QUANTUM LEAP: Werner Heisenberg, one of the inventors of quantum mechanics, invoked a concept of *potentia* to describe the virtual reality of the quantum level of matter as it emerges from energy:

"it is as though the program of Galileo and Locke, which involved discarding secondary qualities (color, taste, etc.) in favor of primary qualities (the quantities of classical mechanics), had been carried a stage further and these primary qualities had themselves become secondary to the property of *potentia* in which they all lay latent" (quoted in J. C. Polkinghorne, *The Quantum World*, p. 81).

62. On SUPERLINEARITY, see *A Thousand Plateaus*, pp. 85, 91, 95 [*108, 115, 121*]. The superlinearity of the abstract machine is also expressed in the phrases "ABSTRACT LINE" and "BROKEN LINE OF BECOMING." The image these phrases invoke is of a set of mutually exclusive linear trajectories through the world coexisting in a state of potential, as if crumpled into a supercharged bundle bristling with energy. When one of those trajectories finds a body to express it, it breaks from the bundle, striking out into the world of actuality. The path the body follows can be represented graphically as an arrow passing between two adjacent points (*A Thousand Plateaus*, p. 294n83). The points represent other actual bodies around which the body in becoming navigates, seen from the point of view of their own pathmaking capacity. The bodily coordinates in the actual world through which the body-in-becoming moves envelop other potential trajectories still crumpled in the ball of virtuality. The line of becoming is "abstract" because its linear directionality can only be conceived or diagrammed in relation to other lines remaining in a state of envelopment (in other words, as an angle on the virtual). It is "broken" because the path taken is a breakaway of potential: a zigzag from the virtual into the actual, from one actual state of a body toward another, and away from the actual and virtual states of certain other bodies. Those bodies, if not passed by, might overpower the body-in-becoming, reenveloping its trajectory—but at *their* coordinates. Every becoming runs the risk of all or part of its transformational potential being annexed to a foreign body through a process of forcible repotentialization (capture). On the abstract line and the broken line, see *A Thousand Plateaus*, pp. 293–94, 294n83, 298, 497–99 [*359–60, 359n67, 365–66, 621–24*], and *Différence et répétition*, pp. 44, 352–54.

63. On the ONE, see *Différence et répétition*, pp. 149, 355, 382; *Logic of Sense*, p. 152 [*178*] ("*on*" is translated in this passage as "they"); *A Thousand Plateaus*, p. 265 [*324*]; and *Foucault* (1986), pp. 17, 26, 62, 122.

64. INFORMATION: *A Thousand Plateaus*, p. 76 [*96*].

65. For the critique of linguistic CONSTANTS, see *A Thousand Plateaus*, pp. 92–100, 103–105 [*116–27, 130–33*]; for the critique of the notion of a STANDARD LANGUAGE, ibid., pp. 100–103 [*127–31*]; on CONTINUOUS VARIATION, ibid. and 108–109, 340, 369 [*137–38, 419, 458*].

66. LINGUISTICS AS INSUFFICIENTLY ABSTRACT: ibid., pp. 90–91 [*115*].

67. Deleuze and Guattari's critique of the SIGNIFIER is developed throughout *Anti-Oedipus* (see esp., pp. 205–209, 241–44 [*243–48, 287–89*]), and in *A Thousand Plateaus*, pp. 65–68, 112–17 [*84–87, 141–47*].

68. NEITHER VISIBLE NOR HIDDEN: Foucault, *The Archaeology of Knowledge*, p. 109 (quoted in Deleuze, *Foucault* [1986], p. 25).

69. Such a rereading of FOUCAULT would, most notably: rehabilitate his much maligned *Archaeology of Knowledge* by helping to clarify its philosophical underpinnings; and correct the impression that Foucault is reducible to a philosopher of language by highlighting the neglected role in his work of "nondiscursive formations" (institutions understood as forms of content) and "visibilities" (what I have called "vertical content"; in this connection, see *Foucault* [1986], p. 117). The appearance of Deleuze's book on Foucault should go a long way toward motivating a reassessment. Unfortunately, the English translation (*Foucault*, trans. Seán Hand [Minneapolis: University of Minnesota Press, 1988]) sometimes obscures key philosophical distinctions Deleuze takes pain to make. Most seriously, it tends to submerge the all-important concept of virtual-actual by such word choices as "particular element" and "particular feature" for "*singularité*," "realization" for "*actualisation*," "evolution" for "*devenir*" (becoming), and by phraseology assimilating virtuality to possibility. Other slippages reintroduce a communicational model of language ("transmission" for "*émission*," "medium" for "*milieu*"), and both mechanism ("machine-like" for "*machinique*," which is conventionally translated as "machinic") and subjectivism (in one passage, "d'après un principe de parcimonie" becomes "begrudgingly" and "le possible" becomes "sense of possibility"). The translation should be used with caution. In the present work, I have chosen to give page references only to the French.

A quick indication of the philosophical overlap between Deleuze and Foucault, as seen from Foucault's side, can be had by referring to *L'Ordre du discours*, pp. 58–61, where Foucault describes his celebrated historical "breaks" as incorporeal "events" and speaks of "cesurae" in a vocabulary similar to the vocabulary of fractalization adopted here. See also Foucault's brilliant review of *Logic of Sense* and *Différence et répétition*: "Theatrum Philosophicum," *Language, Counter-Memory, Practice*, pp. 169–98. For the confluences with Deleuze and Guattari's political thinking, see "Intellectuals and Power" in the same volume. Deleuze and Guattari state their areas of disagreement with Foucault in *A Thousand Plateaus*, p. 531n39 [*175–76n*]: first, force is more fundamentally a phenomenon of DESIRE (which is not a personal phenomenon, but rather the contextual impulsion or unity-in-movement immanent to language) than of POWER (which as we have seen is a network of elaborated forces operating in a certain impulsive mode); and second, RESISTANCE ("escape," becoming other) is primary in relation to power rather than a derived response to it. Both of these points are developed below (although not directly in relation to Foucault).

HABIT

1. DOG VOMIT: Samuel Beckett, *Proust*, p. 8.

2. In "Coldness and Cruelty," Deleuze analyzes two highly elaborated kinds of COLDNESS (that of the masochist, and the sadist's "apathy") as strategies for chilling humanity in order to reconnect with intenser pleasures, in an escape from warmed-over Oedipal normality (Deleuze, "Coldness and Cruelty," in Deleuze and Sacher-Masoch, *Masochism*, esp. pp. 51–52, 117–19 [*50–52, 117–20*]). A third usage of cold (this time involving drugs) as the degree zero of subjective reconstruction is described in *A Thousand Plateaus*, pp. 152–54 [*188–91*]. Deleuze and Guattari's use of terms such as "intensity" and "sensation" should not be mistaken for a back-door return to subjectivity as understood by PHENOMENOLOGY: a field of untamed experience grounding conscious thought. Although intensity and sensation are on the level of the complicated causality from which subjectivity arises, they have nothing to do with the phenomenological concept of originary experience. This will become clearer later in this chapter, in the section comparing subjectivity to inhumanly warm water. For the critique of phenomenology, see *Différence et répétition*, p. 179, and *Foucault* (1986), pp. 116–19.

3. On the ABSTRACT MACHINE as synthesizer, see *A Thousand Plateaus*, pp. 110, 343 [*138–40, 423–24*].

4. On SEDIMENT, see *A Thousand Plateaus*, p. 41 [*55*].

5. On the concept of the INDIVIDUAL, see *Spinoza: Practical Philosophy*, pp. 76–78, 125–26 [*109–11, 169–70*]; *Logic of Sense*, 109–11 [*133–35*]; *Différence et répétition*, p. 317; *A Thousand Plateaus*, p. 254 [*310–11*]; and *Le Pli*, pp. 84–87. The exact terms employed in this discussion ("supple individual," "individual," "superindividual") are extrapolations which do not occur in Deleuze and Guattari's own work.

6. On MOLAR and MOLECULAR, see *Anti-Oedipus*, passim, esp. pp. 279–89, 342–43 [*332–42, 409–11*], and *A Thousand Plateaus*, passim, esp. pp. 208–31 [*253–85*].

7. On the PRODUCTION OF PRODUCTION, see Anti-Oedipus, pp. 6–7 [*12–13*]; the phrase "PRODUCTION OF RECORDING" occurs on p. 16 [*22*].

8. The PERSON as empty category is inscribed in the semantic ambivalence of the French *personne* ("person," "nobody"). Its etymology (from the Latin *persona*, "theater mask") expresses its nature as a generalizing overlay. On the person as "NOBODY," see *A Thousand Plateaus*, pp. 105–106 [*133–34*] and *Différence et répétition*, p. 253; for the genesis of the person as CATEGORY ("general concept," "extensive class") from the individual ("class with one member"), see *Logic of Sense*, pp. 114–18, 138–39, 177–78 [*139–43, 163–64, 208–209*].

9. The MASCULINE PRONOUN is retained here because the function of the judge is patriarchal regardless of the sex of the body fulfilling it. That Man is the model of "molar" (phallocentric) human identity is developed below.

10. The French *consommation* encompasses both "consumption" and "consummation."

11. Deleuze and Guattari recognize several forms of SURPLUS VALUE, including but not limited to surplus value in the Marxist sense. On the human level, the surplus value sensation always takes the form of a "prestige." In the case of economic surplus value, it is the miraculous powers attributed to capital as a fetish, as described by Marx. On Marx, FETISHISM, and surplus value, see *Anti-Oedipus*, pp. 10–12 [*16–18*]. On the varieties of surplus value, ibid., pp. 150, 163–64, 189, 226–28, 232–36 372 [*176, 192–93, 224, 269–70, 276–82, 446–47*], and *A*

Thousand Plateaus, pp. 10, 53, 314, 336, 451, 458, 491–92 [*17, 70, 386, 414, 563, 572, 613–14*].

12. On CODE and MILIEU, see *A Thousand Plateaus*, p. 313 [*384*].

13. On CODE and FORM, see *A Thousand Plateaus*, pp. 41, 338 [*55, 417*].

14. On FOLDING, see *Logic of Sense*, pp. 198, 355–56n3 [*230, 259n*]; *Différence et répétition*, pp. 89, 278–79; *Anti-Oedipus*, pp. 100–101, 177–78, 267–68, 358–59 [*120, 209–10, 319, 430*]; *A Thousand Plateaus*, pp. 41–42, 46–47, 255 [*55–56, 61–62, 312*]; *Foucault* (1986), pp. 101–30, 133–40; and Deleuze, *Le Pli*, passim. Deleuze distinguishes between several kinds of folding. For present purposes, these are reduced to "infolding" (folding resulting in a more or less bounded space).

15. On DOUBLE ARTICULATION in its simplest form, see *A Thousand Plateaus*, pp. 40–41 [*55*].

16. On OVERCODING, see *Anti-Oedipus*, pp. 200–13 [*236–52*], and *A Thousand Plateaus*, pp. 41–42, 135–36, 222–24 [*55–56, 168–70, 271–74*]. The concepts of territorialization/deterritorialization/reterritorialization, and decoding/recoding are developed throughout these two books and *Kafka*.

17. "Every order-word carries a death sentence—a JUDGMENT, as Kafka put it"; "The strata are the judgment of God" (*A Thousand Plateaus*, pp. 76, 41 [*96, 54*]).

18. On the syntheses of CELLULAR BIOLOGY, see François Jacob, *The Logic of Life*, pp. 247–98, and *A Thousand Plateaus*, pp. 42, 58–59, 62 [*57–58, 76–78, 81*].

19. "Ideal yet effective; absolute yet differentiated." *A Thousand Plateaus*, p. 218 [*266*]. Deleuze and Guattari often quote Proust's phrase, "REAL WITHOUT BEING ACTUAL, ideal without being abstract" (abstract in the sense of an empty concept): see *Proust*, p. 57 (translation modified) [*73–74*]; *A Thousand Plateaus*, p. 94 [*119*]; *Différence et répétition*, p. 269; and *Bergsonism*, p. 99 [*96*].

20. PERCEPTION ACTUALIZES: Ilya Prigogine and Isabelle Stengers, *Entre le temps et l'éternité*, p. 163. The process being described here is the "breakaway" of potential discussed in *Force*, note 62, above.

21. For a general treatment of the COLLAPSE OF THE WAVE-PACKET, see Polkinghorne, *The Quantum World*, pp. 34–38.

22. SCIENTISTS PERTURB: Prigogine and Stengers, *Entre le temps et l'éternité*, p. 130

23. The most condensed presentation of Deleuze and Guattari's theories of STRUCTURATION are to be found in *A Thousand Plateaus*, pp. 39–74, 501–16 [*53–94, 626–41*] ("The Geology of Morals" and "Conclusion: Concrete Rules and Abstract Machines"). They rarely use the word "structuration" due to the totalizing connotations it often has. They favor INTEGRATION (especially in earlier works by Deleuze such as *Différence et répétition*; the term should be understood in the mathematical sense, as a function, a curve joining discrete points), and STRATIFICATION (*A Thousand Plateaus*).

24. SEPARATION: "Each level of organization represents a threshold where objects, methods and conditions of observation suddenly change. Phenomena that are recognizable at one level disappear at the lower level; their interpretation is no longer valid at a higher level. . . . Construction in successive stages . . . built by a series of integrations . . . Living beings thus construct themselves in a series of successive 'parcels.' They are arranged according to a hierarchy of discontinuous units." CONNECTION: "From particle to man, there is a whole series of integrations, of levels, of discontinuities. But there is no breach either in the composition of the objects or in the reactions that take place in them; no change in 'essence'. . . . [T]here is no complete break [between cultural levels] and the levels of biology" (Jacob, *The Logic of Life*, pp. 266, 302, 305, 321).

25. On the WHOLE AS APART from the parts it unifies, see *Proust and Signs*, pp. 142–50 [*193–203*].

26. The concepts of SUBJECTED GROUP and SUBJECT-GROUP (see pp. 63ff.) were introduced by Guattari in his essay "La Transversalité" (1964), *Psychanalyse et transversalité*, p. 76 (*Molecular Revolution*, p. 14, where "*groupe assujetti*," or subjected group, is badly translated—as is the rest of the paragraph—as "dependent group"). See Deleuze's preface to that collection, "Trois problèmes de groupe" (translated as "Three Group Problems" by Mark Seem, *Semiotext(e)*, *Anti-Oedipus* 2.3 (1977), pp. 99–109); *Anti-Oedipus*, pp. 64, 280, 348–49, 375–78 [*75, 333, 417–18, 451–54*]; and *A Thousand Plateaus*, p. 116 [*146*].

27. On the PLANE OF TRANSCENDENCE, see *A Thousand Plateaus*, pp. 265–66, 281–82, 454 [*325–26, 345, 567*]. The REDUNDANCY of molarity

should also be distinguished from the redundancy of the event of meaning as discussed above. Molar redundancy is a limitative, imposed meaning-effect.

28. On CELERITAS versus GRAVITAS, see *A Thousand Plateaus*, p. 370 [*460*].

29. On REACTIVE and ACTIVE, see *Nietzsche and Philosophy*, pp. 39–72 [*44–82*]. On AFFIRMATION, ibid., pp. 171–94 [*197–222*].

30. Deleuze and Guattari's favorite example of an UNNATURAL COUPLING are the WASP and the ORCHID. The wasp is an integral part of of the orchid's reproductive system *and* morphology. The orchid's patterning "mimics" a wasp (their forms conjoin); the orchid is hermaphroditic and the wasp heterosexual (they conjoin reproductive systems); the wasp uses the orchid for food, the orchid uses the wasp for fertilization (they conjoin alimentary and reproductive functions). See *Proust and Signs*, p. 120 [*164*]; *Anti-Oedipus*, pp. 39, 285, 323 [*47, 339, 385*]; and *A Thousand Plateaus*, pp. 10, 69, 293–94 [*20, 89, 360*]. See also *A Thousand Plateaus*, p. 258 [*315*] ("unnatural participation").

31. On FREE ACTION, see *A Thousand Plateaus*, pp. 397, 490–91 [*494, 611–13*]. On the DOUBLE-PINCERED DOMINATION OF STRUCTURATION, ibid., pp. 40, 45, 63, 67 [*54, 60, 82, 87*].

32. The science of NONEQUILIBRIUM THERMODYNAMICS is dedicated to just such phenomena. Its founder, Ilya Prigogine, expresses an affinity with Deleuze in Ilya Prigogine and Isabelle Stengers, *La Nouvelle alliance*, pp. 387–89 (the passage in question is not included in the English book based on this work, *Order out of Chaos* (New York: Bantam, 1984). Prigogine was a major influence on Guattari's work in the late eighties: see Guattari, "Les Energétiques sémiotiques," in J.-P. Brans, I. Stengers, P. Vincke, eds., *Temps et devenir: A Partir de l'oeuvre d'Ilya Prigogine*, reprinted in *Cartographies schizoanalytiques*, pp. 67–92. Guattari assimilates the concept of PROCESS in *Anti-Oedipus* (passim, esp. pp. 130–38 [*155–62*] with Prigogine and Stengers' "DISSIPATIVE STRUCTURE" (defined later in this chapter) in *Les années d'hiver: 1980–1985*, p. 293. See also Deleuze, *Pourparlers*, pp. 43, 167–68.

33. This DISSIPATIVE STRUCTURE is called the "Bénard instability": see Prigogine and Stengers, *La Nouvelle alliance*, pp. 214–17, 426–28, and *Entre le temps et l'éternité*, pp. 52–64.

34. On the SENSITIVITY of dissipative structures, see Prigogine and Stengers, *La Nouvelle alliance*, pp. 430–31, and *Entre le temps et l'éternité*, pp. 59–65, 179.

35. On ATTRACTORS, see Prigogine and Stengers, *La Nouvelle alliance*, pp. 11, 191, 203, 212, 347; *Entre le temps et l'éternité*, pp. 71–72; and Guattari, *Cartographies schizoanalytiques*, pp. 134, 158–59.

36. For Prigogine and Stengers on RESONANCE, see *Entre le temps et l'éternité*, pp. 109–20, 130, 185; on AMPLIFICATION, see *La Nouvelle alliance*, pp. 213, 215, 224–25, 259, 428, and *Entre le temps et l'éternité*, pp. 162–63. For Deleuze and Guattari on resonance (as developed in the remainder of the present chapter: the interaction between the actual and the virtual as resonance, interiority as resonance, and striation and molarity as rigidly coordinated resonance), see *Proust and Signs*, pp. 133–38, 140–42 [*181–86, 191–92, 218–19*] (the third set of page references from the revised French edition are not in the earlier English translation); *Différence et répétition*, pp. 154–55, 256, 356, 357, 372; *Logic of Sense*, pp. 103, 174, 179, 226, 229, 239 [*125, 204, 209–10, 263–64, 266–67, 279*]; *A Thousand Plateaus*, pp. 57, 60, 72, 133, 211, 212, 223–24, 295, 433, 498, 506 [*75, 78, 92, 100–101, 166, 257, 259, 261, 272–74, 362, 539–40, 621, 631*]. The instantaneousness of global resonances caused by a local disturbance in a supermolecule means that what Prigogine and Stengers call a level of "nonlinear" (superlinear) or "delocalized" relations has been added to the level of linear amplification from one local subindividual to another. For Deleuze and Guattari on NONLOCALIZABLE LIAISONS, see *Anti-Oedipus*, pp. 286, 309 (translation modified) [*341, 368*], and *Le Pli*, p. 69.

37. On COMPOSSIBILITY (a term from Leibniz), see *Différence et répétition*, pp. 68–69, 339, 351; *Logic of Sense*, pp. 111, 171–72 [*134–35, 200–201*]; *Le Pli*, pp. 79–90.

38. On SUPERMOLECULARITY as a suppression of the duality between the molecular and the molar (the "microscopic" and the "macroscopic"), see Prigogine and Stengers, *La Nouvelle alliance*, pp. 216, 226, 236, 425–26.

39. RESONANCE and RECOGNITION: "As if each molecule . . . were 'informed' of the system's global state. . . . the system begins to behave as a whole": Prigogine and Stengers, *La Nouvelle alliance*, p. 231. See also *Entre le temps et l'éternité*, p. 61.

40. On increased DEGREES OF FREEDOM in dissipative systems, see Prigogine and Stengers, *La Nouvelle alliance*, p. 236, and *Entre le temps et l'éternité*, p. 118.

41. On COCAUSALITY and the suppression of the duality between chance and determinacy, see Prigogine and Stengers, *La Nouvelle alliance*, pp. 13, 230, 260–63, 329, 342, and *Entre le temps et l'éternité*, pp. 60, 95–96.

42. For examples of the theory of self-organizing DISSIPATIVE STRUCTURES applied to what are often considered MOLAR FORMATIONS, see Prigogine and Stengers, *La Nouvelle alliance*, pp. 235–36, 261–65 (animal species, their biochemistry and evolution), ibid. pp. 14–15, and *Entre temps et l'éternité*, pp. 81–84 (climate).

43. On FRACTAL ATTRACTORS and DENSE POINTS (also called "singular points"), see Prigogine and Stengers, *La Nouvelle alliance*, pp. 13, 125–26, 234–35, 362, 398–402, 417–22, and *Entre le temps et l'éternité*, pp. 73–76. The dense points are none other than the mysterious SINGULARITIES Deleuze analyzes (most notably in *The Logic of Sense*). The abstract points of a Deleuze–Guattarian DIAGRAM are expressions of these singularities: see *Logic of Sense*, passim, esp. pp. 50–53, 100–108, 136 [*65–68, 122–32, 161*], and in relation to PART-OBJECTS, pp. 229, 261. See also *Différence et répétition*, pp. 212, 260, 269–74; *Anti-Oedipus*, pp. 286 [*340*], and in relation to part-objects, pp. 309n, 324 [*369n, 387, 475*] (the last page reference to the French edition cites an appendix that was published separately in English as "Balance-Sheet Program for Desiring-Machines," trans. Robert Hurley, *Semiotext(e)*, *Anti-Oedipus*, 2.5 [1977], pp. 117–35); *A Thousand Plateaus*, pp. 11, 156, 372, 405, 408 [*19, 194, 461, 462, 505, 508*]; *Foucault* (1986), pp. 13–14, 18, 21, 29, 33, 80, 82, 84–85, 87 (it is most regrettable that the term "singularity" tends to disappear in the English translation of this book); and *Le Pli*, pp. 28–32, 81, 86–87. For a brilliant post-Deleuzian presentation of the philosophy of singularity, see Giorgio Agamben, *La Communauté qui vient: Théorie de la singularité quelconque*.

44. If all this talk of VIRTUALITY and ACTUALITY and resonance between them sounds mystical or mythic, it may well be, but only to the extent that quantum mechanics and astrophysics are. Prigogine and Stengers apply the coresonance model to the debate on the origin of the universe. They theorize that the virtual is inherently unstable because

it is composed of different particles that are in constant flux, but in ways that do not harmonize. In the absence of matter, at maximum entropy, the turbulence in the virtual is amplified to the point of an explosive contraction releasing an unimaginable amount of pure energy. The energy is as unstable as the void, and immediately dilates, creating matter. A universe is born (and Lucretius is vindicated). The presence of matter muffles the turbulence by giving it an outlet, by providing a dimension rigid enough to limit it but flexible enough to absorb it. What we get in the form of "chance" and indeterminacy is overflow from the actual's absorption of the virtual. After the initial contraction-dilation, the material universe goes on dilating slowly until its future is consumed by its past and it disappears into maximum entropy. Then it all starts over again. There is a time line or "arrow of time" (*clinamen*, or "swerve," in Lucretius's vocabulary) leading out of the void through the material world and back into the void. More accurately, there are many time lines, as many as there are universes that will have been, even more, as many as the phenomena that will have been born and died in those worlds—because the resonance between the virtual and the actual never ends. This amounts to a scientifically derived version of Nietzsche's theory of the ETERNAL RETURN OF DIFFERENCE that is very close to Deleuze's philosophical version. (On the eternal return, see Prigogine and Stengers, *Entre le temps et l'éternité*, pp. 167–68; on RESONANCE between the virtual and actual, pp. 130, 185–86. For references to Deleuze on the eternal return, see *Force*, note 31, above. For Deleuze on Lucretius and the *clinamen*, see "Lucretius and the Simulacrum," *Logic of Sense*, pp. 266–279 [*307–24*], and *A Thousand Plateaus*, pp. 361–62, 489–90 [*446–47, 610–11*].)

Deleuze supplements Nietzsche with Bergson. Following Bergson, he calls the virtual a PURE PAST, a past inaccessible but necessary to personal experience. The virtual is the "past in general that makes possible all pasts" (*Bergsonism*, p. 57 [*52*]). It does not precede the present but is *contemporaneous* with it (pp. 59–61 [*55–57*]). "The 'present' that endures divides at each 'instant' into two directions, one oriented (dilating) toward the past, the other contracting toward the future" (p. 52 [*46*]). The present is the "tightest," most "contracted" level of a future-past that coexists with it at various levels of dilation. The most dilated level of present, the purest level of the pure past, is an inverse image of matter in its most relaxed state: total entropy (see *Différence et répétition*, pp. 367–68). From that "pure past," Prigogine and Stengers add, a new future explodes: the virtual is the end and beginning of everything, at each instance and at the extremes of history. Prigogine and Stengers would probably agree that the virtual can be conceived as having levels (as in Bergson's famous cone diagram, *Matter and Memory*, p. 162 [*181*], reproduced in the English edition of Deleuze's *Bergsonism*, p. 60, and in *Cinema II*, p. 294 [*108*]; each level can be thought of as corresponding to the "phase space" of an actual stratum); that although it is indeterminate in relation to our world, it is far from undifferentiated; and that actualization of the virtual, the contraction of the "pure past," is a "translation" of its mode of differentiation into ours (*Bergsonism*, pp. 63–64 [*60*]).

However, the use of the word "pure" would probably trouble them. The "pure past" at its deepest level is, in Deleuze's words, "impassive," "neutral," "sterile," "eternal" (some of the most frequently repeated words in *Logic of Sense*: see for example pp. 5, 31–32, 95, 100 [*13–14, 44–45, 116–17, 122*]) —in other words, entropic. This is not consistent with Prigogine and Stengers's perpetual turbulence model, according to which the virtual is not just an inverse image of the actual (a dilation of its contraction) but has its own contractions and therefore resonates in its own right. It is more the flipside of matter than its inverse image; it is the same matter plunged into two different dimensions at the same time (on the "rupture of the symmetry" between the actual and virtual, see *Entre le temps et l'éternité*, p. 191). Actualization does not coax virtuality out of its impassivity, but instead holds its explosiveness in check, gingerly perturbing a potential out of it when it needs one. Entropy only applies to the actual (*Entre le temps et l'éternité*, p. 189). "Sterility" would have to be restricted to meaning in its aspect as a culminating end effect, with the understanding that the "effect" can be reinserted into the syntheses, converting to a cause and rejoining the turbulent potential of the virtual at its point of intersection with the actual. This is the strategy used in the present work.

A consequence of Prigogine and Stengers's theories is that there is no "unified field." Deleuze and Guattari's "monism" of matter-energy would have to be interpreted to imply no stasis or homogeneity on any level. The only "unity" would be in the sense of a holding-together of disparate elements (virtual and actual). Holding-together is in fact the predominant definition in Deleuze and Guattari's work, although they are tainted somewhat by Bergson's insistence that the virtual at its "purest" level, the pure past "in itself," is monistic and only the actual has a multiplicity of time-lines on all levels (see *Bergsonism*, pp. 73–83 [*71–83*]). The entire concept of the "in-itself," already discarded by Bergson in relation to the actual, would have to be discarded for the virtual as well, resulting in a thoroughly Heraclitean position. That tendency is expressed in Deleuze and Guattari's definitions of the abstract machine as having no form or substance, only function (see for example *A Thousand Plateaus*, pp. 141, 511 [*176, 637*]). Function with no form or substance to confine it would be a continually changing, turbulent pool of matter–energy. The abstract machine in its virtuality would be indeterminate in position and velocity, outside our space of relatively stable matter and quantifiable energy, but not "in itself": rather than a pure past, it would be a PURE OUTSIDE, an outside so far out that it would have no "itself" of any kind to be "in" (see *Foucault* (1986), passim, esp. pp. 92–93, 129–30; and Foucault, "Maurice Blanchot: The Thought From Outside," *Foucault/Blanchot*, pp. 9–58). Terms like "far," "deep," "distant," would in fact lose all meaning in relation to the virtual, and "level" would have to conceived nonspatially (as a degree of immanent vibratory intensity). If the virtual is a space of pure exteriority, then every point in it is adjacent to every point in the actual world, regardless of whether those points are adjacent to each other (otherwise some actual points would separate the virtual from other actual points, and the virtual would be outside their outside — in other words relative to it and mediated by it). The later Deleuze and Guattari becomes increasingly consistent with this more Blanchotian position.

45. WE NEVER CLOSE: When methods developed to calculate the fractional dimensionality of systems governed by fractal attractors (the weather, for example) are applied to human brainwave patterns, the results are highly suggestive. In deep SLEEP, brainwave patterns are governed by a fractal attractor whose dimension is between four and five, indicating the presence of an open, relatively stable dissipative system whose states can be described probabilistically. In the WAKING state, no fractal attractor can be detected — meaning that waking life is governed by a fractal attractor of a dimensionality so high that it is beyond being an open system. It is a highly unstable dissipative

structure that can never be scientifically described, even probabilistically. See Prigogine and Stengers, *La Nouvelle alliance*, pp. 15–16; *Entre le temps et l'éternité*, p. 84. "PHASE SPACE" diagrams are used extensively throughout both books; for an explanation of what one is, see ibid., p. 71. On the inadequacy of the concept of the integrable system, see *La Nouvelle alliance*, pp. 123–27 and passim.

46. On the BODY WITHOUT ORGANS, see *Anti-Oedipus*, passim, esp. pp. 9–15, 325–29 [*15–21, 389–93*], and *A Thousand Plateaus*, pp. 149–66, 506–508 [*185–204, 632–34*].

47. On BABY BURPS, see *Anti-Oedipus*, p. 41 [*49*].

48. On SENSATION as the CONTRACTION or envelopment of a plurality of levels, see *Différence et répétition*, pp. 296–97, and Deleuze, *Francis Bacon: Logique de la sensation*, vol. 1, pp. 28–29, 30. On HABIT (or "habitus") as CONTRACTION and RESONANCE, see *Différence et répétition*, pp. 11–12, 100–102, 106–107, 128–29, 151, 155, 366–67. See also Deleuze, *Empirisme et subjectivité*, pp. 61–71, 101, 104, 132. On REDUNDANCY and subjectivity, see *A Thousand Plateaus*, pp. 40, 113, 115, 132–33, 183 [*54, 142, 144, 165–66, 224*].

49. On the LARVAL SUBJECT ("dissolved self," "passive self"), see *Différence et répétition*, pp. 107, 116–18, 129, 155, 354, 366. The word translated as "self" is *moi*, "me": at this level, the larval selves are not unified in an "I." The term "FLEDGLING SELF" used below does not occur in Deleuze and Guattari.

50. On PART-OBJECTS, see *Anti-Oedipus*, passim, esp. pp. 5–6, 71–73, 324, 326–27 [*12, 85–87, 387, 390–91*]; on how Deleuze and Guattari's view differs from that of Melanie Klein, the originator of the theory of part-objects, see ibid., pp. 42–46 [*50–54*]; see also *Habit*, note 43, above. On ORGANIC organization, see *Monstrosity*, note 45, below. On MEMORY as virtuality, see *Bergsonism*, ch. 3, pp. 51–72 [*45–70*].

51. On the ATTRACTION-REPULSION between the nonlimitative and limitative bodies without organs (also expressed as the rejection of the organs by the body without organs: the rejection by desire of the organic functioning of part-objects), see *Anti-Oedipus*, pp. 11–12, 325–27 [*17–18, 389–90*].

52. On the ZOMBIE as a quintessential modern myth, see *Anti-Oedipus*, p. 335 [*401*], and *A Thousand Plateaus*, pp. 425–26, 447–48 [*530, 558–59*].

53. On APPLICATION, see *Anti-Oedipus*, passim, esp. pp. 100–101, 177–79, 306–308 [*120–21, 209–11, 314–21, 365–67*]. Application is a form of FOLDING, as discussed above. It is also called "*rabattement*" (usually translated in *Anti-Oedipus* as "falling back on" or "reduction").

54. Deleuze and Guattari analyze the conjunction between religion, early childhood experience, class, and race in terms of FACIALITY (*A Thousand Plateaus*, pp. 167–91). The "face" in question (or "black hole/white wall system") is less a particular body part than the abstract outline of a libidinally invested categorical grid applied to bodies (it is the "diagram" of the mother's breast and/or face abstracted from the maternal body without organs and set to work by the socius toward patriarchal ends): "The face is not a universal. It is not even that of the WHITE MAN; it is White Man himself, with his broad white cheeks and the black hole of his eyes. The face is Christ. The face is the typical European, what Ezra Pound called the average sensual man, in short, the ordinary everyday Erotomaniac. . . . Not a universal, but *facies totius universi*. Jesus Christ superstar: he invented the the facialization the entire body and spread it everywhere. . . . [T]he face is by nature an entirely specific idea, which did not preclude its acquiring and exercising the most general of functions: the function of biunivocalization, or binarization. It has two aspects: the abstract machine of faciality, insofar as it is composed by a black hole / white wall system, functions in two ways, one of which concerns the units or elements, the other the choices. Under the first aspect, the black hole acts as a central computer, Christ, the third eye that moves across the wall or the white screen serving as general surface of reference. Regardless of the content one gives it, the machine constitutes a facial unit, an elementary face in biunivocal relation with another: it is a man *or* a woman, a rich person or a poor one, an adult or a child, a leader or a subject, 'an x or a y.' The movement of the black hole across the screen, the trajectory of the third eye over the surface of reference, constitutes so many dichotomies or arborescences . . . [C]oncrete individual faces are produced and transformed on the basis of these units, these combinations of units. . . . You don't so much have a face as slide into one. Under the second aspect, the abstract machine of faciality assumes a role of selective response, or choice: given a concrete face, the machine judges whether it passes or not, whether it

goes or not, on the basis of the elementary units. This time, the binary relation is of the 'yes-no' type. . . . Racism operates by the determination of degrees of deviance in relation to the White-Man face, which endeavors to integrate nonconforming traits into increasingly eccentric and backward waves, sometimes tolerating them at given places under given conditions, in a given ghetto, sometimes erasing them from the wall, which never abides alterity" (*A Thousand Plateaus*, pp. 176–77 [*216–18*]). "Faciality" organizes systems of BINARY OPPOSITION operating on different levels, and functions as their dynamic point of contact: an abstract plane with which they all intersect, and by virtue of which they can communicate with each other and with the world at large (to continue Deleuze and Guattari's computer metaphor, it is the "central processing unit" through which each binary program runs). It ensures cross-system consistency (the mutual adaptation, for example, of the binary systems regulating the personal and the political: a common "operating system" and "machine language"). It sets up functional correlations between distinctions made on one level and analogous distinctions on another, suggesting a web of standardized symbolic relays between levels. This authorizes one to proceed metaphorically from any given distinction to its counterpart on any level. The family, however, serves as the default reference level to which all symbolic relays automatically return unless otherwise programmed (OEDIPUS). Communication between levels also creates the possibility of a collapse of levels. Hallucination returns the oppositional systems to their plane of contact in faciality—but in a dysfunctional way that sees only the equivalences and erases the differences. Regression and breakdown are when the distance between binarized levels is effaced, leaving only the socius's analogic, now defunctionalized, correlations; they are when society's "is like" becomes a painfully personalized "is."

55. On the PHALLUS as "despotic" agent of BINARIZATION and social control, see *Anti-Oedipus*, pp. 72–73, 205–209, 294–95, 358–59 [*86–87, 242–47, 350–51, 430*]. A connection may be made between the very different vocabularies Deleuze and Guattari use to analyze processes of subjectification in *Anti-Oedipus* and *A Thousand Plateaus* by interpreting the phallus as the operator of FACIALITY (the "cursor," or Christ's eye).

56. On CONATUS, see *Spinoza: Practical Philosophy*, pp. 59–60, 98–104 [*83, 135–43*]; on DESIRING-MACHINE versus ASSEMBLAGE, see *Dialogues*, p. 101 [*121*]; on the WILL TO POWER, see *Nietzsche and Philosophy*, pp. 49–55, 61–64, 171–75 [*56–62, 69–72, 197–201*] ("power" in the sense of potential, "willing" in the sense of affirming: *not* power over something, which is reactive rather than affirmative). The theory of desire and the unconscious is developed throughout *Anti-Oedipus*, in passages too numerous to cite.

57. Some Lacanian psychoanalysts admit that the "LOST OBJECT" is a retrospective illusion, but do not take the next step of questioning the notion that the presence/absence dialectic and resulting splitting is the necessary foundation of human subjectivity. See Serge Leclaire, *Psychanalyser*, p. 73. For Deleuze and Guattari's critique of the mirror stage, see *A Thousand Plateaus*, p. 171 [*210*].

58. On Lacanian psychoanalysis and the METAPHYSICS OF LACK, see *Anti-Oedipus*, passim, esp. pp. 60–61, 71–73, 82–84, 205–17, 294–96 [*71–72, 85–87, 97–100, 242–57, 350–52*]. On desire and the UNCONSCIOUS AS REAL, rather than imaginary or symbolic, see pp. 26–27, 52–53 [*34–35, 61–62*].

59. On the FRAGMENTED BODY, see *Anti-Oedipus*, pp. 326–27 [*390*], and *A Thousand Plateaus*, pp. 164–65 (where the term OwB, "organs without a body," occurs), 171–72 [*203, 210*].

60. Umberto Eco uses a FRAGMENTED BODY paradigm in his lament on the condition of Italian youth in the seventies and Deleuze and Guattari's influence on their Autonomia movement—the young revolutionaries, it seems, are taking "symbols for facts," having regressed to a state of imaginary confusion in which they are no longer capable of perceiving difference (*L'Espresso*, May 1, 1977; translated into French as "Soyez tranquilles, je ne me suiciderai pas," in *Italie '77: Le "Mouvement" et les intellectuels*, pp. 135–44). René Girard gives Deleuze and Guattari credit for trying to break out of the Symbolic/Imaginary alternative, but feels that they fail in their mission, landing back in the Imaginary. In doing so, they are reinforcing a social trend to retire to a fragmented-body state: "Système du délire," *Critique* 306 (November 1972), esp. pp. 988–99.

61. CHILDHOOD BLOCKS are Deleuze and Guattari's answer to the theory of regression. They are unconscious traces of infantile hyper-

differentiation that are still active at some level in the life of the adult, and can serve as keys to unlock a perfectly up-to-date becoming-supermolecular of the adult. On "childhood blocks," see *Kafka*, pp. 4, 67, 78–79 [*9, 122, 141–43*] and *A Thousand Plateaus*, pp. 164–65, 294 [*203, 360–61*].

62. On the DANGERS of returning to the body without organs (inventing a "line of escape") and the need for sobriety, see *A Thousand Plateaus*, pp. 205–206, 227–31 [*251–52, 277–83, 349–51*]. For practical tips on how to do it successfully, see "How Do You Make Yourself a Body without Organs," *A Thousand Plateaus*, pp. 149–66 [*185–203*].

63. FEMINISM AND THE BODY WITHOUT ORGANS: See especially Alice Jardine, *Gynesis*, pp. 208–23. See also Luce Irigary, *This Sex Which Is Not One*, pp. 140–41 (quoted in part in Jardine, p. 213), and Teresa de Lauretis, *Technologies of Gender*, pp. 23–24.

64. On BECOMING-WOMAN, see Guattari, "Devenir femme," *La Révolution moléculaire*, pp. 295–302 (execrably translated as "Becoming a Woman" in *Molecular Revolution*, pp. 233–35; this essay does not appear in the French Recherches edition); and *A Thousand Plateaus*, pp. 271–81, 287–92, 470 [*332–44, 352–58, 587–88*].

65. On WHITE MAN as the STANDARD of identity (the "MAJORITY"), see *A Thousand Plateaus*, pp. 105–106, 176–78, 291–94, 544n82 [*133–34, 216–18, 356–61*]. See also note 54 above and "Monstrosity," below.

66. On the feminist potential of what Mary Anne Doane and other feminist film critics have termed FEMININE MASQUERADE, see Gaylyn Studlar's analysis of Marlene Dietrich: *In the Realm of the Senses: von Sternberg, Dietrich, and the Masochist Aesthetic*. Madonna might be considered a contemporary example; see Susan McClary, *Feminine Endings: Music, Gender, Sexuality*, pp. 148–66. On men being caught in their own identity trap, and on the potential for play with gender stereotypes to yield less constraining alternate identifications for women, see Tania Modleski, *The Women Who Knew Too Much: Hitchcock and Feminist Theory*, especially her analysis of *Rear Window*, pp. 73–86.

67. For the few passages in which Deleuze and Guattari come close to discussing the practicalities of GENDER POLITICS, see *Anti-Oedipus*, pp. 61 [*71–72*], *A Thousand Plateaus*, pp. 469–73 [*586–91*]; Félix Guattari and Toni Negri, *Les Nouveaux espaces de liberté*, pp. 27, 28–29; Guattari, *Les Trois écologies*, p. 46 ("not only should the diverse levels of practice

not be homogenized . . . they should be engaged in a process of HETEROGENESIS. Feminists will never take becoming-woman too far, and there is no reason to demand that immigrants renounce their cultural traits. . . . Particularist cultures should be allowed to develop, at the same time as new contracts of citizenship are invented. Accommodation should be made for the singular, the exceptional, the rare, within the least intrusive state structure possible").

68. For a description of a gay-male BECOMING-MAN (in relation to Fassbinder's film *Querelle*), see Steven Shaviro, "Masculinity, Spectacle, and the Body of *Querelle*," in *The Cinematic Body* (forthcoming). For comparable lesbian strategies, see Pat Califia, "Feminism and Sadomasochism," *Ten Years of Co-Evolution Quarterly: New That Stayed News, 1974–1984*, pp. 206–214), and SAMOIS, *Coming to Power: Writing and Graphics on Lesbian S/M.*

69. There are many kinds of becoming BEYOND THE HUMAN PALE: becoming-animal, -vegetable, -mineral, and best of all, becoming-molecule. These are discussed at length in section 10 of *A Thousand Plateaus*, pp. 232–309 [*284–380*]. On BECOMING-ANIMAL, see also *Kafka*, pp. 12–15, 34–38, 47, 84 [*23–28, 63–69, 87, 150–51*]; on "NONHUMAN" SEX, see *Anti-Oedipus*, pp. 294–96, 354–56 [*350–52, 425–27*], and *A Thousand Plateaus*, p. 233 [*285*]. On HETEROSEXUALITY as a molar containment of becoming, see *Proust*, pp. 119–25 [*163–70, 210–11*] (the second set of French quotes come from a passage in the revised French edition which does not appear in the earlier English translation).

70. BRINGING IT ALL BACK HOME: "Words expressing neighboring ideas reciprocally limit each other . . . the value of a given term is determined by what surrounds it," Ferdinand de Saussure, *Course in General Linguistics*, p. 114 [*160*]. Saussure seems to contradict himself a few pages farther, when he says that a signified or signifier *taken separately* has no positivity, only reciprocal difference, but that the sign formed by a signified–signifier combination is a "positive term." The relation between two such "positive terms" is an OPPOSITION (which is not a difference but a "distinction"). Saussure does not support the idea that an opposition involves positive terms, or explain why oppositional pairs deserve to be validated as scientifically trustworthy "distinctions." He only offers what appears to have been for him a self-evident example: "father/mother" (pp. 118–19 [*166–67*]) The ideological proposition that gender categories are in any sense scientific positivities has

long since been debunked by the feminist movement. I have chosen to ignore — as have most of his followers — Saussure's dubious claim to have found a positivity of language in oppositional pairs. By my reckoning, an opposition is still a negative difference (a reciprocal difference reduced to two contrasting terms), and GENDER ROLES within the family are rendered no more self-evident by linguistics than by biology. The quotes from Saussure can be found on pp. 80, 10, 9–10, 120 [*115, 25, 24, 169*].

71. Many POST-SAUSSURIAN THINKERS have taken his concept of language as a system of reciprocal difference even further, doing away with the referential function mooring meanings to things (even arbitrarily). This is meant as a radicalizing gesture, but more often than not it forbids an adequate treatment of the interconnection of language and power. The prescriptive capacity of language — its ability to directly effect a transformation of a body; the order-word — is usually left by the wayside along with referentiality. Objects can no longer be referents and thus fall outside the purview of language and even of thought (if a concept is a signified and a signified has no positivity, thought is only a network of empty linguistic units in continual metaphoric and metonymic slippage). Because "objective" is confused with "bodily" or "material," the body falls out as well. In order to recover it, it is claimed that the body is only in discourse: the "BODY AS TEXT." Since language is still conceived of as a form (however self-undermining), the body in discourse is a disembodied body ("no substance"). It stands to reason that only a similarly disembodied (formal) power could act on a disembodied body. It all ends in IDEALISM, masked by such "subversive" concepts as *jouissance*, the pleasure of the text, free play: if power is formal, what resists it is formal as well — the revolution in style. Deleuze and Guattari insist on the materiality of both language and the body, without appealing to referentiality as a fundamental function of language and, paradoxically, without positing any other direct mode of relation between discourse and its "objects" (see the preceding chapter).

72. On UNDIFFERENTIATION as the flipside of oppositional difference, and the two together as an Oedipal mechanism, see *Anti-Oedipus*, pp. 78–79, 110 [*93–94, 131*].

73. How an author negotiates the distinction between these distinctions is a good YARDSTICK by which to measure his or her philosophical

confluence with Deleuze and Guattari on the question of difference (although Deleuze and Guattari do not themselves use the term "hyperdifferentiation"). Many of the thinkers they are commonly compared with (Barthes, Althusser, Derrida, Kristeva, Baudrillard) fall more on the side of identity-undifferentiation, and for that reason can still be said to repose in the shadow of Saussure's tree, even if they claim to have closed the door on it, as Lacan did with his counterillustration (*Ecrits*, p. 151 [*499*]). Other authors whose names do not necessarily spring to mind offer a more compatible philosophical constellation (Simondon, Prigogine and Stengers, Bakhtin, Ducrot, Klossowski; in addition to the more obvious names of Spinoza, Bergson, and Foucault).

74. Deconstructive strategies are of great importance in demonstrating the limits of oppositional difference. DECONSTRUCTION, however, does not allow for the possibility of a positive (in the sense just given) description of nonbinary modes of differentiation. It leaves the identity-undifferentiation system basically intact, emphasizing the ineffability, unthinkability, and unsustainability of what subtends identity, and applying overwhelming negative terms to the undermining of binary oppositions (typically analyzed in terms of aporia).

75. Baudrillard can be seen as THE CONSUMMATE PHILOSOPHER OF SHOPPING. He takes the Freudo-Saussurio-capitalist system of identity-undifferentiation to its logical conclusion. He accepts the equation identity = negative difference, and takes the obvious next step of asserting that if identity has no positivity, it does not exist, it is an empty category. He goes on to say that *everything* is therefore undifferentiated, including sign systems. This is the famous "implosion of meaning," according to which one abstract category inexorably slides into the next, in a playing out of the specious conceptual reversibility inherent to oppositional difference: not-X = Y; not-Y = X; Z = not-X not-Y; therefore Z = Y + X . . . . At that point of vicious circularity, the only alternative to cynicism ("everything is everything else, so nothing matters and I'll do what I please") is seduction: affirming the play of empty signifiers, surrendering oneself to the allure of the sign. This takes us from cynicism to what passes these days for sophistication ("I'll still do what I please, but I'll have fun doing it"). Unfortunately, in an "information economy" signs cost money. Surrendering yourself to them means giving yourself over to consumerism. Baudrillardians

never make it past the shopping mall—after the breakdown of the family, a new microcosm to be trapped in (in which movement is still circular but not habitual—being totally lost). *Dawn of the Dead*. Baudrillard's "hyperspace" is eccentric but not exorbital. He fails to go off on a tangent. (For an analysis of shopping-to-be as a consumerized form of affirmation, see Rhonda Lieberman, "Shopping Disorders.")

76. A SCHIZOPHRENIC in the clinical sense is someone who attempted an escape from identity-undifferentiation, but was thwarted by society or otherwise failed. "SCHIZOPHRENIA" in Deleuze and Guattari's is not a malady; it is a process (that of becoming). A diagnosed "schizophrenic" is produced when the process ends in an abrupt impasse. On schizophrenia as a process, see *Anti-Oedipus*, pp. 34–35 [*41–43*] and passim; on clinical schizophrenia, see *Anti-Oedipus*, pp. 113, 123–24 [*134, 147*].

MONSTROSITY

1. DEGREE ZERO: Georges Canguilhem, *La Connaissance de la vie*, p. 160.

2. CANINE LACES: This is a summary of a story by Vladimir Slepian, discussed in *A Thousand Plateaus*, pp. 258–59 [*316–17*].

3. On COUNTERACTUALIZATION, see *Logic of Sense*, pp. 150–52, 161, 168, 178–79 [*176–78, 188, 197, 209–10*] (the French term is "*contre-effectuation*").

4. On ANALOGY, see *Différence et répétition*, pp. 44–52, 345–49, and *A Thousand Plateaus*, pp. 234–37 [*286–90*]; on BECOMING as nonanalogical, ibid., 274 [*336*]; on GOOD SENSE and COMMON SENSE, *Différence et répétition*, pp. 174–75, 291–92; on GENERAL IDEAS, ibid., pp. 7–12, 20–22, 278, and Bergson (on whose work Deleuze bases his own critique), *Matter and Memory*, pp. 156–63 [*173–81*]. On the traditional "IMAGE OF THOUGHT," see *Différence et répétition*, p. 172.

5. On DOGS AS OEDIPAL animals, see *A Thousand Plateaus*, pp. 28–29, 240, 248 [*41, 294, 304*].

6. On LATITUDE and LONGITUDE, see *A Thousand Plateaus*, 157–58, 256–57, 260 [*195, 314, 318*].

7. On BECOMING always passing through the MIDDLE (*milieu*), see *A Thousand Plateaus*, pp. 25, 293, 297–98 [*37, 359–60, 365–66*].

8. On BECOMING-ANIMAL as an attempted escape from Oedipality, see *Kafka*, pp. 9–15 [*17–28*]; on becoming as distinct from METAPHOR, ibid.,

20–22 [*37–41, 65, 127*]: "There is no longer a designation of something by means of a proper name, nor an assignation of metaphors by means of a figurative sense. But *like* images, the thing no longer forms anything but a sequence of intensive states. . . . We are no longer in the situation of an ordinary, rich language where the word dog, for example, would directly designate an animal and would apply metaphorically to other things (so one could say 'like a dog'). . . . [T]here is no longer man or animal, since each deterritorializes the other, in a conjunction of flows, in a continuum of reversible intensities. . . . [T]here is no longer a subject of the enunciation, nor a subject of the statement. It is no longer the subject of the statement who is a dog, with the subject of the enunciation remaining a man. . . . Rather, there is a circuit of states that forms a mutual becoming, in the heart of a necessarily multiple or collective assemblage" (pp. 21–22 [*39–40*]; translation modified). On becoming as distinct from IMITATION based on a structural analogy between relations, see *A Thousand Plateaus*, pp. 274–75 [*335–37*]: "Do not imitate a dog, but make your organism enter into composition with *something else* in such a way that the particles emitted from the aggregate thus composed will be canine as a function of the relation of movement and rest, or of molecular proximity, into which they enter. . . . You become animal only molecularly. You do not become a barking molar dog, but by barking, if it is done with enough feeling, with enough necessity and composition, you emit a molecular dog."

9. On the foundation of thought as a ZONE OF INDETERMINACY filling a gap created by suspending automatic reaction, see *Cinema I*, pp. 61–66 [*90–97*].

10. "What must happen is a HIJACKING OF SPEECH. Creating has always been a different thing from communicating. In order to escape control, the most important thing is perhaps to create VACUOLES OF NON-COMMUNICATION, interrupters": Deleuze, *Pourparlers*, p. 238. This momentary SUSPENSION of circuits of action–reaction is the same process described in *Anti-Oedipus* as the "arrest" of the desiring machine (the BODY WITHOUT ORGANS emerges in the space of suspension): see pp. 7–10 [*13–16*]. This process is also called "ANTIPRODUCTION" in *Anti-Oedipus*.

11. On the IMAGINATION as an ACTUAL–VIRTUAL CIRCUIT, see Deleuze, *Pourparlers*, pp. 91–92, and *Cinema II*, pp. 127 [*166–67*]. For an early

formulation ("The spontaneous imagination 'as originator of arbitrary forms of possible intuitions'"), see *Kant*, p. 49 [*71*]. On imagination as "PURE THOUGHT," see *Différence et répétition*, pp. 187–91.

12. Becoming is a form of SIMULATION: "Simulation must be understood in the same way we spoke of identification. . . . It carries the real [Oedipal actuality] beyond its principle [molar functioning governed by whole attractors] . . . to the point where it is effectively produced by the desiring machine [in the virtual]. The point where the copy ceases to be a copy in order to become the Real *and its artifice* [becoming-other]," *Anti-Oedipus*, p. 87 [*104*]. Molar personhood is a simulation to begin with: "PERSONS ARE SIMULACRA derived from a social aggregate whose code is invested for its own sake" (ibid., p. 366 [*439*]). Since no particular body can entirely coincide with the code (regularized functions) enveloped in its assigned category and in the various images recapitulating it, a molar person is always a bad copy of its model — an unacknowledged, low-level becoming; an undercover simulation. The difference between becoming-other and becoming-the-same is not the difference between a false copy and a true copy. It is a difference in degree of falsity (artifice). Becoming-other is a simulation that overthrows the model once and for all, so that it can no longer be said to be a copy in even approximate terms. It is a declaration of bad will toward sameness, in a full deployment of the powers of the FALSE." It is not an illusion, but a real and potentially politically potent move against dominating forces: the forces of molarity (the powers of the "true"; good/common sense and the institutions that apply it). See *Logic of Sense*, pp. 253–66 [*292–306*] ("Plato and the Simulacrum"); *Anti-Oedipus*, pp. 321–22 [*384*]; and *Cinema II*, pp. 147–55 [*192–202*] and ch. 6 generally ("The Powers of the False").

13. On the nonvisual MAPPING of becoming versus the static TRACING characteristic of analogical, or representative, thought, see *A Thousand Plateaus*, pp. 12–14, 146–47 [*20–22, 182–83*].

14. On MOLARITY as an APPARATUS OF CAPTURE, see *A Thousand Plateaus*, p. 40 [*54*] (the "STRATA" in general), 167–91, 211, 333–34 [*205–34, 256–57, 261, 411–12*] (molar subjectivity as a "BLACK HOLE" sucking in energies), 424–73 [*528–91*] ("Apparatus of Capture," on the State).

15. On the COLLECTIVE NATURE OF ALL BECOMING, see *Kafka*, 17–18, 82–85 [*31–33, 148–53*] and *A Thousand Plateaus*, 337–38, 340–42, 345–46

[*416, 419–22, 426–27*] (all expression as the product of "collective assemblages of enunciation"; artistic expression, or "MINOR LITERA-TURE," as a group becoming anticipating a future population); 105–106, 198, 200, 279–80, 470, 472–73 [*133–34, 242, 244, 342–44, 588, 590–91*] (becoming as a "becoming-(of)-everybody" [*le devenir (de) tout le monde*]).

16. On the INSUFFICIENCY OF BECOMINGS-ANIMAL, see *Kafka*, pp. 14–15, 36–38 [*27–28, 65–69*].

17. On SLOWNESS as a possible strategy of becoming, see *A Thousand Plateaus*, p. 56 [*73–74*]. Speaking in terms of SPEED or slowness can be misleading: the distinction is a qualitative one between kinds of movement, not a quantitative one between rates of movement (ibid., p. 371 [*460*]). Becoming in itself is "absolute speed," a jump from the quality of movement or mode of composition of molarity to a radically different one; but it always occurs relative to molar thresholds of perception. Molarity can only perceive becoming as a change in quantitative rate of movement carrying something across one of its thresholds of tolerance—in other words, it sees becoming only relative to itself, as measured against its own standards of movement. Becoming is THAT WHICH IS BY NATURE IMPERCEPTIBLE, BUT CANNOT NOT BE PERCEIVED: although its absoluteness, its difference in nature, cannot be seen by molarity, the body-in-becoming is nevertheless inevitably felt by molarity as an irritation, as a perturbation in its circuits of regularized movement. See *A Thousand Plateaus*, pp. 280–82 [*344–45*]. The preceding strategy of camouflage and the following one of inhabiting derelict spaces are ways of using this semiblindness of molar formations to political advantage.

18. "BECOMING-MINORITARIAN [what is being called here 'becoming-other'] as the universal figure of consciousness is called AUTONOMY," (*A Thousand Plateaus*, p. 106 [*134*]).

19. A MOTIONLESS VOYAGE may be a becoming (and many travels through space are not: tourism). On motionless voyages, see *A Thousand Plateaus*, pp. 197, 199 [*242, 244*], and *Anti-Oedipus*, pp. 318–19 [*380–81*].

20. On becoming as UNTIMELY, see *A Thousand Plateaus*, p. 296 [*363*].

21. SIMULATE: *Anti-Oedipus*, p. 87 [*104*].

22. The formula "seeming to be what you are" was suggested by Monte Cazazza's definition of "MISDIRECTION": "making something that isn't seem to be what it is" (Interview, *Re/Search* 11, *Pranks* [1987], p. 73).

23. Deleuze and Guattari distinguish between PRECONSCIOUS INVEST-MENT or class interest, and UNCONSCIOUS INVESTMENT or desire. A person or organization with a "revolutionary" or "reactionary" precon-scious investment may be unconsciously dominated by the opposite virtual pole of desire. "MICROFASCISM" is the presence of fascisizing tendencies within avowedly revolutionary individuals or groups. See *Anti-Oedipus*, pp. 255–58, 343–51 [*303–307, 411–20*], and Guattari, "The Micro-Politics of Fascism," *Molecular Revolution*, pp. 217–32 (the original of this essay, "Micro-politique du fascisme," occurs in both French versions of *La Révolution moléculaire*: pp. 44–67 [1977], pp. 35–60 [1980]).

24. The concept of TRANSVERSALITY was introduced by Guattari in his early investigations into the "SUBJECT-GROUP" (defined in the preced-ing chapter—what I have called a "supermolecule"). See Guattari, "La Transversalité" (1964), *Psychanalyse et transversalité*, pp. 72–85 (trans-lated as "Transversality" in *Molecular Revolution*, pp. 11–23). See also: Deleuze's preface to *Psychanalyse et transversalité*, "Three Group Prob-lems," esp. pp. 99–109) [*vi*]; *Proust*, pp. 110–15, 149–59 [*150–57, 201–203, 210–11*] (the last passage cited does not appear in the earlier edition, on which the English translation is based); *Anti-Oedipus*, pp. 36–39, 43–44, 69–70, 280, 286–87 [*44–47, 51–52, 81–82, 333, 341*]; and *A Thousand Plateaus*, pp. 10–11, 239, 296–98, 335–36 [*18, 292, 363–67, 414–15*].

25. On the PROBLEM as the objective condition of open-ended becom-ing, rather than a logical investigation of being leading to the closure of a solution, see *Différence et répétition*, pp. 88–89, 205–13, 218–21, and *Logic of Sense*, pp. 52–57 [*67–73*].

26. GUARANTOR OF THE GOOD: On the segregative operation of thought as a moral imperative, see Deleuze, "Plato and the Simulacrum," *Logic of Sense*, pp. 253–65 [*292–306*].

27. The emphasis on the "thisness" of things is not to draw attention to their solidity or objecthood, but on the contrary to their transitoriness, the singularity of their unfolding in space-time (being as flux; metasta-bility). It is meant as a reference to Deleuze and Guattari's concept of

HAECCEITY. See *A Thousand Plateaus*, pp. 253, 260–65, 271–72, 273, 276–77, 296, 378, 408 [*310, 318–24, 332, 334, 343–44, 363, 469, 505*].

28. The IDENTIFICATION OF THE OUTSIDE (others with a small "o") as Other (an enemy identity, or rival sameness) is a particular instance of what Deleuze and Guattari see as one of the fundamental operations of Oedipus: the interiorization and DISPLACEMENT OF THE LIMITS of the socius. This is the mechanism by which the distinction between identity-undifferentiation and hyperdifferentiation (limitative and nonlimitative body without organs) is translated into a distinction between identity and undifferentiation (normally functioning and abnormally functioning molarized body). See *Anti-Oedipus*, passim, esp. pp. 102, 135, 165–66, 175–77, 230–33, 266–67, 307, 372–73 [*121, 161, 195, 207–209, 273–77, 317–18, 366, 447–48*]. A terminological reminder: a BODY WITHOUT ORGANS (BwO) is a body from the point of view of its potential dynamism. The BwO can be thought of as the constellation of part-objects governing a given body's tendencies in becoming, or its desire (the attractor states it invents for itself in response to its perceptions of deterministic constraint; the "degrees of freedom" it claims; its virtuality). The SOCIUS (or "full body") is the interaction between the limitative and nonlimitative BwOs functioning in a society (between BwOs governing bodies moving toward the anarchist-schizophrenic pole versus BwOs governing bodies moving toward the fascist-paranoid pole). Each BwO (whether the body it governs is a human individual or an institution) is a deterritorialization of the socius (superabstracted as pure function; as grasped from the point of view of its potential dynamism—but from the necessarily limited perspective of one of the bodies within it). The BwO is an expression of individual desire in its social dimension. This is another way of saying that all becomings (which consist in the invention of a BwO) are fundamentally collective: they are selective evaluations and translations of potentials enveloped in society. Their individuality is a derivation of a collectivity. A socius has its own BwO (its potential dynamism in itself, rather than for a particular body; often called the PLANE OF CONSISTENCY of a society: the sum total of a society's BwOs). In *A Thousand Plateaus*, the term "socius" is all but replaced by "plane of consistency." On the socius as full body in relation to the BwO, see *Anti-Oedipus*, pp. 32 [*40–41*]. The term "socius" occurs on pp. 150, 333 [*186, 411*] of *A Thousand Plateaus*.

29. The PLANE OF TRANSCENDENCE (also called a "PLANE OF ORGANIZA-TION") is the dimension proper to the limitative BwOs governing bodies-in-being (bodies caught in becoming-the-same). The PLANE OF IMMANENCE (also called a "PLANE OF CONSISTENCY" or "plane of composition") is the infinitely more encompassing dimension proper to the nonlimitative BwOs governing bodies opting for a becoming-other. (Nonlimitative BwOs include the limitations of becoming-the-same in the pool of potentials they draw upon and counteractualize; they effect inclusive conjunctive syntheses rather than exclusive disjunctive ones.) Planes of transcendence are associated with bounded interiorities; planes of immanence, with fields of exteriority. See *A Thousand Plateaus*, pp. 154, 156, 254–56, 265–72 [*191, 194, 310–13, 325–33*].

30. IMAGE is used here broadly, to encompass words, thoughts, perceptions and visual "representations" (such as films, photographs, and paintings). An image can be defined as the translation of a dynamism from one level of reality to another of different dimensionality (contraction). This always involves a transposition from one space or substance — medium, sphere of operation — to another. For convenience, that transposition may be likened to the projection of a volume onto a surface. This definition of the image as surface of contraction is derived from Bergson. According to Bergson, the human body does not just produce or consume images: like all things, THE HUMAN BODY *IS* AN IMAGE (a perceptual mechanism of contraction): "I see plainly how external images influence the image I call my body: they transmit movement to it. And I also see how this body influences external images: it gives back movement to them. My body is, then, in the aggregate of the material world, an image which acts like other images, receiving and giving back movement, with, perhaps, this difference only, that my body appears to choose, within certain limits, the manner in which it shall restore what it receives" (Bergson, *Matter and Memory*, pp. 19–20 [*14*]). The world is the sum total of images in reciprocal presupposition.

In no case does an image exist *in* a body or a mind. Minds, like the body they are associated with, are themselves images. An image is a center of dynamic exchange whereby movement steps up (is contracted) or steps down (is redilated) from one dimension of reality to another, and is therefore always in the middle (it is a site of passage and exchange in a field of exteriority; it is a milieu). Minds are always outside the bodies that have them, in another dimension (the virtual as Idea). *Language* is less a medium of communication than the *milieu* of Ideas, the site of exchange where actuality gives up its movement to virtuality, which then sends it back translated (thought and imagination as a virtual-actual circuit). For Bergson, as for Deleuze and Guattari, the ideas and images belonging to a given body are fundamentally *impersonal*, outside any structure of interiority such as an identity or personality (which instead derive from them, secondarily, as a regularization of ideas and images arriving from outside: *habit*). "Images can never be anything but things" (ibid., p. 125 [*139*]). Images "are not in the brain; it is the brain that is in them. This special image which persists in the midst of the others, and which I call my body, constitutes at every moment, a transversal section of the universal becoming. It is then the *place of passage* of the movements received and thrown back, a hyphen, a connecting link between the things which act upon me and the things upon which I act—the seat, in a word, of the sensori-motor phenomena" (ibid., pp. 151–52 [*168–69*], translation modified to restore the word "transversal"). On the impersonality of "memories" (pure thought), and on habit as autonomic sensorimotor response endowed with impersonality (ideality) by an overlay of memory, see pp. 79–90 [*83–96*]. The PERSONAL is understood as the empty site of passage between the subpersonal (nerve firings) and the suprapersonal (Ideas)—compare the derivation of the person in *Habit*. A body has "free choice" to the exact degree to which it disposes of impersonality (can access a wide variety of Ideas for overlay on the habitual situations in which it finds itself). Molarity, as overcoding (the overlay of a category), is impersonality at its lowest power (confined to weakly abstract general ideas): the "personal" dimension of existence is the systematic limitation of the inhuman potential for deviation contained in every body. "Normality is the degree zero of monstrosity."

A familiarity with Bergson's theories of the image are indispensable for understanding Deleuze's *Cinema I* and *Cinema II* and their usefulness for media theory.

31. It is inaccurate, but necessary for purposes of presentation, to divide the DOUBLE MOVEMENT OF THE PLANE OF TRANSCENDENCE into steps or moments: on the one hand, abstraction, elevation, generalization; and on the other reconcretization, application, descent. It is

important to keep in mind that the two moments of this "circuit," like those of becoming-other, are strictly simultaneous. It all happens in the time it takes to perceive an image, think a thought, or have a desire.

32. It is striking that there is at least one other film, and from a society quite distant from France's, where WINE functions in almost identical fashion: *Red Sorghum*, directed by Zhang Yimou (China, 1988).

33. On the QUASICAUSE, see *Anti-Oedipus*, pp. 11–12, 141, 147, 194, 227 [*17–18, 165, 172, 230, 269–70*], and *Logic of Sense*, pp. 8, 33, 86, 94, 124–25, 147, 144–47, 169–70 [*18, 46, 106, 115, 149–50, 169–72, 198–200*]. The usage in *Logic of Sense* differs from that of *Anti-Oedipus*. In the former, the incorporeal efficacy of all meaning is called quasicausality; in the latter, the term is reserved for despotic meaning production. Deleuze and Guattari's notion of the quasicause in relation to political forma-tions derives from Marx's analysis of the mystifying powers of capital as FETISH. See *Capital*, vol. 1, pp. 163–77, 1003–1004 (commodity as fetish), and esp. pp. 1020–22, 1056–58 and *Capital*, vol. 3, pp. 515–18 (capital itself as fetish).

34. It is crucial to distinguish between CODE and LANGUAGE. DNA is a convenient model for the functioning of a code. In order to replicate, DNA must leave its characteristic double-helix shape. It unwinds and parts its strands: its functioning is *linear*. Its unified three-dimensional structure is in excess of its workings (it is an evaporative surplus value effect). Deleuze and Guattari, following Jacob, emphasize that the genetic code has none of the essential qualities of a language: "neither emitter, receiver, comprehension, nor translation, only redundancies and surplus-values" (*A Thousand Plateaus*, p. 62 [*81*]). The genetic code is inextricable from its territory (the chemical medium of the cell). It has a single substance of expression (DNA), which is of the same nature as its contents. DNA is a protein molecule which works with protein molecules to produce protein molecules. It directly, physically, reorders molecular components (see Jacob, *The Logic of Life*, pp. 273–76). If this can be called "translation," it is not at all in the sense in which a language can translate. Any transformations that occur as a result of DNA's workings are not a function of the code itself, but of the successive syntheses its reorderings are taken up by (metabolism, reproduction of the species, natural selection, viral transfer, and so on). This is true of all molar codes. This is the sense in which a cultural

image is a code: it contracts a reality of a higher dimension into a structurally integrated unity-effect which cannot function without stepping down to a molecular level.

Language functions in a very different way. Its form of expression can be translated into an almost infinite variety of substances (media). Not only is its form of expression alienable from its substance, but it can alienate the forms of its contents from their substances and translate them into its own substance (meaning). Further, it can retranslate those forms of content from its substance into other substances (incorporeal transformation). Language is highly deterritorialized and deterritorializing. It is active; it is transformational; its actions straddle many levels; it is superlinear. Language may convey codes in the form of identity categories or general ideas. To the extent that it does, it can be said to function ideologically (language as a vehicle for good/common sense). In addition, language itself can be coded. For example, a given language's ever-changing continuum of sounds can be abstracted into a static phonetic system which is then reapplied to the language in disciplinary fashion, in an attempt to rein in its range of variation. Such codings of language are always in the service of the institution of a *standard language*. The distinction between a code and a language is an important one that it is not often made in semiotics. What is lost when it is not made is the whole political dimension of language. Codes are always power mechanisms associated with molar organization. They are never neutral or objective. Any science of codes is a science of domination, however subtly masked.

35. The quantities between which the "EQUIVALENCE" is established (suffering and surplus value) are incommensurable: they operate on different levels of reality. The "EXCHANGE" — all exchange — is unequal by nature. The forced correspondence between parallel series of incommensurable quantities is imposed precisely for the purpose of assuring their uneven distribution: some bodies will be in a position to manipulate the differential between the two series to their own advantage, others will not; some bodies will hurt more than others, and they are not the ones who will collect the most compensation. This is as true of capitalism as it is of so-called primitive societies, although both the suffering and the surplus value take a different form. In "primitive" societies, the suffering takes the form of explicit ritual torture, and the surplus value is bestowed by the collectivity as prestige accruing to a

chief, dominant clan, or religious-political elite. The equation established is "wrong committed = pain suffered," with the corollary "pain suffered with no prior wrong = credit against society" (as in rites of passage after which an individual has a right to a share of the social product). Everyone, even the "good," are placed in a posture of DEBT toward society: in order to get something from society, you must first pay up; if you don't play by the rules, you pay anyway. In capitalism, the suffering is personal and is implicit in one's "natural" "right" to work; surplus value takes the form of private capital (the ability to make money with money). In "primitive" societies the arbitrary equivalence between incommensurable levels and the distribution of their respective quantities is accomplished with the help of magic (shamanistic leadership; magical kingship). In capitalism, it happens as if by miracle: both the equivalence and the distribution seem to be self-establishing. The quasicause seems to function as a full cause, without stepping down to the level of its content—labor—which is perceived as an impediment to profit rather than a producer of value. (The capitalist miracle is most graphically illustrated in the institution of interest, where money seems to lie in the bank begetting itself in a bourgeois version of immaculate conception.) Capitalism infinitizes a body's debt to society: all but the richest must slave away being "productive members of society," everyone must "pay back her debt to society," day in and day out, or starve. The unequal equivalence that is set up operates on a continual basis rather than punctually (rites of passage) or serially (punishments for particular crimes): it is institutionalized as the everyday equation between habitual suffering and regular paychecks (work). In "primitive" societies, the position in the circuit of unequal exchange a body will hold is formally marked in its flesh (tattooing, circumcision, and so on). In capitalism, the MARKING also operates day to day, on an informal and haphazard basis (work-related injuries and disorders, access to fashion and prestige commodities according to income, neurosis, despair, and so on).

Ideologies and philosophies that give privileged status to concepts of equivalence ("social equality") and exchange ("social contract") mask a caste or class-stratified society. Mechanisms of "exchange" are apparatuses for capturing bodily energies and their channeling them into a system of surplus-value creation favoring a minority. Institutions of "equality," as systems for the imposition of a social "consensus," play into the hands of mechanisms favoring the uneven distribution of surplus value, if only by failing to challenge the miraculous agency credited for all production (in other words, by failing to dismantle the dominant quasicause and shatter the sameness it nurtures). On the "wrong committed = pain suffered" equation and the INFINITIZATION OF DEBT, see Nietzsche, *The Genealogy of Morals*, pp. 57–96 (Second Essay); on CRUELTY AND DEBT in "primitive" societies as compared to capitalism, see *Anti-Oedipus*, pp. 184–98, 217, 222 [*218–34, 256–57, 263*]; for the CRITIQUE OF EXCHANGE, see *Anti-Oedipus*, pp. 184–88 [*218–22*], and *A Thousand Plateaus*, pp. 437–48 [*545–60*]. On UNEQUAL EXCHANGE as a characteristic of global capitalism, see *A Thousand Plateaus*, pp. 468–69 [*584–86*].

36. Once again, it is artificial to divide the functioning of the PLANE OF TRANSCENDENCE into separate moments. It is more accurate to think of it reinventing itself each time a general idea is thought or a molar desire produced. Each reinvention is a momentary transformation of the body producing the general idea or molar desire into a "person." A body can be said to have an identity when it produces a steady stream of such thoughts and desires. As more bodies become identified, they congregate in institutions obliging others to identify themselves in like manner (channelization). The speed and frequency of the reinvention of the plane of transcendence increases. Speaking in terms of "circuits" and "life cycles" is a convenient short-hand used to express the paradoxical ability of the plane of transcendence to spread and reproduce itself—paradoxical because it has no being to reproduce and its very existence is a contradiction in terms. It is *"rare"* in Foucault's sense in *The Archaeology of Knowledge*: its spread is a dissemination of events that are empty in themselves, but nevertheless produce effects (it is a distribution of incorporeal transformations). When the reinventions of the plane of transcendence have spread to every corner of society, it can be said to have become immanent.

37. The term UBIQUITOUS ENEMY is used here to designate the fascist version of what, in relation to capitalism, Deleuze and Guattari, inspired by Paul Virilio, call the "UNSPECIFIED ENEMY" (*ennemi quelconque*): see *A Thousand Plateaus*, pp. 421–22, 466–69, 471–72 [*524–26, 583–84, 589*].

38. On the FASCIST-PARANOID POLE of desire (the "despotic body without organs"), see *Anti-Oedipus*, pp. 192–221, 276–83, 340–41 [*227–*

62, 329–36, 406–409], and (in relation to the "signifying regime"), *A Thousand Plateaus*, pp. 112–17 [*141–47*]; on FASCISM PROPER, see *A Thousand Plateaus*, pp. 163–64, 214–15, 462–63 [*201–202, 261–62, 578*], and *Anti-Oedipus*, pp. 257–58 [*306–307*]. On the attractor state of the fascist-paranoid pole as a virtual absolute State, the URSTAAT (complete social stability and order), see *Anti-Oedipus*, pp. 217–22, 260–62, 314, 374 [*257–62, 309–11, 374, 449*] and *A Thousand Plateaus*, pp. 360, 427–31 [*445, 532–38*].

39. On ANARCHY-SCHIZOPHRENIA as a virtual pole of collective desire, see *Anti-Oedipus*, passim, esp. pp. 273–82 [*325–36*]. Deleuze and Guattari are more comfortable calling this the "nomadic" pole of desire rather than the "anarchist" pole, although both terms occur (they disassociate themselves from traditional anarchism, considering themselves Marxist instead: see note 53, below). On NOMADIC DESIRE, see Deleuze, "Nomad Thought," pp. 142–49 [*159–90*]; Deleuze and Guattari, *A Thousand Plateaus*, pp. 351–423 ("Treatise on Nomadology"), 492–99 [*434–527, 614–24*]; and *Anti-Oedipus*, pp. 105, 278, 292, 318–20 [*125, 330, 348, 381–83*]. "Anarchy" as a synonym of "nomadic desire" usually comes up in connection with Artaud: see for example, *A Thousand Plateaus*, p. 158 [*196*].

40. On the MIXITY of all actual social formations, see *A Thousand Plateaus*, pp. 119, 145–46, 474–75 [*149, 181–82, 593*].

41. On VALUE as a differential of force productive of meaning, see Deleuze, *Nietzsche and Philosophy*, pp. 1–8 [*1–9*].

42. On the FASCIST STATE as a SUICIDE STATE, see *A Thousand Plateaus*, 230–31 [*281–83*], and Paul Virilio, *L'Insécurité du territoire*, pp. 23–50.

43. The FASCIST-PARANOID POLE of desire can be correlated with Freud's DEATH DRIVE; see *Anti-Oedipus*, pp. 8, 62–63, 358–59 [*14–15, 74, 430*]. Deleuze and Guattari's concepts of EROS and LIBIDO, however, have no counterpart in Freud. For Deleuze and Guattari, eros is the impulse behind becoming, rather than a regressive satisfaction bound up with the death drive. Its tendency is toward a heightening of tension (complication; the unstable equilibrium of supermolecularity), not a discharge of it (reestablishment of an ideal stable equilibrium whose ultimate image is death). Freud's eros is part of the fascist-paranoid pole, not the anarchist-schizophrenic one. The "JOY" of becoming is different in nature from "pleasure." Becoming is *not* in any way a

PLEASURE PRINCIPLE (its "joy" can be as painful as the whip against the masochist's skin; it is indeterminate in relation to the affective categories of molarity). For an extended discussion of eros, libido (in Deleuze and Guattari's vocabulary, energy dedicated to the connective syntheses at the basis of becoming) and the death drive in "schizoanalysis" versus psychoanalysis, see *Anti-Oedipus*, pp. 331–38 [*396–404*]; for the critique of "pleasure" (and *jouissance*), see *A Thousand Plateaus*, pp. 154–55, 156–57 [*191–92, 194*]; on libido, see *Anti-Oedipus*, pp. 13 [*19*].

44. On the REACTIVITY ("*ressentiment*") endemic to identity, see *Nietzsche*, pp. 111–46 [*127–68*]. On becoming as "JOY," or "AFFIRMATION," ibid., pp. 180–94 [*207–26*], *Anti-Oedipus*, pp. 16–21 [*22–29*], and *A Thousand Plateaus*, p. 155 [*192*].

45. Deleuze and Guattari's frequent use of the terms "machine" and "machinic" (as in "desiring machine") are often misinterpreted as a metaphor between the body as organism and the machine as technological apparatus. Deleuze and Guattari, however, make a basic distinction between the "machinic" and the "mechanical." Both the organic and the mechanical belong to the molar, as does representation. The MECHANICAL refers to a structural interrelating of discrete parts working harmoniously together to perform work; the ORGANIC is the same organizational model applied to a living body. REPRESENTATION is a mode of expression operating in this same structural fashion. A system of representation is a system of image production whose elementary units are signs (arrested images; images as evaporative meaning effects) grasped as wholes composed of working parts, between which analogical relations are established by rhetorical transference (metaphor, synecdoche, allegory—any "figurative" meaning mechanism). Deleuze and Guattari reserve the term "concrete machine" (as opposed to abstract machine) for technological apparatuses (not all of which are mechanical, of course—anymore than all systems of image production are representative). By MACHINIC they mean functioning immanently and pragmatically, by contagion rather than by comparison, unsubordinated either to the laws of resemblance or utility. By PRODUCTION they mean the process of becoming (production in the usual sense, as the production of objects or use values, is a special type of production). Living bodies and technological apparatuses are machinic when they are in becoming, organic or mechanical when they are functioning in a state of stable equilibrium. On machinic

versus mechanical, see *Anti-Oedipus*, pp. 283–89 [*337–44*], and the appendix, "Bilan-Programme pour machines désirantes," pp. 463–87 (translated separately as "Balance-Sheet Program for Desiring Machines, *Semiotext(e)*, 2.5, *Anti-Oedipus*, pp. 177–35), and *A Thousand Plateaus*, p. 256 [*313*]; on the organic as a specific, limitative mode of bodily functioning, see ibid., pp. 158–59 [*196–97*], and *Anti-Oedipus*, pp. 325–27 [*389–90*]; on the "machinic phylum" as abstract machine of technological becoming (the inventive and selective agency for technical machines), see *A Thousand Plateaus*, pp. 395–403, 409–11 [*491–502, 509–12*].

46. Only one thing can rival the BOREDOM of this endless reproduction of representations of the unrepresentable: endless deconstructions of them.

47. On FASCISM-PARANOIA AS CANCER of the socius, see *A Thousand Plateaus*, pp. 163–64 [*201–202*].

48. The "MAJORITY" is called here "Molar Man" or "Standard Man." "Minority" or "becoming-minor" is called here "becoming-other." On BECOMING-MINOR, see *Kafka*, "What Is a Minor Literature," pp. 16–27 [*29–50*]; Deleuze, "Un Manifeste de moins," in Deleuze and Bene, *Superpositions*, pp. 94–102, 119–31; *A Thousand Plateaus*, pp. 104–107, 272–86, 291–98, 338–50, 469–73 [*131–35, 333–51, 356–67, 417–33, 586–91*] and ch. 10 generally ("Becoming-Intense, Becoming-Animal, Becoming-Imperceptible . . ."). Deleuze and Guattari often use the word MINORITARIAN to emphasize that the distinction is not numerical, but qualitative, a difference in mode of composition: "it is obvious that 'man' holds the majority, even if he is less numerous than mosquitoes" (*A Thousand Plateaus*, p. 105 [*133*]). Becoming-woman, -child, -animal, -mineral, -vegetable, and so on, are varieties of becoming-minoritarian. BECOMING-IMPERCEPTIBLE is the process taken to its highest power. Deleuze and Guattari call the point of contagion at which becoming-imperceptible destroys identity as such, sweeping the majority itself into becoming, "becoming everybody/everything" (*devenir tout le monde*): see *Monstrosity*, note 15, above.

49. On BECOMING AS VIRAL, see *A Thousand Plateaus*, pp. 10–11, 465 [*17–18, 580*].

50. On the ATTRACTION-REPULSION between the nonlimitative and limitative bodies without organs, see *Habit*, note 51, above. On becom-

ing as "COSMIC" process, see *A Thousand Plateaus*, pp. 326–27, 338–50 [*401–402, 416–33*].

51. A MODE OF PRODUCTION, for Deleuze and Guattari, is not determining, in the first or last instance. It is codetermining, like any other social formation. Social formations are defined by virtual modes of composition or consistency. These are actualized as interrelations of heterogeneous components operating on every level, from the most concrete to the most abstract (bodies, objects, words, thoughts, perceptions). Actual formations are always mixed. An economic system cannot be isolated from its virtuality (the modes of desire it expresses) or from other actual formations with which it is reciprocal presupposition (its field of exteriority). The principle of MIXITY extends to the possibility of different formations of the same nature—even modes of production—coexisting in the same social field (though at different coordinates in it, or actualized to different degrees). There is fundamentally NEITHER BASE NOR SUPERSTRUCTURE in a society. There are, however, STRATIFICATIONS: statistical accumulations of regularized functions of many kinds which interlink to form a self-reproducing mechanism preserving and disseminating certain balances of forces (an apparatus of capture). Mode of production, base and superstructure are concepts which belong to the realm of stratification or institutionalized molar functioning (power). Deleuze and Guattari question less their existence than their centrality. They are end products, derivations of more encompassing processes (of *the* process: becoming as dissipative structure—as captured by conservation-oriented structuration). Like every formation, they are *in between*: sites of passage that gather up movement and send it back translated. They have no logical, historical or teleological priority over any other type of actual formation. On mode of production, base and superstructure, see *A Thousand Plateaus*, pp. 89–90, 435 [*113–14, 542*]; on stratification, see ibid., pp. 40–42, 49–50, 335–37 [*54–56, 65–66, 413–16*], and ch. 3 generally ("The Geology of Morals").

52. For the SOCIAL TYPOLOGIES developed by Deleuze and Guattari, see *A Thousand Plateaus*, pp. 208–31, 448–73 [*254–83, 560–91*] (on State and anti-State forms) and 111–48 [*140–84*] (on molar organizations of expression, or "REGIMES OF SIGNS").

53. Deleuze and Guattari's prime example from earlier historical periods of a social formation at the anarchist-schizophrenic extreme

are the NOMADS of the steppes. See *A Thousand Plateaus*, pp. 351–423 [*434–527*] ("Treatise on Nomadology"). As previously mentioned, they do not often use the term "anarchy" for this pole, preferring "nomadism" instead. Deleuze and Guattari still characterize their own thought as MARXIST (an assessment with which many Marxists disagree). For Deleuze's most recent reaffirmation of his Marxism, see *Pourparlers*, p. 232.

There is an extensive and growing literature on the Situationists and May 1968. For a quick account of the SITUATIONISTS and further references, see Edward Ball, "The Great Sideshow of the Situationist International," *Yale French Studies*, 73 (1987), pp. 21–37. A useful collection of documents from MAY 1968 is Alain Schnapp and Pierre Vidal-Naquet, eds., *The French Student Uprising: November 1967–June 1968, An Analytical Record*. On PROVOS AND KABOUTERS, see Roel van Duyn, "The Kabouters of Holland," in Marshall S. Shatz, ed., *The Essential Works of Anarchism*, pp. 569–74. For a Green perspective on the German movements of the early eighties, see Rudolf Bahro, *Building the Green Movement*; for a broader range of approaches, see *The German Issue*, *Semiotext(e)* 4.2 (1982); for Guattari on ECOLOGY, see *Les Trois écologies*. The classic collection of essays from the current within the FEMINIST MOVEMENT closest to the perspective being advanced here (anticensorship feminists defending "deviant" sexualities) is Carol S. Vance, ed., *Pleasure and Danger: Exploring Female Sexuality*. On the CATALONIAN ANARCHISTS, see Murray Bookchin, *The Spanish Anarchists*.

Some English and French sources on the too little-known AUTONOMIST MOVEMENT in Italy: *Autonomia: Post-Political Politics*, *Semiotext(e)* 3.3 (1980); *Autonomy and the Crisis. Italian Marxist Texts of the Theory and Practice of a Class Movement: 1964–1979*; Antonio Negri, *Marx Beyond Marx: Lessons on the Grundrisse* (contains a chronological summary of Negri's work by Michael Ryan); Negri, *Revolution Retrieved: Selected Writings on Marx, Keynes, Capitalist Crisis and New Social Subjects: 1967–83*; Brian Massumi, "Harbinger or Hiccup? Autonomy in Exile," and Brian Massumi and Alice Jardine, "Interview with Toni Negri," both in *Copyright* 1 (Fall 1987), pp. 64–89; *Les Untorelli, Recherches* 30 (November 1977) (contains an article by Guattari, "Masses et minorités à la recherche d'une nouvelle stratégie," pp. 113–22); Fabrizio Calvi, ed., *Italie '77: Le "Mouvement" et les intellectuels*; Marie-Blanche Tahon and André Corten, eds., *L'Italie: Le Philosophe et le gendarme, Actes du colloque de Montréal*; Guattari, *La Révolution moléculaire* (1980), pp. 121–213. Guattari and Negri, in *Communists Like Us*, sketch a green-influenced, post-autonomist, libertarian communist position on politics in the eighties.

A word of warning on slavish dedication to any model of action: The conviction that even recent examples of revolutionary rupture (in particular May 1968 and Autonomy) are obsolete and should not necessarily be taken as models for future activism is growing even among even their most unrepentant veterans. Toni Negri, responding to certain patterns he sees emerging from such disparate events as the French student movement of 1986, Tiananmen Square, and the upheavals in Eastern Europe in 1989, sees the emergence of a new mode of collective action for change — one that is the radically anti-ideological and nonpolemical (even silent: the French students not only refused to delegate media spokespeople or negotiators, but in their largest demonstration carried no placards and shouted no slogans): "Any reformist approach is impossible. . . . Utopia is impossible. . . . Only a void of determinations, the absolute lack of the social bond, can define an alternative. Only the practice of the inconsistency of the social bond is capable of revolution. Tiananmen and Berlin represent masses of disaggregated individuals asserting themselves, in untimely fashion, on the stage of power. They constitute a potential, void of positive determinations, presenting itself as a radical alternative. They have nothing to say. . . . Pure potential. . . . Democracy as the *constituent power of the multitude*," "Polizeiwissenschaft," *Future antérieur* 1 (1990), pp. 85–86. In a similar vein, see Agamben, *La Communauté qui vient*, pp. 87–90. On the French student movement of 1986, *La Nouvelle vague: Novembre–décembre 1986, Libération*, special supplement, January 1987 (includes short articles by Baudrillard, Bourdieu, and Virilio).

54. On SOCIAL DEMOCRACY, see *A Thousand Plateaus*, pp. 463–64 [577–78].

55. On KEYNESIANISM and CORPORATISM, see Toni Negri, "Keynes and the Capitalist Theory of the State Post-1929," *Revolution Retrieved*, pp. 5–42, and Alliez and Feher, "The Luster of Capital," *Zone* 1/2 (1987), pp. 318–26.

56. The distinction between FORCED MOVEMENT and REAL MOVEMENT is not the same as the opposition between "illusory" and "real," despite the misleading terminology. Both "forced movement" and "real move-

ment" are "real," in the sense that they are material, actually occur, and have causal force. They are less in opposition than in tension, in the same way that the limitative and nonlimitative poles governing a virtual–actual circuit are. The forced movement of democracy parodies the virtual at a certain level of actuality, limiting the perception of its potential and thereby keeping the amplitude of systemic change to a minimum without risking civil war. The distinction between them might be better stated as that explained earlier between the *mechanical* (organ-ized, cyclic movement contained in an artificial milieu of interiority and functioning primarily to preserve or reproduce molar entities) and the *machinic* (having to do with the transformational potential of part-objects in a field of exteriority).

This definition of "forced movement" corresponds to what Deleuze and Guattari call the OBJECTIVE APPARENT MOVEMENT proper to the quasicause (in this case, the quasicause is the general idea "democracy," as applied by nonfascist governmental institutions). They define objective apparent movement as "the true perception of a movement produced on a recording surface" (as opposed to a "false consciousness"): see *Anti-Oedipus*, p. 10 [*16*]. What Deleuze calls "forced movement" (*Différence et répétition*, pp. 154–56, 356; *Proust and Signs*, pp. 141, 148 [*191, 200*]; *Logic of Sense*, pp. 239–40 [*279–80*]) is a different concept entirely.

57. Michel Foucault describes the PROLIFERATION OF MINIDESPOTISMS in *Discipline and Punish*. Foucault calls the mechanisms of the miniaturization of molarity and its application to the human body "biopower," and outlines them in *The History of Sexuality I: An Introduction*.

58. FASCISTS IN THE GRASS: For an account of these groups, see James Coates, *Armed and Dangerous: The Rise of the Survivalist Right*. It is striking that the fascist philosophy of the eighties and nineties is often localist in ideology as well as in actual functioning. Many of the groups argue for political autonomy on the county level (as the name of one of the most notorious suggests: the Posse Comitatus). They are more anarcho-capitalist than State-fascist, as were Hitler and Mussolini. This is perhaps a reflection of the power of the quasicause "democracy," which has apparently been compelling enough even to force fascism itself into hybridizing with it to form a peculiar miniaturization of the State-form that still defines itself in terms of political sovereignty but claims it as a right extending over an area only a few miles in diameter.

59. Novelists such as Thomas Pynchon and Philip K. Dick point to the ubiquity of fascism-paranoia in modern American "democracy."

60. Deleuze's most sustained pre-*Anti-Oedipus* analyses of the ANOEDIPAL FORCE OF SEXUAL BECOMINGS are "Coldness and Cruelty," in Deleuze and Sacher-Masoch, *Masochism*, and *Proust and Signs*.

61. On FORMAL SUBSUMPTION of labor to capital, versus the REAL SUBSUMPTION of society to capital, see Marx, *Capital*, vol. 1, pp. 1019–25. Negri's analyses of the "social worker" are an investigation into the mechanisms of real subsumption. See "Archaeology and Project: The Mass Worker and the Social Worker," *Revolution Retrieved*, pp. 203–228, and Alliez and Feher, "The Luster of Capital," *Zone* 1/2, pp. 341–50.

Deleuze and Guattari describe real subsumption as a bipolar process of MACHINIC ENSLAVEMENT and SOCIAL SUBJECTION, which together define capitalism's mode of *capture* of bodily energies: "There is enslavement when human beings themselves are constituent pieces of a machine that they compose among themselves and with other things (animals, tools), under the control and direction of a higher unity. But there is subjection when the higher unity constitutes the human being as a subject linked to a now exterior object, which can be an animal, a tool, or even a machine.... [T]he modern State, through technological development, has substituted an increasingly powerful social subjection for machinic enslavement. . . . Capital acts as a point of subjectification that constitutes all human beings as subjects; but some, the 'capitalists,' are subjects of enunciation that form the private subjectivity of capital, while the others, the 'proletarians,' are subjects of the statement, subjected to the technical machines in which capital is effectuated.... We are now in the immanence of an axiomatic, not under the transcendence of a formal Unity.... A small amount of subjectification took us away from machinic enslavement, but a large amount brings us back.... For example, one is subjected to TV insofar as one uses and consumes it, in the very particular situation of a subject of the statement that more or less mistakes itself for a subject of enunciation ('you, dear television viewers, who make TV what it is . . .'); the technical machine is the medium between two subjects. But one is enslaved by TV as a human machine insofar as the television viewers are no longer consumers or users, nor even subjects who supposedly 'make' it, but intrinsic component pieces, 'input' and 'output,' feedback or recurrences that are no longer connected to the machine in such a way as to produce or use it. In machinic enslavement, there is nothing but transformations and exchanges of information, some of which are mechanical, others human. . . . Rather than stages, subjection and enslavement constitute two coexistant poles" (*A Thousand Plateaus*, pp. 456–58 [*570–73*]).

62. This is NEOCOLONIAL CONTROL because the First World nations do not attempt direct political sovereignty over the "developing" nations. "Third World" countries are left wide latitude with regard to their social and political systems (as long as they are not overly socialist; fascisms are just fine, however), and their domestic economies do not have to be fully subsumed right away (the world economy is not strong enough to accomplish this yet). Deleuze and Guattari emphasize the heterogeneity of the formations existing within capitalism on the world scale. "Peripheral" countries may be "polymorphous" with respect to their internal social and political organization, but must be "isomorphic" in their relations with the "center": see *A Thousand Plateaus*, pp. 455–56 [*569–70*]. What have been dubbed the East European "revolutions of 1989" by the media is the sudden and total subsumption of the "Second World" after seventy years of relentless pressure to join the center or be relegated to the periphery.

63. On ENDOCOLONIZATION, see Paul Virilio, *L'Insécurité du territoire*, passim, esp. pp. 51–64, 71, 100, 158, 161, and Virilio and Sylvère Lotringer, *Pure War*, pp. 95–99.

64. DESPOTIC OVERCODING functions by exclusive disjunctive synthesis (application; segregation); LIBERAL RECODING functions by inclusive disjunctive synthesis (arbitration; integration). Coding, functioning by connective synthesis, is characteristic of "primitive" societies (SEGMENTARITY). On the CAPITALIST AXIOMATIC, see *A Thousand Plateaus*, pp. 451–56, 460–73 [*563–70, 575–91*], and *Anti-Oedipus*, pp. 244–47, 335–39, 372–76 [*291–93, 400–406, 446–51*].

65. On the WANING OF AFFECT in postmodernism, see Fredric Jameson, "Postmodernism, or The Cultural Logic of Late Capitalism," *New Left Review* 146 (July–August 1984), pp. 61–62.

66. A useful way of expressing the change in the functioning of capitalism in the information age is that *circulation* of objects replaces their *production* as the motor of the economy. In other words "use value"

(the ability of an image to be inserted into a molar apparatus and do work for it: reterritorialization) has been subordinated to "exchange value" (its ability to foster extramolar flow and transformation: deterritorialization). This shift in capitalism's center of gravity necessitates an overhaul of Marx's theory of SURPLUS VALUE, according to which surplus value can only be derived by the direct exploitation of "living labor."

The change in the nature of surplus-value can be explained as an extension of Marx's famous inversion of the commodity–money equation marking the birth of industrial capitalism. The equation begins as C-M-C′ ("commodity–sum of money–second commodity": "selling in order to buy," in other words production of a commodity, its sale, and the purchase of a second commodity-object with use value). That equation is inverted to become M-C-M′ ("sum of money–commodity–second sum of money": "buying in order to sell"; production of a commodity for turnover; capital accumulation). See *Capital*, vol. 1, pp. 247–57. Now a similar inversion has taken place in the relation of the commodity to itself, or rather to its image (in the narrow sense of a coded image or model): C-I-C′ (replication of a commodity-object that has use value on the basis of an image or model of it: production of production) becomes I-C-I′ (the elision of use value in the movement from one commodity-image to the next: self-turnover, production of consumption for consumption's sake). The commodity has become a form of capital with its own motor of exchange (fashion, style, "self-improvement") and cycle of realization (image accumulation / image shedding; Kruger's "buying in order to be"). Its value is now defined more by the desire it arouses than by the amount of labor that goes into it.

This implies the existence, in fact the predominance, of a kind of surplus value that is created in the process of circulation itself. The value of commodity-images (defined broadly this time, to encompass objects, bodies, representations and information: decoded sites of force conversion) is attached more to their exchange and inclusive disjunction (the production of recording accompanying the singular acts of consumption made possible by the inclusive conjunctions of the capitalist axiomatic) than to their material production. Deleuze and Guattari call this form of surplus value SURPLUS VALUE OF FLOW. It has two aspects, corresponding to the consumer/capitalist dense points of the capitalist relation: it continues to feed into capital accumulation in the hands of the capitalist, but wherever capital surplus value is extracted in an act of purchase, an evanescent double of what accrues to the capitalist is deposited in the hands of the consumer. This GHOST SURPLUS VALUE has a noncapital form; it is even reminiscent of precapitalist surplus value. It is more on the order of a prestige, an "aura" — style, "cool," the glow of self-worth, "personality." Subjectivity itself has not simply been subordinated to the commodity relation. It has become the product of consumer exchange, a derivative of decoded commodity-images (as opposed to being a product of overcoding: the despotic application of a coded image in a fundamentally political rather than economic operation). Subjectivity is the IMMATERIAL GROSS PRODUCT of the neoconservative state: the ghost in the axiomatic machine of capital accumulation. However, the farther both forms of surplus-value production develop, the harder it is to tell which is "derivative" and which "determining." The ghost surplus value of subjectivity, like capitalist surplus value as a means of investment, is reinserted into states of things and begins to produce its own effects (it develops into a supplementary feedback level of causality, following a process similar to the one described in the last chapter, but freed from molarity). It gets to the point that it becomes necessary to speak of two interlocking axiomatics, the capitalist and the subjectifying, both of which constitute transpersonal modes of desire (or abstract machines) coextensive with the social field, and neither of which taken separately is determining of anything.

The two-sidedness of surplus value accounts for the "schizophrenia" of postmodernity: the flowering of desire in play and experimentation, side by side with enormously widening social inequality and constant reminders of economic exploitation of the grimmest sort (homelessness, the "permanent underclass" of the ghettoes, higher infant mortality in some city centers than in the "Third World," and so on). On surplus value of flow versus surplus value of code (the subjective prestige value bestowed upon a body by the despotic quasicause in the process of overcoding), see *Anti-Oedipus*, pp. 150, 228, 248–49 [*176, 270, 295–96*], and *A Thousand Plateaus*, p. 451 [*563*]. On the obsolescence of Marx's theory of surplus value explained from a still Marxist perspective, see

Negri, *Revolution Retrieved*, pp. 219–20. The terms "ghost surplus value" and "immaterial gross product" are extrapolations that do not occur in Deleuze and Guattari or Negri.

67. On SIMULATION AS REAL movement, see note 12, above.

68. On the DISPLACEMENT OF LIMITS of capitalism, see *Anti-Oedipus*, pp. 230–33, 266–67, 372–73 [*273–77, 317–18, 447–48*].

69. The trend in the nineties for government to contract out social services to private enterprise underlines the fact that even the unemployed now participate in the economy, if only as stimuli for the continued expansion of the tertiary sector, the capital for which is being drawn in part from formerly "unproductive" tax monies.

In spite of the fact that inequality is exacerbated under present-day capitalism, it cannot be said to be a class system. CLASS is a molar concept. It is homologous to individual identity, only it applies to a group of individuals. For there to be *class consciousness*, there must be a population of individuals in the same situation of exploitation, who have, or have the potential for, molar identity, and *whose identities are or can be made to coincide with that exploitation*, in other words are subsumable under that general idea (proletarian overcoding: the despotic imposition of an anticapitalist countermolarity by the "vanguard"). This is only possible in a capitalist system producing the form of surplus value described in note 66 as obsolete. When this capital surplus value is doubled by a "ghost surplus value" taking the form of subjective prestige or "aura," a second axis of potential self-definition is introduced that escapes molar confines. A body can define itself by a mode of *individual desire* absolutely particular to it (its specific way of inclusively conjoining images, their consumption and production), rather than defining itself by the exploitation it has in common with other bodies. Bodies have become radically *singularized*. People no longer define themselves primarily by what they do for a living, but by what they love, what they eat or wear and where they go. This is not simply a ruse of Power to prevent people from realizing their commonality ("false consciousness"). It is a real production of difference as a real dimension of people's lives. *Class no longer exists* in anything resembling what it was in the nineteenth and early twentieth centuries. Which is not to say that disparities do not exist, or that everyone is now a capitalist. Every body is still positioned in the social field according to which dense point dominates their activities (consumer, worker/ commodity, or capitalist). But the situation is infinitely more complicated than it was, because even though not every body is a capitalist, every body visibly consumes—and in postmodernity that means that every body accumulates surplus value, at least in its ghost form of subjective "prestige." The poor are neither those who do not receive surplus value, nor necessarily those who have less money to spend— in one month more money passes through the hands of a small-time drug dealer of the inner city underclass than many a bourgeois makes in a year. A body's relative social position is defined more by *how* money flows through it, not how much money flows through it, and by *what kind* of surplus value its flow allows the body to accumulate, not whether it accumulates any. The poor are those who are only in a position to receive surplus value predominantly in the form of subjective prestige value (the importance of style in the ghetto).

The dense points of the capitalist relation do not define a contradiction or an opposition, but a differential (more or less surplus value, or this kind or that, with or without the possibility of capital accumulation). When the capitalist relation is actualized, the particular content it receives displays an almost infinite variety of concrete forms. Rather than being defined by its class, a body helps define a continuum of variation. Worker and capitalist are two of the many variables entering into the definition of this continuum. They constitute just one of its axes. They, like other constituent variables of the continuum, superabstract poles that do not exist in actuality in their pure forms. A body cannot be assigned a determinate class—only a position on a superabstract continuum. Since the continuum is in constant self-transformation, a body's social position is more a vector (an immanently determined direction and mode of movement) than an enduring state of being correlated to an enduring consciousness (a transcendent quality belonging to a self-same entity). Class as such no longer exists because "it is no longer possible to define quantities of exploitation. . . . [T]he productive routes within society, the interactions among laboring subjects, is by definition immeasurable. . . . [t]he distinctions between 'productive labor' and 'unproductive labor,' between 'production' and 'circulation,' between 'simple labor' and 'complex labor' are all toppled" (Toni Negri, "Crisis of Class"). Negri is convinced that politics can no longer be described as a dialectical process, quite simply because CONTRADICTION HAS BEEN ABOLISHED: see *Revolution Retrieved*, pp. 222–25.

It follows that no anticapitalist politics whose goal is to revive class consciousness will succeed. All such strategies can revive is despotic overcoding.

70. According to Deleuze and Guattari, all social formations are DEFINED BY WHAT ESCAPES THEM—the "lines of escape" or becomings running through them—not by their *contradictions*. In other words, they are defined by how they try to contain escape (their apparatuses of capture). See *A Thousand Plateaus*, pp. 90, 216–17 [*114, 263–64*]. From the perspective of the present work, the closer a formation comes to the fascist-paranoid pole, the closer it comes to defining itself by its contradictions.

71. On ARCHAISMS WITH A CONTEMPORARY FUNCTION within capitalism, see *Anti-Oedipus*, pp. 177, 208–209, 232, 257–58, 261 [*209, 247, 276, 306–308, 311*].

Works Cited

Agamben, Giorgio. *La Communauté qui vient: Théorie de la singularité quelconque*. Paris: Seuil, 1990.

Alliez, Eric and Michel Feher. "The Luster of Capital." *Zone* 1/2 (1987): 318–26.

Austin, J. L. *How To Do Things with Words*. Cambridge, Mass.: Harvard University Press, 1962.

Autonomia: Post-Political Politics, Semiotext(e) 3.3 (1980).

Autonomy and the Crisis: Italian Marxist Texts of the Theory and Practice of a Class Movement, 1964–1979. London: Red Notes and CSE Books, 1979.

Bahro, Rudolf. *Building the Green Movement*. Philadelphia: New Society Publishers, 1986.

Bakhtin, Mikhail. *See* Volosinov, V. N.

Ball, Ed. "The Great Sideshow of the Situationist International." *Yale French Studies* 73 (1987): 21–37.

Beckett, Samuel. *Proust*. New York: Grove Press, 1957.

Benveniste, Emile. *Problems in General Linguistics*. Coral Gables, Fla.: University of Miami Press, 1971.

Bergson, Henri. *Matter and Memory*. Translated by N. M. Paul and W. S. Palmer. New York: Zone Books, 1988. French ed.: *Matière et mémoire*. Paris: PUF, 1939.

Bookchin, Murray. *The Spanish Anarchists*. New York: Free Life Books, 1977.

Brans, J. P., I. Stengers and P. Vincke, eds. *Temps et devenir: A Partir de l'oeuvre d'Ilya Prigogine*. Geneva: Patiño, 1988.

Califia, Pat. "Feminism and Sadomasochism." In *Ten Years of Co-Evolution Quarterly: New That Stayed News, 1974–1984.* San Francisco: North Point Press, 1986.

Calvi, Fabrizio, ed. *Italie '77: Le "Mouvement" et les intellectuels.* Paris: Seuil, 1977.

Canguilhem, Georges. *La Connaissance de la vie.* 2nd ed. Paris: Vrin, 1980.

Cazazza, Monte. Interview. *Re/Search* 11, *Pranks* (1987): 72–74.

Coates, James. *Armed and Dangerous: The Rise of the Survivalist Right.* New York: The Noonday Press, 1987.

Deleuze, Gilles. *Bergsonism.* Translated by Hugh Tomlinson and Barbara Habberjam. New York: Zone Books, 1988. French ed.: *Le Bergsonisme.* Paris: PUF, 1968.

Deleuze, Gilles. *Cinema I: The Movement-Image.* Translated by Hugh Tomlinson and Barbara Habberjam. Minneapolis: University of Minnesota Press, 1986. French ed.: *Cinéma I: L'Image-mouvement.* Paris: Minuit, 1983.

Deleuze, Gilles. *Cinema II: The Time-Image.* Translated by Hugh Tomlinson and Robert Galeta. Minneapolis: University of Minnesota Press, 1989. French ed.: *Cinéma II. L'Image-temps.* Paris: Minuit, 1985.

Deleuze, Gilles. *Différence et répétition.* Paris: PUF, 1968.

Deleuze, Gilles. *Empirisme et subjectivité.* Paris: PUF, 1953.

Deleuze, Gilles. *Expressionism in Philosophy: Spinoza.* Translated by Martin Joughin. New York: Zone Books, 1990. French ed.: *Spinoza et le problème de l'expression.* Paris: Minuit, 1968.

Deleuze, Gilles. *Foucault.* Translated by Seán Hand. Minneapolis: University of Minnesota Press, 1986. French ed.: *Foucault.* Paris: Minuit, 1986.

Deleuze, Gilles. *Francis Bacon: Logique de la sensation.* 2 vols. Paris: Editions de la Différence, 1981.

Deleuze, Gilles. "I Have Nothing to Admit." Translated by Janis Forman. *Semiotext(e)* 2.3, *Anti-Oedipus* (1977). French ed.: "Lettre à un critique sévère" in *Pourparlers* (Paris: Minuit, 1990).

Deleuze, Gilles. *Kant's Critical Philosophy*. Translated by Hugh Tomlinson and Barbara Habberjam. Minneapolis: University of Minnesota Press, 1984. French ed.: *La Philosophie critique de Kant*. Paris: PUF, 1963.

Deleuze, Gilles. *The Logic of Sense*. Translated by Mark Lester with Charles Stivale. Edited by Constanin V. Boundas. New York: Columbia University Press, 1990. French ed.: *Logique du sens*. Paris: Minuit, 1969.

Deleuze, Gilles. *Nietzsche and Philosophy*. Translated by Hugh Tomlinson. New York: Columbia University Press, 1983. French ed.: *Nietzsche et la philosophie*. Paris: PUF, 1962.

Deleuze, Gilles. "Nomad Thought." Translated by David B. Allison. In Donald B. Allison, ed. *The New Nietzsche*. Cambridge, Mass.: MIT Press, 1985. Originally published as "La Pensée nomade" in *Nietzsche aujourd'hui?* vol. 1. (Paris: 10/18, 1973).

Deleuze, Gilles. *Le Pli: Leibniz et le Baroque*. Paris: Minuit, 1988. Translation forthcoming from University of Minnesota Press.

Deleuze, Gilles. *Pourparlers: 1972–1990*. Paris: Minuit, 1990. Translation forthcoming from Columia University Press.

Deleuze, Gilles. *Proust and Signs*. Translated by Richard Howard. New York: Braziller, 1972. French ed.: *Proust et les signes*. Paris: PUF, 1964. 2d ed. 1970. (The English translation is of the first edition. The second French edition contains a new conclusion and has different chapter divisions.)

Deleuze, Gilles. *Spinoza: Practical Philosophy*. Translated by Robert Hurley. San Francisco: City Lights, 1988. French ed.: *Spinoza: Philosophie pratique*. Paris: Minuit, 1970. 2d expanded ed. 1981.

Deleuze, Gilles. "Three Group Problems." Translated by Mark Seem. In *Semiotext(e)*, 2.3, *Anti-Oedipus* (1977): 99–109. Originally published as "Trois problèmes de groupe," a preface to Guattari, *Psychanalyse et transversalité* (Paris: Maspero, 1972).

Deleuze, Gilles and Carmelo Bene. *Superpositions*. Paris: Minuit, 1979.

Deleuze, Gilles and Michel Foucault. "Intellectuals and Power." Translated by Donald Bouchard and Sherry Simon. In Michel Foucault. *Language, Counter-Memory, Practice*. Donald Bouchard, ed. Ithaca, N.Y.: Cornell University Press, 1977. Originally published as

"Les Intellectuels et le pouvoir," *L'Arc* 49: *Gilles Deleuze* (1972; 2d. expanded ed. 1980): 3–10.

Deleuze, Gilles and Félix Guattari. *Anti-Oedipus: Capitalism and Schizophrenia*. Translated by Robert Hurley, Mark Seem, and Helen R. Lane. Minneapolis: University of Minnesota Press, 1983. French ed.: *L'Anti-Oedipe: Capitalisme et schizophrénie*. Paris: Minuit, 1972. 2d. expanded ed. 1974.

Deleuze, Gilles and Félix Guattari. "Balance-Sheet Program for Desiring-Machines." Translated by Robert Hurley. *Semiotext(e)*, 2.5, *Anti-Oedipus* (1977): 117–35. Originally published as "Bilan-Programme pour machine désirantes," appendix to Deleuze and Guattari, *L'Anti-Oedipe*, 2d ed. (Paris: Minuit, 1974).

Deleuze, Gilles and Félix Guattari. *Kafka: Toward a Minor Literature*. Translated by Dana Polan. Minneapolis: University of Minnesota Press, 1986. French ed.: *Kafka. Pour une littérature mineure*. Paris: Minuit, 1975.

Deleuze, Gilles and Félix Guattari. *A Thousand Plateaus: Capitalism and Schizophrenia*. Translated by Brian Massumi. Minneapolis: University of Minnesota Press, 1987. French ed.: *Mille Plateaux: Capitalisme et schizophrénie*. Paris: Minuit, 1980.

Deleuze, Gilles and Claire Parnet. *Dialogues*. Translated by Hugh Tomlinson and Barbara Habberjam. New York: Columbia University Press, 1987. French ed.: *Dialogues*. Paris: Flammarion, 1977.

Deleuze, Gilles and Leopold von Sacher-Masoch. *Masochism*. Contains Deleuze, "Coldness and Cruelty" and Sacher-Masoch, "The Venus in Furs." Translated by Jean McNeil. New York: Zone Books, 1989. French ed.: *Présentation de Sacher-Masoch*. Paris: Minuit, 1967.

Ducrot, Oswald. *Dire et ne pas dire: Principes de sémantique linguistique*. Paris: Herman, 1972.

Eco, Umberto. "Soyez tranquilles, je ne me suiciderai pas." In *Italie '77: Le "Mouvement," les intellectuels*. Fabrizio Calvi, ed. Paris: Seuil, 1977. Reprinted from *L'Espresso*. May 1, 1977.

Feher, Michel and Eric Alliez. *See* Alliez, Eric and Michel Feher.

Foucault, Michel. *The Archaeology of Knowledge*. Translated by A. M. Sheridan Smith. New York: Pantheon, 1972.

Foucault, Michel. *Discipline and Punish*. Translated by Alan Sheridan. New York: Vintage, 1979.

Foucault, Michel. *The History of Sexuality I: An Introduction*. Translated by Robert Hurley. New York: Pantheon, 1978.

Foucault, Michel. *L'Ordre du discours*. Paris: Gallimard, 1971.

Foucault, Michel. "The Thought from Outside." Translated by Brian Massumi. In Maurice Blanchot and Michel Foucault, *Foucault/Blanchot*. New York: Zone Books, 1987.

The German Issue, Semiotext(e) 4.2 (1982).

Gil, José. *Métamorphoses du corps*. Paris: Editions de la Différence, c. 1985.

Girard, René. "Système du délire." *Critique* 306 (November 1972): 957–96.

Gleick, James. *Chaos: Making a New Science*. New York: Viking, 1987.

Guattari, Félix. *Les Années d'hiver: 1980–1985*. Paris: Barrault, 1986.

Guattari, Félix. *Cartographies schizoanalytiques*. Paris: Galilée, 1989.

Guattari, Félix. *L'Inconscient machinique*. Paris: Editions Recherches, 1979.

Guattari, Félix. *Molecular Revolution: Psychiatry and Politics*. Translated by Rosemary Sheed. New York: Penguin, 1984. (A collection of essays drawn from *Psychanalyse et politique* and the two editions of *La Révolution moléculaire*.)

Guattari, Félix. *Psychanalyse et transversalité*. Paris: Maspero, 1972. (Essays 1965–1970.)

Guattari, Félix. *La Révolution moléculaire*. Paris: Editions Recherches, 1977. (Essays 1971–1977.)

Guattari, Félix. *La révolution moléculaire*. Paris: Union Générale d'Editions (10/18), 1980. (Essays 1972–1979. The two collections of essays entitled *La Révolution moléculaire* differ substantially in content. The English collection entitled *Molecular Revolution* corresponds to neither.)

Guattari, Félix. *Les Trois écologies*. Paris: Galilée, 1989.

Guattari, Félix and Gilles Deleuze. *See* Deleuze, Gilles and Félix Guattari.

Guattari, Félix and Toni Negri. *Communists Like Us: New Spaces of Liberty, New Lines of Alliance.* Translated by Michael Ryan. New York: Semioext(e), 1990. French ed.: *Les Nouveaux espaces de liberté.* Paris: Dominique Bedou, 1985.

Histoires de La Borde, Recherches 21 (March–April 1976).

Irigary, Luce. *This Sex Which Is Not One.* Translated by Catherine Porter. Ithaca, N.Y.: Cornell University Press, 1985.

Jacob, François. *The Logic of Life.* Translated by Betty E. Spillmann. New York: Pantheon, 1973. 2d ed 1982.

Jameson, Fredric. "Postmodernism, or The Cultural Logic of Late Capitalism." *New Left Review* 146 (July–August 1984): 53–92.

Jardine, Alice. *Gynesis.* Ithaca, N. Y.: Cornell University Press, 1985.

Jeffrey, Tom. "Mimicking Mountains." *Byte* 12. 14 (December 1987): 337–344.

De Lauretis, Teresa. *Technologies of Gender: Essays on Theory, Film, and Fiction.* Bloomington, Ind.: Indiana University Press, 1987.

Lacan, Jacques. *Ecrits.* Translated by Alan Sheridan. New York: Norton, 1977. French ed.: *Ecrits.* Paris: Seuil, 1966. (The English translation is only a selection.)

Leclaire, Serge. *Psychanalyser.* Paris: Seuil, 1968.

Lieberman, Rhonda. "Shopping Disorders." In *The Politics of Everyday Fear,* edited by Brian Massumi. Minneapolis: University of Minnesota Press, forthcoming.

Lotringer, Sylvère and Paul Virilio. *See* Virilio, Paul and Sylvère Lotringer.

Lyotard, Jean-François. *The Postmodern Condition: A Report on Knowledge.* Translated Geoff Bennington and Brian Massumi. Minneapolis: University of Minnesota Press, 1984.

Mandelbrot, Benoit. *Fractals: Form, Chance, and Dimension.* San Francisco: Freeman, 1977.

Marx, Karl. *Capital,* vol. 1. Translated by Ben Fowkes. New York: Vintage, 1977.

Marx, Karl. *Capital,* vol. 3. Translated by David Fernbach. New York: Vintage, 1981.

Massumi, Brian. "Harbinger or Hiccup? Autonomy in Exile." *Copyright* 1 (Fall 1987): 64-73.

McClary, Susan. *Feminine Endings: Music, Gender and Sexuality*. Minneapolis: University of Minneapolis Press, 1991.

Modleski, Tania. *The Women Who Knew Too Much: Hitchcock and Feminist Theory*. New York: Methuen, 1988.

Negri, Toni. "Crisis of Class." In *Open Marxism*, vol. 2, *Theory and Practice*, edited by Werner Bonefeld, Richard Gunn, and Kosmas Psychopedis. London: Pluto Press, forthcoming.

Negri, Toni. "Interview with Toni Negri." *Copyright* 1 (Fall 1987): 74–89.

Negri, Toni. *Marx Beyond Marx: Lessons on the Grundrisse*, ed. Jim Fleming. Translated by Harry Cleaver, Michael Ryan, and Maurizio Viano. New York: Autonomedia, 1991.

Negri, Toni. "Polizeiwissenschaft." *Future antérieur* 1 (1990): 77–86.

Negri, Toni. *Revolution Retrieved: Selected Writings on Marx, Keynes, Capitalist Crisis and New Social Subjects. 1967–83*. London: Red Notes, 1988.

Negri, Toni and Félix Guattari. *See* Guattari, Félix and Toni Negri.

Nietzsche, Friedrich. *The Genealogy of Morals*. Translated by Walter Kaufmann. New York: Vintage, 1967.

Nietzsche, Friedrich. *The Will to Power*. Translated by Walter Kaufmann and R. J. Hollingdale. New York: Vintage, 1968.

La Nouvelle vague: Novembre–Décembre 1986, Libération special supplement (January 1987).

Orbach, R. "Dynamics of Fractal Networks." *Science* 231.4740 (February 21, 1986): 814–19.

Polkinghorne, J. C. *The Quantum World*. London: Penguin Books, 1984.

Prigogine, Ilya and Isabelle Stengers. *Entre le temps et l'éternité*. Paris: Fayard, 1988.

Prigogine, Ilya and Isabelle Stengers. *La Nouvelle alliance*. Paris: Gallimard, 1979. 2d. expanded ed. 1986.

Prigogine, Ilya and Isabelle Stengers. *Order out of Chaos*. New York: Bantam, 1984.

Pynchon, Thomas. *Vineland*. Boston: Little, Brown, 1990.

SAMOIS, ed. *Coming to Power: Writing and Graphics on Lesbian S/M*. 3d. ed. Boston: Alyson, 1987.

Saussure, Ferdinand de. *Course in General Linguistics*. Translated by Roy Harris. La Salle, Ill.: Open Court, 1983. French ed.: *Cours de linguistique générale*. Paris: Payot, 1972.

Schnapp, Alain and Pierre Vidal-Naquet. *The French Student Uprising: November 1967–June 1968. An Analytical Record*. Boston: Beacon, 1971.

Shatz, Marshall S., ed. *The Essential Works of Anarchism*. New York: Bantam, 1971.

Shaviro, Steven. *The Cinematic Body*. Palo Alto, Cal.: Stanford University Press, forthcoming.

Silverman, Kaja. *The Subject of Semiotics*. Oxford: Oxford University Press, 1983.

Stengers, Isabelle. *See* Prigogine, Ilya and J. P. Brans.

Stewart, Ian. *Does God Play Dice? The Mathematics of Chaos*. Cambridge, Mass.: Basil Blackwell, 1989.

Studlar, Gaylyn. *In the Realm of Pleasure: Von Sternberg, Dietrich, and the Masochistic Aesthetic*. Urbana, Ill.: University of Illinois Press, 1988.

Tahon, Marie-Blanche and André Corten, ed. *L'Italie: Le Philosophe et le gendarme. Actes du colloque de Montréal*. Montreal: VLB, 1986.

Trois milliards de pervers, *Recherches* 12 (March 1973).

Les Untorelli, *Recherches* 30 (November 1977).

Vance, Carol S., ed. *Pleasure and Danger: Exploring Female Sexuality*. Boston: Routledge & Kegan Paul, 1984.

Virilio, Paul. *L'Insécurité du territoire*. Paris: Stock, 1976.

Virilio, Paul and Sylvère Lotringer. *Pure War*. New York: Semiotext(e), 1983.

Volosinov, V. N. (Mikhail Bakhtin). *Marxism and the Philosophy of Language*. Translated by Ladislav Matejka and I. R. Titunik. Cambridge, Mass.: Harvard University Press, 1986.

Index

incorporeal transformation, 28–29, 32–
34, 50, 76, 91, 98, 104, 116, 119,
190n36
capital and, 128–29
indeterminacy
objective, 62–63, 66, 68, 73, 84, 87,
91, 95, 110, 168n44
subjective, 79
zone of, 99–101, 104–105
See also Differentiation, un-; Identity,
confusion
indirect discourse, 29
free, 33
individual, 91
super-, 48–49, 52, 54–55, 162n5
supple, 48–49, 52, 61, 70, 77, 162n5
See also Person
infinitive, 18–20, 25, 158n60
inhibition, 103
insistence. *See* Subsistence
institution, 18–19, 24–26, 101
disciplinary, 57, 114–15, 125–26, 133,
139
See also Despotism; Fascism; Liberal
nation-state; Overcoding
institutional psychotherapy, 3
integration, 14, 18, 19, 22, 54, 68, 69,
70, 164n23
political, 101–102, 104, 121–29
intellectual, role of, 2
"intension," 66, 157n56
intensity, 7–8, 47, 60, 66, 69–71, 73,
161n2
intensity = 0, 70
zone of, 70
intention, 11, 28, 81. *See also* Will
interference, 64, 66, 69, 95
interiority, 2, 80, 84, 111, 115, 121,
122, 136, 137, 184n28. *See also*
Milieu, bounded; Subject; System,
closed
interpretation, 11, 17
invention, 41, 67, 89, 92, 100, 137, 138
investment, preconscious vs. unconscious, 183n22

Irigaray, Luce, 5, 175n63

Jacob, François, 163n18, 164n24, 187–
88n34
Jameson, Fredric, 199n65
Jardine, Alice, 175n63, 195n53
jargon, 41, 157n55
Jeffrey, Tom, 150n30
jouissance, 177n71, 192n43
joy, 2, 72, 151n31, 191n43
judgment, 49–51, 57, 76–77, 88,
145n24, 163n17
justice, 4

Kabouters, 121, 195n53
Kafka, Franz, 163n17
Kant, Immanuel, 2, 158n60
Keynesianism, 122, 128
Khmer Rouge, 120
Klein, Melanie, 171n50
Klossowski, Pierre, 157n56, 178n73
Koch curve, 22–23
Kristeva, Julia, 178n73
Kruger, Barbara, 84, 200n66

Lacan, Jacques, 2, 155n45, 178n73.
See also Psychoanalysis, Lacanian
lack, 85
Laing, R. D., 3
language
vs. code, 107, 187n34
communication and, 41, 186n30
constants of, 41–42
as deterritorializing, 188n34
elementary unit of, 34, 40
as impulsion, 30–31
limits and, 149n23
power and, 154–55n45
as prescriptive, 90
as reductive, 90
standard, 188n34
as structure, 82
as superlinear, 46, 188n34
unity of, 90
See also Connotation; Content;

Context; Indirect discourse; Order-word; Signification; Superlinearity
langue, 41, 43
latitude, 98
Lauretis, Teresa de, 175n63
Leclaire, Serge, 174n57
Leibniz, G. W., 156n53, 166n37
lesbian movement, 89, 103, 127, 176n68
liberalism, 5
liberal nation-state, 121–27, 131, 132, 134
libido, 191–92n43
Lieberman, Rhonda, 179n75
limit, 22, 67, 86, 106, 107, 116–17
  absolute vs. relative, 36–40, 57–58, 140
  of capitalism, 137
  displacement of, 184n28
  language and, 149n23
  of liberal nation-state, 126
  See also Threshold
linearity, 40, 46, 187n34. See also Superlinearity
local-global, 62–63, 65–66, 69, 141, 166n36
logos, 4, 6, 30
Lotringer, Sylvère, 199n63
love, 78, 87, 97, 108, 109
Lucretius, 2, 168n44
Lyotard, Jean-François, 144n14

machine
  concrete, 192n45
  technical, 193n45, 198–99n61
  See also Abstract machine; Machinic; Mechanical
machinic
  assemblage, 27
  enslavement, 198–99n61
  vs. mechanical, 160n69, 192–93n45, 197n56
  phylum, 193n45
majority, 122, 193n48. See also Man, Standard; Standard

mall, 133
Mallarmé, Stéphane, 151n31
Man
  as general idea, 97
  Standard (Molar), 4, 86, 103, 121–22, 135, 162n9, 172n54, 193n48
  White, 172–73n54
Mandelbrot, Benoit, 150n30
mapping, 22, 101, 114, 181n13
marginality, 106. See also Middle; Limit
marking, of body, 189n35
marriage, 28–29, 32, 39–41
Martinet, André, 153n37
Marx, Karl
  on fetishism, 162n11, 187n33
  on real subsumption, 198n61
  on surplus value, 200–202n66
Marxism, 113, 195n53
  Deleuze and Guattari and, 3, 191n39, 195n53
mask, 105, 162n8. See also Camouflage
mass media, 134, 186n30, 198–99n61
Massumi, Brian, 195n53
matter, 21, 23, 25, 52–55, 169–70n44
matter of content, 25–26, 152n36
matter of expression, 152n36
May 1968, 2, 3, 120–21, 196n53
McClary, Susan, 175n66
meaning
  essence and, 17–19, 33
  evaluation and, 56
  as "evaporative" effect, 20–22, 27
  force and, 6, 10–46, 155n45
  "implosion" of, 178n75
  linguistic, 27, 30, 90
  as nonrelation, 16
  separation and, 20
  subject of, 17, 26–27, 33, 40, 43, 113
  as translation, 14–17
  See also Good/common sense
mechanical, vs. machinic, 160n69, 192–93n45, 197n56
memory, 49, 72–75, 186n30
metaphor, 44–45, 82–84, 98, 101, 113, 173n54, 177n71, 179–80n8, 192n45